'As matters of religion become more contentious in Australia, Beck's thorough, clear and insightful analysis of the religion provisions of the Australian constitution is welcome and timely. This book provides a fascinating history of the legal, political and social aspects of one of the few rights provisions of the Constitution.'

Carolyn Evans, The University of Melbourne, Australia

'The Australian Constitution's references to religion have long been misunderstood. This work of meticulous and engaging scholarship uncovers their true historical origins and explains their foundational meaning. In doing so, it throws light on Australia's historical culture, underlining its significance for both legal and popular understanding of law and religion today. Beck's book will change minds.'

Helen Irving, The University of Sydney, Australia

'Does Australia's Constitution protect religious freedom? Does it separate religion and state? Luke Beck has given us a genuinely original, meticulously-researched and eye-opening take on how the Constitution's religion clauses got there, and what they mean – with potentially far-reaching consequences. More, it's thoroughly readable!'

Marion Maddox, Macquarie University, Australia

Religious Freedom and the Australian Constitution

This book examines the origins of Australia's constitutional religious freedom provision. It explores, on the one hand, the political activities and motives of religious leaders seeking to give the Australian Constitution a religious character and, on the other, the political activities and motives of a religious minority seeking to prevent the Australian Constitution having a religious character. The book also interrogates the argument advanced at the Federal Convention in favour of section 116, dealing with separation of religion and government, and argues that until now scholars and courts have misunderstood that argument. The book casts new light to show how the origins of the provision lead to section 116 being conceptualised as a safeguard against religious intolerance on the part of the Commonwealth. Written in an accessible style, the work has potential to influence the development of constitutional doctrine by the High Court through its challenge of historical assumptions on which the High Court's current doctrine is based. Given the ongoing political debates concerning the interaction of discrimination law and religious freedom, the book will be of interest to academics and policy-makers working in the areas of law and religion, constitutional law and comparative law.

Dr Luke Beck is Associate Professor at Monash University, Australia.

ICLARS Series on Law and Religion

Series Editors:

Silvio Ferrari, University of Milan, Italy, Russell Sandberg, Cardiff University, UK, Pieter Coertzen, University of Stellenbosch, South Africa, W. Cole Durham, Jr., Brigham Young University, USA, and Tahir Mahmood, Amity International University, India

The *ICLARS Series on Law and Religion* is a new series designed to provide a forum for the rapidly expanding field of research in law and religion. The series is published in association with the International Consortium for Law and Religion Studies, an international network of scholars and experts of law and religion founded in 2007 with the aim of providing a place where information, data and opinions can easily be exchanged among members and made available to the broader scientific community. The series aims to become a primary source for students and scholars while presenting authors with a valuable means to reach a wide and growing readership.

Other titles in this series:

Islam, Law and the Modern State: (Re)imagining Liberal Theory in Muslim Contexts
Arif A. Jamal, National University of Singapore, Singapore

Free Exercise of Religion and the United States Constitution: The Supreme Court's Challenge
Mark P. Strasser, Capital University Law School, USA

Law and International Religious Freedom: The Rise and Decline of the American Model
Pasquale Annicchino, European University Institute, Italy

Proportionality, Equality Laws, and Religion: Conflicts in England, Canada, and the USA
Megan Pearson, University of Southampton, UK

Islam and Women's Income
Farah Deeba Chowdhury, Queen's University, Canada

Blasphemy, Islam and the State
Stewart Fenwick, University of Melbourne, Australia

Religions and Constitutional Transitions in the Muslim Mediterranean
Edited by Alessandro Ferrari, University of Insubria, Italy and James Toronto, Brigham Young University, USA

Religion, Pluralism, and Reconciling Difference
W. Cole Durham, Jr and Donlu Thayer, both at Brigham Young University, USA

https://www.routledge.com/ICLARS-Series-on-Law-and-Religion/book-series/ICLARS

Religious Freedom and the Australian Constitution

Origins and Future

Luke Beck

Routledge
Taylor & Francis Group
LONDON AND NEW YORK

First published 2018 by Routledge

2 Park Square, Milton Park, Abingdon, Oxfordshire OX14 4RN
52 Vanderbilt Avenue, New York, NY 10017

Routledge is an imprint of the Taylor & Francis Group, an informa business

First issued in paperback 2019

British Library Cataloguing-in-Publication Data
A catalogue record for this book is available from the British Library

Library of Congress Cataloging-in-Publication Data
Names: Beck, Luke, author.
Title: Religious freedom and the Australian Constitution : origins and future / Luke Beck.
Description: New York : Routledge, 2018. | Series: ICLARS series on law and religion | Includes bibliographical references and index.
Identifiers: LCCN 2017046192 | ISBN 9780815367260 (hardback)
Subjects: LCSH: Freedom of religion—Australia. | Constitutional law—Australia.
Classification: LCC KU2162 .B43 2018 | DDC 342.9408/52—dc23
LC record available at https://lccn.loc.gov/2017046192

ISBN: 978-0-8153-6726-0 (hbk)
ISBN: 978-0-367-89374-3 (pbk)

Typeset in ITC Galliard
by Apex CoVantage, LLC

Contents

Foreword

*The Hon Robert S French AC**

This excellent book is also timely. It concerns section 116 of the *Constitution* which provides:

> The Commonwealth shall not make any law for establishing any religion, or for imposing any religious observance, or for prohibiting the free exercise of any religion, and no religious test shall be required as a qualification for any office or public trust under the Commonwealth.

The provision, which applies only to the exercise of Commonwealth powers, is oddly located in Chapter V of the *Constitution* entitled 'The States.' That location is part of the fossil record of a convoluted but interesting history. It is a piece of sloppy editing of the draft Constitution Bill. On the evidence presented in this book, revision itself was the product of confused understanding by delegates of what section 116 was all about and inattention to its precise terms.

Luke Beck has teased out of the Australian Convention Debates and other historical records a finely grained account of the activities of the religious pressure groups, and the responses of the leading delegates engaged in the religious establishment and freedom debates which led to section 116. The account in the work of the political and ecclesiastical currents and cross-currents underpinning the Convention Debates about section 116 and its draft precursors, makes fascinating reading. He has also offered a theoretical characterisation of the section and a critical review of the exposition of its history and purposes disclosed in judgments of the High Court.

The book begins in the late nineteenth century when there was strong advocacy from the organised Christian churches against the notion that the State had nothing to do with religion. In Chapter 2 of the book an account is given of the activities of the Scottish-born Victorian Congregationalist leader, Alexander Gosman. At a convention organised by the Australasian Federation League in Bathurst in 1896 known as the 'People's Federal Convention', Gosman unsuccessfully proposed a motion acknowledging the 'existence of a widespread belief in the government of the world by Divine Providence' and commending the cause of Federation to the wisdom and piety of the people and that 'the Supreme Ruler may be invoked to further, if it please Him, the Federal movement . . .' There was 'fierce discussion' and 'strong resentment' in opposition. The Mayor of Wickham suggested

* Former Chief Justice of the High Court of Australia.

that declarations of religious belief should be left to the clerics 'who might as a preliminary federate the churches.' A member of the New South Wales Parliament said that delegates 'might as well be called upon to express belief in a solar system.' Gosman's motion however, had at least procedural support, from John Quick. On the last day of the Convention a watered-down motion was adopted:

> That this Convention, acknowledging the government of this world by Divine Providence, commends the cause of Australian Federation to all those who desire to promote the material, moral, and social advancement of the people of Australia.

The Bathurst Convention is identified by Dr Beck as the beginning of a serious movement seeking to achieve constitutional recognition of God.

In 1897, the New South Wales Council of Churches, including representatives of the largest Protestant denominations in the colony, met to consider an approach to the pending Federal Convention to obtain formal acknowledgment, in the *Constitution*, of God as the ruler of nations. A petition campaign was initiated and supported by Councils of Churches in the other colonies. A similar initiative was undertaken by the Catholic Archbishop of Sydney, Cardinal Patrick Moran. However, Moran also stood for election as a New South Wales delegate to the Federal Convention, a candidature which caused a 'sectarian explosion' from the Protestant leaders who would have been sympathetic to his aim of securing an acknowledgment of religion in the *Constitution*.

There was much debate about the Churches' proposition. Andrew Inglis Clark thought it was a Roman Catholic idea in pursuit of a 'horrible purpose.' Moreover, any 'doctrine of a corporate responsibility of all the members of a community for the religious opinions of each of them' was the antithesis of Protestantism. That was what the idea of a constitutional recognition of God involved. Christian opposition to the whole idea was led by the Seventh Day Adventists. Their Sabbath being on Saturday, they were opposed to Sunday observance laws which existed in a number of the colonies. In March 1897, they began their own counter petition campaign. They argued that the recognition of God in the *Constitution* would place that document upon a religious basis and lay the foundation for religious legislation. The feared effects of preambular recognition of the Deity upon the substance of the *Constitution*, has parallels in more recent times, reflected in some arguments against constitutional recognition of Australia's Indigenous people.

Dr Beck suggests that what the Adventists feared most was legislative power to enact and enforce Sunday observance laws. This, they believed, was the chief motive of the Council of Churches' recognition campaign. The fear was fuelled in part by a decision of the Supreme Court of the United States.[1] The Adventists attributed to the Supreme Court a holding that the Christian character of the United States gave rise to a rule of statutory interpretation that it was presumed that a statute was not intended to hinder religion. The Court had held that the *Alien Contract Labour Law 1885* (US), which prohibited the importation of foreigners to perform labour or service in the United States, did not apply to the importation of a minister of religion. As Dr Beck points out, however, the Court had not said the Christian character of the nation gave rise to any power to pass laws concerning religion.

1 *Church of the Holy Trinity v United States* 143 US 457 (1892).

There is an interesting discussion of the Adventists' theological reasoning and the conclusion is offered that both their campaign and that of the Council of Churches were religio-political in character, with objectives reflecting their different theologies.

Chapter 4 explores debates at the Federal Convention session in Adelaide in March 1897 so far as they related to attempts to secure constitutional recognition of God. A variety of petitions had been received. John Quick suggested that the preamble of the *Constitution* should include the words 'Whereas the people, invoking Divine Providence, have agreed . . .' The motion was negatived and the minutes do not record any debate on it.

A few weeks later in April 1897, Patrick Glynn, a delegate from South Australia, moved that the words 'invoking Divine Providence' be inserted into the preamble. Barton opposed the motion and suggested that Glynn withdraw it. He said, inter alia:

> the whole mode of government, the whole province of the State, is secular. The whole business that is transacted by any community – however deeply Christian, unless it has an established church, unless religion is interwoven expressly and professedly with all its action – is secular business as distinguished from religious business. The whole duty is to render unto Caesar the things that are Caesar's, and unto God the things that are God's.

The Adelaide session of the Convention ended without God in the preamble.

To put the debate in the context of the drafting history, it may be noted that Inglis Clark's first draft constitution for the 1891 Convention had contained two wide-ranging clauses relating to the non-establishment and free exercise of religion. One of them, clause 46, proposed a limit on Commonwealth power. It provided:

> The Federal Parliament shall not make any Law for the establishment or support of any religion, or for the purpose of giving any preferential recognition to any religion, or for prohibiting the free exercise of any religion.

The other provision, clause 81, was directed to the States and provided 'No Province shall make any law prohibiting the free exercise of any religion.' The Bill that emerged from the 1891 Convention contained only one provision, the former clause 81 now renumbered clause 16 of Chapter V, headed 'States.' It provided '[a] State shall not make any law prohibiting the free exercise of any religion.' When the constitution-making process was revived in Adelaide in 1897 the first draft contained only that restriction. It had become clause 109. God was not in the preamble. The position did not change at the Sydney session in 1897. However, the petitions kept coming.

At the close of the 1897 session, the draft Constitution Bill was to be referred to the colonial parliaments for consideration of recommended changes for subsequent discussion by the Convention. The Protestant leaders and the Adventists then turned their attention to those colonial legislatures. They did this through petitions, public meetings and lobbying of colonial politicians. In the event, the parliaments of the five participating colonies, which at that time did not include Queensland, were all persuaded to support an amendment to the preamble.

In the Melbourne session of the Convention on 2 March 1898, the Protestant churches' campaign yielded a result. The South Australian delegate, Glynn, again sought to have

God recognised in the preamble. He moved the insertion of the words 'humbly relying on the blessing of Almighty God.' He described his proposed insertion as 'simple and unsectarian' and 'expressive of our ultimate hope of the final end of all our aspirations, of the great elemental truth upon which all our creeds are based, and towards which the lines of our faiths converge.'

Henry Higgins opposed the motion, arguing that there was no provision to obviate its bad effect. He said that he would seek to insert a clause to provide 'a sufficient safeguard against the passing of religious laws by the Commonwealth.' Quick supported Glynn's motion. Barton noted that Glynn had consulted the Drafting Committee of the Convention about the precise form of words to be used and that those were seen as the least objectionable. Barton expressed the view, however, that it would be 'a danger to insert words of this kind in the preamble' because of the potential implications which a court might draw. Nevertheless, Glynn's amendment was agreed to and the amended preamble agreed to. Dr Beck refers to contemporary commentary and characterises the decision of the Convention as essentially political rather than religious. He offers a critical view of the discussion of the meaning of the religious words in the preamble in Quick and Garran's *Annotated Constitution of the Commonwealth of Australia.*

It is against the background of the recognition of God in the preamble that section 116 can be seen as an 'antidote or counter-balance' and its insertion as a success for the Seventh Day Adventists. When Glynn's amendment to the preamble was accepted, Higgins told the Convention that he would again seek to insert a clause to provide what he called 'a sufficient safeguard against the passing of religious laws by the Commonwealth.' The debate is dealt with in Chapter 5. Higgins' preferred position was to limit the powers of the States as well. However, as the author observes, the consensus among other delegates was that the existing powers of the States should not be altered. Higgins was prepared to accept a partial victory limiting only the powers of the Commonwealth in respect of religion. On 2 March 1898, he moved the insertion of a clause in substantially the same terms of what became section 116.

In Chapter 6 the book deals with what the author calls the 'standard account' of the argument advanced in favour of section 116 as the prevention of an implied power arising from the religious words of the preamble. He concludes, after close examination of the historical record and Higgins' arguments, that Higgins was seeking to do more than simply have the *Constitution* operate as if God had not been recognised in the preamble. He wanted to ensure that the Commonwealth could not make religious laws at all pursuant to any of its express powers, at least not laws of the kind mentioned in section 116. Indeed, the author goes further and suggests there is reason to suppose the Federal Convention as a whole misunderstood what Higgins was getting at. His aim was a denial to the Commonwealth of power to make laws 'on the subject of' religion, as he understood that concept. The language adopted in section 116 was more limited and focussed in its terms than a simple denial of power in respect of religion. That theme is taken up in Chapter 7.

The author points, in Chapter 7, to a discordance between the expressed general purpose of section 116, which was to deny the Commonwealth power to make laws 'on the subject of religion' and the actual language of the provision. Its language does not effect a complete denial of Commonwealth legislative power in respect of religion. It is suggested that the discordance results from the pragmatic political need on Higgins' part to persuade Convention delegates that the clause was necessary in the first place. The author goes further and proposes that the language was not the result of a careful drafting choice, that neither Clark nor Higgins was particularly thoughtful in their choice of it, and that neither the 1891 nor the 1897–1898 Conventions carefully considered and debated the precise language. The language used in section 116 is said to be 'rather haphazard.'

Chapter 8 discusses what the delegates at the Convention understood to be the meaning of section 116. This discussion is placed in the context of a critical view of High Court judgments about what the framers of the *Constitution* were doing, for example, when they used the word 'for' in section 116, rather than the word 'respecting' in the First Amendment of the United States Constitution which provides:

> Congress shall make no law respecting an establishment of religion, or prohibiting the free exercise thereof; or abridging the freedom of speech, or of the press; or of the right of the people peaceably to assemble, and to petition the Government for a redress of grievances.

That examination leads to the conclusion that the Convention delegates did not give close attention to the meaning of the provision it was adopting as section 116. They were giving effect to pragmatic concerns about unintended consequences.

Chapter 9 moves on to consideration about the purpose of section 116 and discusses two contending theories. One, designated 'the neutrality theory', sees section 116 as reflecting a 'general conception of State neutrality towards religion.' It is characterised as a constitutive theory of the foundations of section 116. The concept of neutrality as understood in American jurisprudence is discussed and expanded by reference, inter alia, to a paper by the former Solicitor-General of Victoria, Stephen McLeish.[2]

Dr Beck proposes an alternative constitutive theory which he calls the 'safeguard against religious intolerance theory.' It is linked to the theme of pragmatism and caution underpinning the history of section 116. Under this conception, section 116 is a shield not a sword and it looks to the avoidance of a particular state of affairs, namely religious intolerance. The author takes the view that the neutrality theory cannot be accepted as a coherent and convincing constitutive theory of the origins of section 116. He argues for the safeguard against intolerance theory.

Chapter 10 refers to the interesting history of Doctor H V Evatt's attempt to expand section 116 in the 1940s. In 1942, he proposed the insertion of a new section 60A into the *Constitution* which would confer plenary power on the Commonwealth Parliament including, unnecessarily, power to make laws with respect to a number of specified matters, one of which was 'religious freedom.' His Bill did not proceed past the first reading stage and was passed over to a special conference comprising 24 members to discuss it and the broader question of Commonwealth powers necessary for post-War reconstruction. This initiative did not succeed. Evatt made another attempt in February 1944 to propose an amendment to the *Constitution*, including the extension of section 116 to the States. His Bill failed at the referendum held on 19 August 1944.

Chapter 11 looks to post-War attempts to amend section 116. In this context it discusses the Australian Constitutional Convention 1973–1985, attempts by Gough Whitlam to extend section 116 to the States, the Constitutional Commission of 1985–1988 and the 1988 Rights and Freedoms Referendum.

2 S McLeish, 'Making Sense of Religion and the *Constitution*: A Fresh Start for Section 116' (1992) 18 *Monash University Law Review* 207.

Chapter 12, which discusses the future of section 116, poses the question whether it provides a safeguard against religious intolerance. The author contends that the High Court has misunderstood the point of section 116 and that its reasoning in section 116 cases is 'seriously flawed.' Whether that is so or not is a matter for the reader to judge. He concludes, only partly provocatively:

> Section 116 has the potential to provide a pragmatic safeguard against religious intolerance on the part of the Commonwealth, if only the High Court understood its history. This book provides that history.

The concluding critique of the High Court's approach to section 116 does not require any argumentative response in this Foreword. Whether one agrees or disagrees with it or falls somewhere in between, the book itself provides a rich and detailed history of an important provision of the *Constitution* and food for thought about its purpose and meaning. It also points up the futility of attempts to define original intentions or purposes on the part of those who drafted the *Constitution* except at high levels of generality appropriate to the nature of the document which they were drafting. I commend the book to its readers.

Acknowledgements

This book commenced life as a doctoral thesis at the University of Sydney supervised by Professor Helen Irving and Professor Anne Twomey. I am indebted to both for their guidance and mentoring.

This book also reproduces with permission some material that first appeared in some of my previously published scholarly articles in *Melbourne University Law Review* (volume 41), *Federal Law Review* (volumes 41 and 44) and *Australian Journal of Politics and History* (volume 64).

Luke Beck
Sydney

1 A sabbath breaker in the stocks

The presence of a provision in the *Australian Constitution* separating religion and government and offering some protection of religious freedom in Australia owes much to the civil disobedience – or perhaps wilful criminality – in 1894 of a bricklayer.[1]

In the early afternoon of 29 July 1894, Constable Thomas Burke of the Sydney police witnessed a shocking crime. The constable saw Robert Shannon, later described by a newspaper as 'an undersized man', building a house on Albion Street in Leichhardt, in what is now the inner west of Sydney. The particulars of the crime were that Shannon was mixing mortar and laying bricks. It was a Sunday. Robert Shannon was a bricklayer by trade.

As was his duty, the constable remonstrated with the bricklayer. The constable asked the bricklayer if he knew the day was a Sunday and if he knew he was breaking the law by working in his usual calling on the Sabbath. Even though 29 July 1894 was indeed a Sunday, the bricklayer denied the day was the Sabbath. Shannon told the constable, 'I don't care about the law. I work here every Sunday, and will continue to do so.'

The law in question was a statute passed in England during the reign of Charles II and which was in force in New South Wales in 1894. The *Sunday Observance Act 1677*,[2] required that 'all and every person and persons whatsoever shall on every Lords day apply themselves to the observation of the same by exercising themselves thereon in the dutyes of Piety and true Religion publiquely and privately.'[3] Unfortunately for Robert Shannon, the Act also required that no 'Tradesman, Artificer Workeman Labourer or other Person whatsoever shall doe or exercise any worldly Labour, Busines or Worke of their ordinary Callings upon the Lords day or any part thereof (Workes of Necessity onely excepted).'[4] In other words, working on Sundays was a crime.

1 This account is taken from newspaper reports. See 'Sentenced to the Stocks', *National Advocate* (Bathurst), 11 August 1984, 2; 'Sunday Labor Prosecution', *Evening News* (Sydney), 9 August 1894, 4; 'The Stocks Case – Some Departmental Correspondence', *Newcastle Morning Herald and Miners' Advocate* (Newcastle), 11 August 1894, 5; 'Sentenced to the Stocks. The Sentence to be Remitted', *The Age* (Melbourne), 14 August 1894, 6; 'The Stocks Case. Sentenced Remitted', *Evening News* (Sydney), 13 August 1894, 5; 'Sunday Observance. The Seventh Day Adventists', *The Australian Star* (Sydney), 20 August 1894, 2.

2 29 Car II c 7.

3 Ibid s 1.

4 Ibid s 1.

On 9 August 1894, Shannon was prosecuted at the Glebe Police Court before Mr G H Smithers, Stipendiary Magistrate. Given that a police officer had caught Shannon in the act, one might think that the case was open and shut and that the best course of action would be for Shannon to plead guilty. Shannon, representing himself, defended the charge.

Shannon admitted in court that he was indeed working on 29 July. However, he was not guilty, Shannon told the magistrate, because there is nothing in the Bible to justify calling Sunday the Lord's Day. 'I believe in keeping the seventh day', Shannon told the magistrate, explaining that the Sabbath was actually Saturday. The magistrate told Shannon that the court would not be entering into a theological debate about which day was the Sabbath.

Shannon was one of about 80 members of a Seventh Day Adventist congregation that met at Chippendale. As a Seventh Day Adventist, Shannon believed that Saturday rather than Sunday was the Sabbath. The Seventh Day Adventists knew Shannon's case was important. A number of them, including the head of the denomination in New South Wales, were present in the public gallery for Shannon's trial.

Shannon had a second argument in his defence. He gave the magistrate a copy of a proclamation issued in 1858 by Queen Victoria. In part, the proclamation declared:

> Firmly relying, ourselves, on the truth of Christianity, and acknowledging with gratitude the solace of religion, we disclaim alike the right and the desire to impose our convictions on any of our subjects. We declare it to be our royal will and pleasure that none be in any wise favored, none molested or disquieted, by reason of their religious faith or observances, but that all shall alike enjoy the equal and impartial protection of the law; and we do strictly charge and enjoin all those who may be in authority under us that they abstain from all interference with the religious belief or worship of any of our subjects, on pain of our highest displeasure.

The magistrate told Shannon that the proclamation could not alter the Act. In any case, the proclamation was a 'Proclamation to the Princes, Chiefs, and People of India' and was never intended for New South Wales.

Shannon then asked the magistrate to postpone the case. The magistrate declined and brought the trial to its inevitable conclusion. Newspapers carried part of the trial's transcript:

Shannon:	Will you postpone the case?
The Magistrate:	I cannot. You have practically admitted the offence.
Shannon:	Not on the Lord's Day.
The Magistrate:	I can only administer the law, but no doubt you were actuated by conscientious scruples. You are fined 2 shillings 6 pence and costs, or in default to be set publicly in the stocks for two hours.
Shannon:	I will prefer the stocks to paying.
Police Sergeant:	All right, you will find them ready for you!

The old legislation prescribed a penalty of a fine or 'in default . . . or in case of insufficiency or inability of the said offender to pay . . . then the party offending shall be set publicly in the stocks by the space of two hours.' Outside court, Shannon told reporters he was determined not to pay the fine.

The authorities faced a significant problem in carrying out the sentence. The use of stocks had fallen into disuse by 1894. No stocks were available. Unsure of what to do, officials at the courthouse wrote to the Department of Justice for advice.

Departmental officials had a solution. Stocks would be made. The Sydney *Evening News* described the solution:

> [I]nstructions were issued to have a pair of what were known as trestle stocks prepared. These are simple in design, similar to the trestles used by carpenters, but in the middle of each there is a cavity about the size of a man's ankle. Secured by bolts at one end, and working on hinges, are two hasps, semi-circular in shape, which can be padlocked over the cavity in question, thereby effectually securing a man's ankles or hands in their iron grasp.[5]

Departmental officials also had ideas about where they would carry out the sentence. The *Evening News* reported: 'It was proposed to carry the sentence into effect by seating the culprit on a form outside the Glebe Court and fastening his ankles in the manner described.'

Not surprisingly, there was public consternation at the prospect of the authorities placing a person in stocks. Public concern extended even to other colonies. In Melbourne, the leader of Australasian Union Conference – the governing body of the Seventh Day Adventists in Australia – an American called A G Daniells gave a protest speech before a large audience at Prahran Town Hall. In that speech, Daniells explained that Seventh Day Adventists like Robert Shannon could not pay fines for working on Sundays because paying would be admitting that they had done something wrong. It was wrong and contrary to scripture, Daniells said, for government to enact and enforce religious laws and right for people of conscience to ignore such laws.

Daniells also travelled to Sydney to continue his protests, including speaking at a public meeting at Leichhardt Town Hall. That public meeting was attended by a member of parliament. The politician complained that Shannon was a hypocrite because Shannon required the men who worked for him not to work on Saturdays. Daniells replied that the situation was entirely different. Shannon's workers were not compelled by law to observe any Sabbath and had freely entered into Shannon's employment knowing his business did no work on Saturdays.

Newspapers described the law as 'odious.' The Under-Secretary of the Department of Justice issued a public denial that there was ever any plan to construct stocks.

Ignoring the plans drawn up by officials, the government had its own solution to the problem of Robert Shannon's sentence. The government advised the Governor to remit Shannon's sentence. Shannon was let off.

Robert Shannon was not the only person prosecuted under the old Sunday laws. Enforcement of the law was, however, highly selective. What motivated the New South Wales government in enforcing the law was not any sense of religious piety or even any sense that the law should be obeyed simply because it is the law. Indeed, as newspapers pointed out, the government itself was among the worst offenders. Government railway services

5 'The Stocks. Shannon's Case', *Evening News* (Sydney), 11 August 1894, 4.

operated on Sunday, for example. Other habitual offenders included newspaper publishers who worked on Sundays preparing their Monday editions.

The leader of the Seventh Day Adventists in New South Wales complained in a letter to the editor of *The Australian Star* newspaper about why the law was being enforced in a selective manner. It was hardly a coincidence, Pastor M'Cullagh wrote, that the government began to enforce the Sunday observance laws shortly after a deputation of Protestant church leaders met with the Premier demanding enforcement of the law.[6]

The Seventh Day Adventists were not just small in number with little electoral clout. They also offended the religious sensibilities of Protestant church leaders. Adventists like Shannon were far from alone in working on Sundays but their crime was compounded in a way that Sabbath breaking by others was not. The Adventists took Saturday as the Sabbath and this offended some Protestant leaders even more than working on Sundays.[7] Seventh Day Adventists like Shannon were convenient targets: prosecuting those most disliked by officious Protestant church leaders would give politicians some reprieve from lobbying and complaints by church leaders.

Constable Burke is unlikely to have just happened to come across Robert Shannon laying bricks and mixing mortar. After all, Shannon's business practices were sufficiently well known that even a member of parliament knew the terms of the contracts under which Shannon's employees worked. Constable Burke was almost certainly sent to catch Shannon in the act.

* * *

Federation occurred less than six years after Robert Shannon nearly found himself sitting in stocks on the steps of a Sydney courthouse because he did not conform to the religious observances endorsed by government. What if the new Federal Government had power to enact religious observance laws or other laws concerning religion? And what if the Federal Government could be persuaded to actually enforce laws concerning religion Australia-wide? The force of federal law would repeat the Robert Shannon story all over the country, potentially with worse consequences.

Robert Shannon's story is a small story. Yet the contours of the much larger story of the separation of religion and government provision of the *Australian Constitution* – section 116 – parallel those of Shannon's story.

The colonial churches – including some of the very same individuals who called on the New South Wales Premier urging the enforcement of Sunday observance laws shortly before Robert Shannon was prosecuted – were keen on the new Federal Government having power to enact laws concerning religion. During the period of the *Australian Constitution's* drafting, they worked towards ensuring that the Federal Government would have a constitutional power to enact laws concerning religion.

Not surprisingly, the prospect of federal laws concerning religion alarmed the Seventh Day Adventists. They knew it was possible to pressure even governments who did not particularly believe in such laws to enforce them. The Seventh Day Adventists – including

6 S M'Cullagh, 'Religious Persecution', *The Australian Star* (Sydney), 17 August 1894, 3.
7 Ibid.

some of the same individuals who led the protests against the prosecution of Robert Shannon – worked towards ensuring that the Federal Government would have no power to enact laws concerning religion.

It is that story, and its implications, that this book tells.

The story is important not just as matter of history and politics but also as a matter of constitutional law. The history and motivations behind section 116, or rather what judges have assumed to be the history and motivations behind section 116, have played an important role in the High Court's interpretation of the provision. This can be seen in the High Court's 1981 decision in *Attorney-General (Vic); Ex Rel Black v Commonwealth*,[8] in which a majority of the High Court rejected an argument that federal funding of religious schools violated the establishment clause of section 116.

To take just two of the judgments in that case, the judgments of Justice Sir Ninian Stephen (who later became Governor-General) in the majority and Justice Lionel Murphy (who was previously Attorney-General in the Whitlam Labor Government) in dissent demonstrate the way in which the history and motivations behind section 116 have influenced the interpretation of the provision. Justice Stephen took the view that the provision was based on English legal experience and interpreted the provision accordingly. He wrote that section 116 'contains four quite distinct restrictions, each concerned with one aspect of the relationship between church and state and each recalling phases of that relationship as it has evolved through centuries of English history.'[9] He also wrote that the language of establishment was at the time of the drafting of the *Australian Constitution* 'then much in vogue in connexion with the current disestablishment debate in the United Kingdom.'[10]

Justice Murphy took an opposite view. He wrote that '[i]n this part of the *Constitution* [i.e. section 116], the framers obviously looked for guidance to the United States, not to the United Kingdom.' The logic behind this comment is not difficult to discern when the language of section 116 is compared with language of the *United States Constitution.*

Section 116 provides:

> The Commonwealth shall not make any law for establishing any religion, or for imposing any religious observance, or for prohibiting the free exercise of any religion, and no religious test shall be required as a qualification for any office or public trust under the Commonwealth.

The First Amendment to the *United States Constitution* provides: 'Congress shall make no law respecting an establishment of religion, or prohibiting the free exercise thereof . . .' Article IV of the *United States Constitution* provides: '. . . no religious Test shall ever be required as a Qualification to any Office or public Trust under the United States.'

Justice Murphy took the view that '[t]he United States' decisions on the establishment clause should be followed. The arguments for departing from them (based on the trifles of differences in wording between the United States and the Australian establishment

8 (1981) 146 CLR 559.
9 Ibid 605.
10 Ibid 608.

clauses) are hair-splitting.'[11] 'The purpose of our establishment clause', Murphy said, 'is the same as that in the United States' Constitution.'[12]

Both approaches – Stephen's British view and Murphy's American view – are problematic. If historical matters are relevant to the meaning of section 116, then surely the starting point is not phases of English history or American purposes. The starting point must be Australian history: how and why section 116 was included in the *Australian Constitution.*

* * *

The Australian history of section 116 has a broader Australian context. The history of section 116 can be understood properly only in the context of Federation Australia's broader constitutional and legal culture. In his work on South Africa's legal culture, Martin Chanock described this culture as

> a set of assumptions, a way of doing things, a repertoire of language, of legal forms and institutional practices. As with all aspects of culture, it changes in response to new situations, but it also reproduces itself; its new responses fit into its existing forms . . . A legal culture embodies . . . a narrative, encompassing both past and future, which gives meaning to thought and actions.[13]

The relevant thought and action in this book concerns the inclusion of section 116 in the *Australian Constitution.*

The American angle to the story is not just that section 116 adopts American constitutional language. As this book explains in some detail, the leading Seventh Day Adventists who led the public debate in favour of a constitutional provision limiting the Federal Government's power in respect of religion were Americans and made arguments based on American experience. American experience and precedents also feature heavily in the legal argument for adopting section 116 made in the Federal Convention that drafted the *Australian Constitution.*

Despite the American angle to the story of section 116, Australian legal culture at the time of Federation was very different to American legal culture at the time of the American Revolution and the drafting of the *United States Constitution* in the 1780s. Three important contrasts in cultural values help explain the Australian cultural context of section 116's history. Australian constitutionalism did not give conceptual primacy to individual rights in the way that American constitutionalism did. Australian constitutionalism was not deeply suspicious of governmental power in the way that American constitutionalism was. Australian constitutionalism was more pragmatic than the theorised American constitutionalism.

In a classic history of the American Revolution, Edward Countryman wrote of the prevailing ideology of rights among Americans of the time.[14] Other scholars have written

11 Ibid 631–2.

12 Ibid 632.

13 Martin Chanock, *The Making of South African Legal Culture, 1902–1936: Fear, Favour and Prejudice* (Cambridge University Press, 2001) 23.

14 Edward Countryman, *The American Revolution* (Hill and Wang, 1985) 218.

of how the revolution was justified 'by appealing to a powerful language of rights'[15] and how the concept of rights was the 'central political philosophy' of the Revolution.[16] Moreover, the framers of the *United States Constitution* understood that a central purpose of a written constitution was protecting rights.[17]

Whilst the *United States Constitution* arose from a constitutional culture giving primacy to individual rights and in which rights discourse was prominent, the same was not true of the *Australian Constitution.* William Harrison Moore wrote in one of the first works on the *Australian Constitution*, entitled *The Constitution of the Commonwealth of Australia*: 'The great underlying principle is that the rights of individuals are sufficiently secured by ensuring, as far as possible, to each a share, and an equal share, in political power.'[18]

Even taking into account the experiences of people like Robert Shannon, there was nothing in recent Australian history at the time of drafting the *Australian Constitution*, as there was in recent American history at the time of drafting the *United States Constitution*, to encourage any widespread concern for individual rights.

Books like A V Dicey's *Introduction to the Study of the Law of the Constitution*[19] and James Bryce's *The American Commonwealth*,[20] read by the framers of the *Australian Constitution*, also dismissed the importance of rights discourse. Dicey was dismissive of constitutional declarations of rights, writing that the 'proclamation in a constitution or charter of the right to personal freedom, or indeed of any other right, gives of itself but slight security that the right has more than a nominal existence.'[21] For Dicey, 'the dominant characteristic of our [i.e. British] political institutions'[22] was parliamentary sovereignty, and it was the rule of law and the common law that served to protect the rights of individuals not constitutional declarations.

Bryce's work has been described as '[b]y far the most influential text that the framers digested' and as 'a vehicle by which the opinions of many members of the Conventions were shaped.'[23] In *The American Commonwealth*, Bryce dealt only briefly with the United States Bill of Rights and considered it an anachronism.[24] He thought that Americans had an unnecessary 'fondness for the enunciation of the general maxims of political freedom.'[25] Bryce also considered that a Bill of Rights would be 'inconvenient' in the British system of parliamentary government,[26] which the Australians were concerned to adopt.

15 Eric Slauter, 'Rights' in Edward G Gray and Jane Kamensky, *The Oxford Handbook to The American Revolution* (Oxford University Press, 2013) 447, 447.
16 Ibid 456.
17 Howard Gillman, Mark A Graber and Keith E Whittington, *American Constitutionalism* (Oxford University Press, 2013) vol 1, 55; Howard Gillman, Mark A Graber and Keith E Whittington, *American Constitutionalism* (Oxford University Press, 2013) vol 2, 83.
18 William Harrison Moore, *The Constitution of the Commonwealth of Australia* (John Murray, 1902) 329.
19 A V Dicey, *Introduction to the Study of the Law of the Constitution* (Macmillan, 4th ed, 1893).
20 James Bryce, *The American Commonwealth* (Macmillan, 2nd ed, 1891).
21 Dicey, above n 19, 194.
22 Ibid 37.
23 John Williams, 'The Emergence of the Commonwealth Constitution' in HP Lee and George Winterton (eds), *Australian Constitutional Landmarks* (Cambridge University Press, 2003) 1, 24.
24 James Bryce, *The American Commonwealth* (Macmillan, 2nd ed, 1891) vol 1, 423.
25 Ibid.
26 Ibid.

A second and related difference between Australian and American constitutionalism was the suspicion with which governmental power was viewed. American constitutionalism was broadly suspicious of governmental power, viewing it as inherently dangerous, whereas Australian constitutionalism did not view governmental power as inherently dangerous, seeing it rather as a vehicle for social progress. In 1902, the New Zealander William Pember Reeves published a two-volume work entitled *State Experiments in Australia and New Zealand* giving an account of what were for the time radical and experimental laws enacted in the Australian colonies and New Zealand. In it, he contrasted what he called the 'colonial governmentalism'[27] of the nineteenth century Australian colonies and New Zealand, involving demands for governmental activity and interference in economic and social activity, with the individualism of the North American colonies in the eighteenth century, involving 'that distrust of a strong, interfering central authority which has been so marked a feature of American democracy.'[28]

The third relevant feature of American constitutionalism that stands out for its contrast with Australian constitutionalism is that American constitutionalism was theorised or philosophical in nature whereas Australian constitutionalism was more pragmatic than theorised. In the classic *The Framing of the Constitution of the United States*, Max Farrand wrote that the *United States Constitution* was written during 'a time when men indulged in philosophical speculation and in political theorizing.'[29] One scholar has written that '[i]deas were the weapons with which Englishmen and Americans fought for a decade before they resorted to arms.'[30] The success of the Revolution meant that, as Alexander Hamilton wrote in *The Federalist No 1* (written to advocate in favour of ratification of the *United States Constitution*), Americans were 'establishing good government from reflection and choice' rather than continuing a form of government brought about by 'accident and force.'[31]

In contrast to the American situation, Australian constitutionalism was more pragmatic than theorised. As Leslie Zines has written, those who framed the *Australian Constitution* 'did not engage in theorising about the nature of the federation they were creating.'[32] Kennett bluntly explains that '[a] random dip into the volumes of the Convention Debates . . . is more likely to reveal intense debate about railways or revenue than political philosophy.'[33] Even if these are broad generalisations, they reflect a key feature of Australian constitutional culture that contrasts with the deep philosophical thinking undertaken by many of those who framed the *United States Constitution.*

It is in this constitutional cultural context that the story of section 116 takes place.

27 William Pember Reeves, *Social Experiments in Australia and New Zealand* (Cambridge University Press, first published 1902, 2011 ed) vol 1, 61.

28 Ibid 61–2.

29 Max Farrand, *The Framing of the Constitution of the United States* (Yale University Press, 1913) 52.

30 John C Miller, *Origins of the American Revolution* (Stanford University Press, 1966) 167.

31 Alexander Hamilton, 'Federalist No 1' in Terence Ball (ed), *The Federalist with Letters of 'Brutus'* (Cambridge University Press, 2003) 1, 1.

32 Leslie Zines, 'Changing Attitudes to Federalism and its Purpose' in Robert French, Geoffrey Lindell and Cheryl Saunders (eds), *Reflections on the Australian Constitution* (Federation Press, 2003) 86, 86.

33 Geoffrey Kennett, 'Individual Rights, the High Court and the Constitution' (1994) 19 *Melbourne University Law Review* 581, 581–2.

2 Arguing for a religious character to the Australian Constitution

A vague craving for official recognition of the authority of God

'I found some of my friends uneasy on account of what they describe as the secular character of the Australian State', Robert William Dale wrote in *Impressions of Australia*, a book describing his visit to Australia in 1887.[1] Dale was a leading English Congregationalist church leader and by 'friends' Dale meant the Australian church leaders of various denominations he met with during his trip. 'They would strongly resist any attempt to establish or endow a Church', Dale told his readers, 'but they have a vague craving for what they describe as a formal and public recognition by the State of the authority of God.'

That vague craving had manifested itself in many ways in colonial Australia.[2] It included agitation and lobbying directed to colonial politicians for the appointment of days of humiliation and days of prayer for the relief of drought. Such approaches were sometimes acceded to, though mostly to placate persistent church leaders rather than out of any genuine official support for the idea. As Robert Shannon found out, it included lobbying for the enforcement of old Sunday observance laws. It also included agitation that the opening of significant public celebrations should commence with prayers; the celebration of Queen Victoria's jubilee in 1887 and the 1888 Centennial International Exhibition in Victoria celebrating the centenary of the arrival of the First Fleet are examples.

Among the church leaders agitating that the Centennial International Exhibition be opened with a religious ceremony was the Scottish-born Victorian Congregationalist leader Alexander Gosman. In address to the Congregational Union in Geelong in 1888, Gosman suggested opening the Exhibition with 'some simple and comprehensive religious ceremony' in which the representatives of the churches would 'act for the time being as the high priests of the nation.' 'While then we are opposed to all forms of State churchism', Gosman told his audience, 'we are as firmly convinced that State religion is not only desirable but necessary.'[3]

1 Robert William Dale, *Impressions of Australia* (Hodder and Stoughton, 1889) 261–2.

2 See Walter Phillips, *Defending "A Christian Country": Churchman and Society in New South Wales in the 1880s and After* (University of Queensland Press, 1981) ch 9.

3 'State Education', *Christian Colonist* (Adelaide), 29 June 1886, 6.

Gosman made a similar argument in a paper he presented at the 1887 conference celebrating the jubilee of Congregationalism in South Australia.[4] In part, the paper discussed 'the relation of the State to religion and to the Churches', a distinction that was important for Gosman. Gosman rejected the idea that the state had nothing to do with religion. He thought it proper that the state had 'disestablished that portion of the Church formerly endowed and exclusively recognized by it.' However, in Gosman's view, this was not a reason for the state to cease being religious. Indeed, Gosman said that should the churches withdraw from political affairs, it might result in 'the tide of atheistic secularism that is threatening to engulf the nations of Europe com[ing] in upon us like a flood and sap[ping] the foundations of civilization that has taken centuries to build up.' It was dangerous, Gosman said, 'to claim that "the State has nothing to do with religion"' because a state that was not religious was not simply '*non*-religious' but '*ir*-religious.'

Gosman also saw a political benefit in a religious state. '[I]f the State is religious,' Gosman explained, 'the existence of the Churches cannot be ignored, and if the Churches cannot be ignored, we cannot be ignored.' The 'we' to whom Gosman referred were religious leaders.

Gosman sought to put theory into practice at the Bathurst's People Convention in November 1896. The Bathurst branch of the Australasian Federation League organised a 'People's Convention' to popularise the cause of Federation and invited leading politicians and religious leaders, including Gosman, to participate. The Convention's task was to write and debate a draft constitution for Australia.

Before the start of the Convention, Gosman wrote to the organisers asking that a motion he had prepared about the authority of God be dealt with as part of the Convention's opening formalities.[5] Gosman's motion read:

> That this Convention of the people, acknowledging the existence of a widespread belief in the government of the world by Divine Providence, desires to commend the cause of Australian Federation to the wisdom and piety of the people; that the Supreme Ruler may be invoked to further, if it please Him, the Federal movement, and so to guide and direct the course of events that Australian Unity may rest upon an enlightened public opinion, and on a solid foundation of righteousness, the only guarantee for the creation and continuance of national prosperity and peace.[6]

'I beg to submit the above resolution to be disposed of in any way the Committee may determine', Gosman wrote to the organising committee. 'My own opinion is that it should be read by the *chairman* – approval to be indicated by standing, either before or immediately after the national anthem. It would be better to be divested of any *personal* aspect.'

4 Alexander Gosman, 'Imperial Federation and Congregationalism' in *Jubilee of Congregationalism in South Australia: Report of the Intercolonial Conference Held in Adelaide, September 1887* (WR Thomas & Co, 1887) 82–5.

5 Gosman to Organising Committee, 'The Recognition of the Supreme Being – Resolution as Originally Drafted', undated, Astley Papers, CY3431, Mitchell Library, Sydney.

6 *Proceedings of the People's Federal Convention, Bathurst, November 1896* (Gordon and Gotch, 1896) 20–1.

Gosman suggested the unusual procedural manoeuvre because he was fully aware that the substance of his motion would be controversial. Gosman's plan was clever. As one historian has put it, '[i]n one step, critics would be utterly disarmed by not wishing to appear unpatriotic [since opposing the motion would require people to sit down when everyone else was standing for the national anthem], while the 'recognition' proposal would at once acquire a patriotic and national aura.'[7] Unfortunately for Gosman, the Convention organisers did not agree to his proposal and Gosman was left to move the motion himself in the ordinary way when an opportunity arose.

That opportunity presented itself on the second day of the Convention. The report of the Convention's proceedings simply notes: 'A point of order having been raised, and some discussion following, the motion was withdrawn.'[8] The report put the situation somewhat mildly. Gosman was right to assume that his motion would stir a strong reaction. The *Sydney Mail and New South Wales Advertiser* described 'fierce discussion' and the 'strong resentment' of many delegates that Gosman had sought to move such a motion.[9] The Mayor of Ballarat 'disgustedly described the convention as "wasting time with frivolous talk."' The Mayor of Wickham 'objected in a loud voice of deadly fluency' to Gosman's motion suggesting that declarations of religious belief 'should be left to the clerics, who might as a preliminary federate the churches.' To applause, a member of the New South Wales Parliament said that delegates 'might as well be called upon to express belief in a solar system.'[10] The *Sydney Morning Herald* called Gosman's motion a 'debating society question.'[11]

Before Gosman withdrew his motion, John Quick, a lawyer, Federation activist and former Victorian politician, offered his opinion that Gosman's motion was in order and a matter relevant to the drafting of a constitution.[12] Quick's opinion is noteworthy because Quick would later find himself at the Australasian Federal Convention of 1897–8 and in a similar position to Gosman with the failure of his own attempt to officially recognise God.

The failure of Gosman's motion at the Bathurst People's Convention did not completely eliminate religion from the proceedings. On the final day of proceedings, one of the other religious leaders in attendance succeeded in having his motion adopted unanimously by the approximately one quarter of delegates who remained in attendance.[13] That motion read: That this Convention, acknowledging the government of this world by Divine Providence, commends the cause of Australian Federation to all those who desire to promote the material, moral, and social advancement of the people of Australia.[14]

7 Richard Ely, *Unto God and Caesar: Religious Issues in the Emerging Commonwealth, 1891–1906* (Melbourne University Press, 1976) 10.
8 *Proceedings of the People's Federal Convention, Bathurst, November 1896* (Gordon and Gotch, 1896) 21.
9 'The People's Federal Convention. A Week at Bathurst' *Sydney Mail and New South Wales Advertiser* (Sydney) 28 November 1896, 1140.
10 Untitled Article, *Sydney Morning Herald* (Sydney) 18 November 1896, 7; 'The People's Federal Convention. A Week at Bathurst' *Sydney Mail and New South Wales Advertiser* (Sydney) 28 November 1896, 1140.
11 Untitled Article, *Sydney Morning Herald* (Sydney) 18 November 1896, 7.
12 Ely, above n 7, 11.
13 Ibid.
14 *Proceedings of the People's Federal Convention, Bathurst, November 1896* (Gordon and Gotch, 1896) 39.

There is an important difference between this motion and Gosman's motion. The successful motion did not *invoke* God in connection with government as Gosman's motion had done. Invoking God in connection with government or the *Constitution* might imply that religion and God had some official or legal significance. Concern about the idea of invoking God in connection with government would later also prove important at the Federal Convention of 1897–8.

The subheading in the report of the Convention's proceedings under which Gosman's motion is recorded is 'Recognition of a Supreme Being.' This, it seems, is one of the first references to the 'recognition' of God in respect of the *Constitution*. Gosman's letter to the organising committee was headed 'The Recognition of the Supreme Being.'[15] Although not fully successful at Bathurst, a serious movement seeking to achieve constitutional recognition of God had begun.

The New South Wales Council of Churches and the campaign for constitutional recognition of God

One of the most symbolic issues in the church leaders' craving for public recognition was the question of Sunday observance laws. The lax enforcement of Sunday laws prompted church leaders, acting across denominational boundaries, to form various lobby groups.

That there was a proliferation of such organisations demonstrates a firm desire on the part of religious leaders that they should be heard in public policy debates and their views respected and adopted in public policy. Indeed, in large measure the concern of religious leaders about Sunday observance reflected not only their beliefs about the Sabbath but also the 'seeming decline in church power over public morality' resulting from a 'widening gap between a secular society and a socially conservative religious establishment.'[16] As Gosman had indicated, official recognition of religion was partly a question concerning the status and influence of religious leaders.

Concern about the lax enforcement of Sunday observance laws was one of the key drivers behind the establishment of the New South Wales Council of Churches. It was the New South Wales Council of Churches that was ultimately responsible for the successful campaign to have God recognised in the Constitution and which in turn prompted the successful campaign for a provision separating religion and government.

The New South Wales Council of Churches was formed in 1889 'chiefly to resist all further attempts to secularize Sunday and, if possible, to have existing infringements of the Sunday laws suppressed.'[17] The formation of the New South Wales Council of Churches was an initiative of the Presbyterian General Assembly and the council included representatives of the Anglican, Presbyterian, Wesleyan, Primitive Methodist, Congregationalist and Baptist denominations, which were the largest Protestant denominations in the colony. In the following years, similar councils were established in the other colonies.

15 Gosman to Organising Committee, 'The Recognition of the Supreme Being – Resolution as Originally Drafted', undated, Astley Papers, CY3431, Mitchell Library, Sydney.

16 Michael Hogan, *The Sectarian Strand: Religion in Australian History* (Penguin Books, 1987) 97.

17 Walter Phillips, *Defending "A Christian Country": Churchman and Society in New South Wales in the 1880s and After* (University of Queensland Press, 1981) 188.

Elections were scheduled for early 1897 to elect delegates to the official Australasian Federal Convention that would first meet in late 1897 and be tasked with drafting a Constitution for a federated Australia. For the New South Wales Council of Churches, a new Constitution was an opportunity for a formal and public recognition by the state of the authority of God. The council had ideas about putting religion in the Constitution.

At its regular meeting in January 1897, the Council of Churches decided to schedule a special meeting for February to discuss approaching the Federal Convention to secure a formal acknowledgment of God as the ruler of nations in the Constitution.[18] '[T]his Council considers it of utmost importance', the council resolved, 'that in the Constitution for a federated Australia there should be a recognition of God as the Supreme Ruler, and that provision be made for such acts of common worship as should be deemed suitable for a legislative body.'

The council also established a subcommittee to inquire into American and Canadian practice and to suggest a way forward.[19] The sub-committee reported at another special meeting in March. The sub-committee reported that in both jurisdictions chaplains recited prayers at the start of each day's sitting of the legislature.[20] The sub-committee also recommended that the Council begin a campaign to obtain signatures for a petition to be sent to the Federal Convention.[21] The text of the petition would read:

1 That in the preamble of the Constitution of the Australian Commonwealth it be recognised that God is the Supreme Ruler of the World, and the ultimate source of all law and authority in nations.
2 That there also be embodied in the said Constitution, or in the standing orders of the Federal Parliament, a provision that each daily session of the Upper and Lower Houses of the Federal Parliament be opened with a prayer by the President and Speaker, or by a chaplain.
3 That the Governor-General be empowered to appoint days of national thanksgiving and humiliation.

The council unanimously adopted the recommendation. The subcommittee also made recommendations about strategies to maximise the number of signatures obtained. Pro forma petitions should be sent to ministers of religion throughout New South Wales who would be asked to obtain signatures at Sunday church services and to the heads of denominations in other colonies asking them to circulate similar petitions.

The petition campaign was enthusiastically supported by the Councils of Churches in the other colonies. Having received correspondence from the New South Wales Council of Churches with a copy of the petition, the South Australian Council of Churches, for example,

18 'The Council of Churches', *Sydney Morning Herald* (Sydney), 4 March 1897, 6.
19 Ibid.
20 Ibid.
21 'Council of Churches. Some Recommendations', *The Inquirer & Commercial News* (Perth), 5 March 1897, 16; 'Meeting of the Council of Churches. Recommendations to the Convention', *The Advertiser* (Adelaide), 3 March 1897, 6; 'The Council of Churches', *Sydney Morning Herald* (Sydney), 4 March 1897, 6.

resolved at its meeting on 18 March 1897 also to circulate the petition.[22] It resolved to forward a copy of the New South Wales petition to all the ministers of its various member denominations as well as other religious groups not affiliated with the Council.

Along with the pro forma petitions, the South Australian Council wrote to ministers with instructions. 'Rev. and Dear Sir', the letter read, '[t]he Council of the Churches in New South Wales has initiated a movement for securing the national recognition of God in the Federal Constitution, and the Council of the Churches in South Australia, and the Bishop of Adelaide have promised hearty co-operation.' The letter continued: 'Feeling sure of your sympathy in this very important matter we forward herewith a petition, and desire to ask you to use every effort to get it signed by as many as possible of the members and adherents of your Church.' 'Any adult can sign', ministers were helpfully told. 'Kindly return it not later than Monday, March 29 to Mr H.J. Holden, Hon. Secretary of the Council of Churches, as above. We are, yours in the service of Christ, [Signed].'

The plan for obtaining signatures was straightforward, and the short return time was therefore no problem. Signatures would be solicited by ministers either during or at the close of services. Because this is precisely the time at which worshippers would be least likely to decline an invitation by their minister to sign, the strategy involved 'a mild but real form of situational duress.'[23] That strategy was highly effective in obtaining large numbers of signatures. However, the strategy had a built-in weakness: the situational duress involved 'weakened [the petitions'] validity as an indicator of electoral feeling.'[24]

The idea that recognising God should occur in the preamble was not an original idea on the part of the New South Wales Council of Churches. The Catholic Archbishop of Sydney, Cardinal Patrick Moran, had suggested it sometime before. Moran had stood unsuccessfully for election as a New South Wales delegate to the Federal Convention. In an 'Address to Electors' published in the Sydney Catholic newspaper the *Freeman's Journal*, Moran explained that he wanted the preamble to assert the supremacy of religion. Moran wrote:

> I would wish, therefore, to see inserted in the preamble to our Constitution that 'Religion is the basis of our Commonwealth and of its laws.' And I would add that, 'In accordance with the spirit of religion, a genuine liberty of conscience is the birthright of every Australian citizen, and the free exercise of Divine worship, insofar as may be consistent with public order and public morality, shall be accorded to all.'[25]

Moran's candidature caused a 'sectarian explosion', with Protestant leaders, who would have been sympathetic to Moran's stated aim of securing an acknowledgment of religion in the *Constitution*, actively campaigning against him.[26] Others, including Catholics, were

22 'National Recognition of the Supreme Being. The Council of Churches', *The Australian Register* (Adelaide) 19 March 1897, 3.

23 Ely, above n 7, 22.

24 Ibid 22.

25 Patrick Moran, 'Address to Electors', *Freeman's Journal* (Sydney), 20 February 1897, 17.

26 Patrick O'Farrell, *The Catholic Church and Community: An Australian History* (New South Wales University Press, 1992) 268.

doubtful about the propriety of a church leader being elected.[27] Moran was not elected, polling fourteenth of 50 candidates for 10 available positions.

The New South Wales Council of Churches might well have borrowed Moran's idea for the constitutional recognition of God to occur in the preamble. The sub-committee which developed the proposal was instructed to look to American and Canadian practice, but neither the *United States Constitution* nor the *British North America Act 1867* contains a reference to God. Indeed, the sub-committee's report of American and Canadian practice, which was reproduced in the *Daily Telegraph* of 3 March 1897, deals only with the issue of legislative prayer.[28] So the idea must have come from elsewhere.

Public commentary at the time attributed it to Moran. When one attempt at the Federal Convention to insert a recognition of God in the constitutional preamble failed, one proponent of that course suggested in a public lecture that it failed because the idea had first been raised by Moran.[29]

The church leaders' motives

There is something odd about Protestant church leaders seeking a constitutional recognition of God. In an unpublished piece of writing,[30] Andrew Inglis Clark wrote that the whole idea was Roman Catholic in nature and was pursuing a 'horrible purpose.' Clark was Tasmanian Attorney-General when the New South Wales Council of Churches decided to embark on its campaign for constitutional recognition and later the author of an important early commentary on the *Australian Constitution.*

Clark pointed out that the way in which the Roman Catholic Church 'determines the truth or falsity of any theological doctrine or proposition is the vote of the majority of the persons who are alleged to be divinely appointed guides and instructors of the faithful members of the Church.' Protestantism, on the other hand, emphatically rejects this notion. 'The fundamental doctrine of Protestantism', Clark wrote, 'is the essentially and absolutely individualistic character of relations of each human soul to its creator.' Even though many Protestant countries have violated this principle throughout history, Protestantism does not 'recognize any power or authority in any majority of men to impose any confession or declaration of religious doctrine or belief upon a minority of the same nation or community.'

Clark explained that any 'doctrine of a corporate responsibility of all the members of a community for the religious opinions of each of them' is the antithesis of Protestantism. Yet, this is exactly what the idea of a constitutional recognition of God involves.

27 See Ely, above n 7, ch 2; O'Farrell, above n 26, 267–71.

28 'The Council of Churches', *Daily Telegraph* (Sydney), 3 March 1897, 8.

29 'The Commonwealth Bill. Lecture by Professor Harper', *Sydney Morning Herald* (Sydney), 3 August 1897, 5.

30 Andrew Inglis Clark, 'The Preamble to the Constitution of the Commonwealth of Australia', Clark Family Papers, University of Tasmania Archives, C4/H13. The essay is printed in Richard Ely, 'Andrew Inglis Clark on the Preamble of the Australian Constitution' (2001) 75 *Australian Law Journal* 36.

In pointing out the inconsistency of Protestants advocating for constitutional recognition of God, Clark sounded a warning:

> When a single person or any number of persons being a minority of the members of a Protestant church differ in opinion from the majority, the principle of Protestantism justifies their secession from the Church with whose doctrines they have ceased to be in sympathy. But to require a single citizen or a minority of citizens to expatriate themselves in order to escape from membership of a nation or community which by a vote of a majority of its members undertakes to make a corporate confession of any religious doctrine or belief is to use political, and consequently physical, force in the name of religion as clearly and directly as it was at any time used for the burning or expulsion of heretics.

For Clark, the fact that constitutional recognition of God did not involve using physical force against those who did not agree with constitutional recognition of God did not lessen the objection. He explained:

> The fact that physical force is not used in this instance for any such horrible purpose as that for which it has been used in other cases does not remove the objection to the use of it in the service of religion, because if the use of it in the service of religion is admitted to be justifiable in any case, the use of it for persecution of heretical opinions on religion will depend entirely on the extent to which the passions and prejudices of a community may at any time become excited and alarmed upon questions of religious belief and doctrine.

The theological inconsistency Clark pointed out is an example of what a modern Australian historian describes as 'civic Protestantism.'[31] Throughout modern Australian history, including in the late nineteenth century when the constitutional recognition of God debate was taking place, civic Protestantism – the idea 'that the marriage of law and morality was made in heaven' – has been the dominant form of Protestant social thinking. Civic Protestantism sometimes finds it difficult 'to distinguish between morality and legality.' For this reason, it is not surprising that Australian social and political history is littered with examples of Protestant religious groups seeking to influence the law in areas of 'morality' where their own rights to freely practise their own religion are not at stake.[32] The campaign for constitutional recognition of God is an instance of this sort of civic Protestantism in practice.

None of this is to say that Protestant church leaders opposed the idea of religious freedom. At least at a superficial level, they fully supported the idea. The draft constitution produced by the Bathurst People's Convention included a prohibition on the States making laws prohibiting the free exercise of religion, but not on the Federal Government making

31 Richard Ely, 'Protestantism in Australian History: An Interpretative Sketch' (1989) 5 *Lucas: An Evangelical History Review* 11, 15. See also Richard Ely, 'The Forgotten Nationalism: Australian Civic Protestantism in the Second World War' (1987) 11(20) *Journal of Australian Studies* 59.

32 Ely, 'Protestantism in Australian History', above n 31, 19.

such laws.[33] The provision was adopted without debate. Gosman and other church leaders at the People's Convention did not object to such a provision. It was uncontroversial. In his paper at the 1887 conference celebrating the jubilee of Congregationalism in South Australia, Gosman claimed that a state religion – which is part of what Gosman was trying to achieve by a constitutional recognition of God – was 'by no means opposed to a liberal and enlightened nonconformity.'

Of course, what people like Gosman understood to be religious freedom might not accord with what is nowadays understood as religious freedom. Gosman was, unsurprisingly, very much in favour of Sunday observance laws and agitated for their enactment and enforcement. The point, however, is that Gosman did not appear to view either constitutional recognition of God or a state religion as inconsistent with religious freedom. Given the Councils of Churches led the campaign for constitutional recognition of God and were made up of representatives from different denominations, the same was generally true of other Protestant church leaders.

What Clark's analysis confirms is that the constitutional recognition of God campaign was not the result of any deep theological convictions or deep intellectual thought. The campaign was about politics, status and power: another instance of what Dale described as church leaders' vague craving for formal and public recognition of the authority of God. Dale was not convinced that such recognition would be meaningful. Dale told readers of his *Impressions of Australia* that 'such a "formal and public" recognition would leave the State just as secular as it is now' unless there was 'practical recognition of the spirit and the laws of Christian ethics in the actual business of the State.'[34] The churches knew this too, and saw constitutional recognition of God as a step in that direction.

As the South Australian Council of Churches circular indicated, the question of constitutional recognition of God was a 'very important matter' to the churches. There were mixed motives. For some it was a matter of ensuring the success of the Constitution and the Commonwealth. At a public meeting in Sydney, one Anglican church leader, Archdeacon Langley, said it was 'of the utmost importance that the foundations of [the] nation should be laid broad, wide, deep, and sound so that sound principles and ripe Government might follow.' He said that the success of England was 'associated with the recognition of God and true religion', commenting additionally that what he called the failure of the French Revolution was 'because the people of France failed to recognise God'.[35] This was not a completely eccentric view since religious leaders often believed that a lack of religiosity was a cause of adversity, and the failure of the French Revolution was regularly referred to in the public debates about constitutional recognition of God. As one historian observes:

> Religious men of that age generally believed in the overruling providence of God, and some churchmen did not hesitate to link the drought, depression and social

33 The draft is published in *Proceedings of the People's Federal Convention, Bathurst, November 1896* (Gordon and Gotch, 1896) 46–76.

34 Dale, above n 1, 261.

35 'The Commonwealth Constitution. Recognition of God', *Sydney Morning Herald* (Sydney), 6 July 1897, 6.

> unrest of the early 1890s with man's neglect of God . . . [This] belief in divine providence was sufficiently strong for religious people to expect some blessing from God on their nation, or at least to be genuinely concerned at a refusal to acknowledge his might.[36]

Similarly, an Anglican newspaper in Adelaide, the *Church News*, wrote that Australian Anglicans desired the constitutional preamble to include words 'setting forth our national creed.'[37]

To some extent and for some people constitutional recognition of God was about 'national' identity. The 26 March 1897 edition of the *Church News* in Adelaide quoted from a variant form of the standard petition which desired 'that in the preamble of the Bill which frames the Federal Constitution, some words may be inserted setting forth our national creed.'[38] There was, such comments show, a concern among some for 'the endorsement of religious values and moral standards' through constitutional recognition of God.[39]

For at least one of the recognition campaign leaders, constitutional recognition of God was about setting 'the tone of national life.'[40] In a speech, later published as a pamphlet, the Presbyterian Andrew Harper, who was one of the leaders of the recognition campaign in Victoria, rejected the notion that matters like the opening of parliaments with prayers and acknowledging God in the *Constitution* were 'mere externalities, which neither represent accurately, nor can alter the real state of things' and could not function to make a nation Christian. They are not 'neutral', Harper said. Rather, for Harper, such things 'have power, which cannot be disregarded, to shape and mould the future. They influence most potently men's conception of what they are and ought to be.' In other words, for Harper recognition of God was about 'national' identity.

For others, constitutional recognition of God was to be pursued for reasons much closer to Gosman's thinking. The *Presbyterian Monthly* editorialised that each of the Australian colonies 'has a history which runs back always to some point at which the supremacy of God was acknowledged in some way.'[41] Without a constitutional recognition of God, the Commonwealth 'will have absolutely no traditions of this kind.' If an 'explicit reference to God in the Constitution was not insisted on the omission will in the future be the ground for asserting that our new Constitution was deliberately founded on the negation of God.'

There was also, in the minds of some of the proponents, the belief that a religious preamble would have actual legal effect and not only amount to establishing a state religion but also authorise federal legislation concerning religion. In this vein was the *Australian*

36 Phillips, *Defending "A Christian Country"*, above n 17, 260.

37 Quoted in W A Colcord, *The Rights of Man, Or Religion and the State: An Exposition of the Province of Civil Government and Religion, and a Plea for Civil and Religious Liberty* (Echo Publishing Company, 1913) 163.

38 Quoted in Colcord, above n 37, 163.

39 Phillips, *Defending "A Christian Country"*, above n 17, 261.

40 Andrew Harper, *Australia Without God: An Appeal to the Churches of Australia to Secure an Acknowledgement of God in the Australian Constitution* (Hutchinson, 1897) 6.

41 Quoted in Ely, *Unto God and Caesar*, above n 7, 38.

Christian World's comment that in seeking constitutional recognition of God, 'we simply ask the Commonwealth to formally say that God is the great Governor-General.'[42] For Harper, constitutional recognition of God would be a preventative measure against 'the danger of permitting the secularisation of our laws.'[43]

In far stronger terms the *Australian Christian World* commented that recognition would amount to the union of church and state as a constitutional principle. Following an early refusal by the Federal Convention to accede to the churches' request for a constitutional recognition of God, that newspaper editorialised: '[O]ur Federationists seem unable to acknowledge that God is the Supreme Ruler of all Nations, not to speak of framing a Constitution with the union of the Church and State as one of its planks.'[44]

The belief that constitutional recognition of God would authorise legislation concerning religion was also held by the chief opponents of recognition, the Seventh Day Adventists, but in their case not as a hope.

42 *Australian Christian World*, 21 May 1897 quoted in Ely, *Unto God and Caesar*, above n 7, 39.

43 Harper, above n 40, 19.

44 Quoted in Phillips, *Defending "A Christian Country"*, above n 17, 258.

3 Arguing against a religious character to the Australian Constitution

The Seventh Day Adventists sound a warning

'Let the people beware. There is danger here', exclaimed the *Bible Echo* newspaper of 22 February 1897.[1] 'Both are in favour of uniting church and state.' The newspaper was sounding a warning about the consequences of the New South Wales Council of Churches' announcement that it would campaign for constitutional recognition of God and Cardinal Moran's earlier speeches supporting the same idea.

The *Bible Echo* was a Seventh Day Adventist newspaper whose target market was Seventh Day Adventists rather than the general population.[2] The Seventh Day Adventists originated in the United States.[3] They were a small fringe Protestant denomination with fewer than 2,000 adherents in the Australian colonies in 1897 compared to a total population of about 3.6 million people.[4] Their influence in their eventually successful campaign for a provision in the *Australian Constitution* limiting the Federal Parliament's power in respect of religion was rather out of proportion to their numbers in colonial Australia. Census statistics record many more adherents for the larger Protestant denominations. In 1901, there were 1,234,213 Anglicans, 351,920 Presbyterians, 397,366 Methodists, 72,278 Baptists, 72,715 Congregationalists, and 70,826 Lutherans in Australia. There were also 705,407 Roman Catholics in 1891. Jews and people listing 'no religion' on their census forms also significantly outnumbered the Seventh Day Adventists.

The Seventh Day Adventists had what many people considered peculiar beliefs about various matters. One of the more famous of those beliefs concerns the religious importance of healthy eating, which led the Seventh Day Adventists to establish the food manufacturer now known as Sanitarium, the maker of popular breakfast cereals. One of the Adventists' more problematic beliefs concerns the observance of Saturday and not Sunday as the Sabbath. What caused them particular trouble – as Robert Shannon could attest – was their additional strong belief in freedom to work on Sundays.

1 'The Council of Churches', *Bible Echo* (Melbourne), 22 February 1897, 60.

2 'Religious Legislation or Religious Liberty: Which Shall it Be?', *Bible Echo* (Melbourne), 29 March 1897, 97. Page numbers in the *Bible Echo* continue from the previous edition.

3 Interestingly, Ellen White, a prophet-type figure in the Seventh Day Adventist church, who is said to have received a divinely-inspired vision of God's plans for humanity and whose writings occupy an important place in Adventist thinking, moved to Australia in 1891: Richard Ely, *Unto God and Caesar: Religious Issues in the Emerging Commonwealth, 1891–1906* (Melbourne University Press, 1976) 26.

4 Australian Bureau of Statistics, *Australian Historical Population Statistics 2014* (cat. no. 3105.0.65.001), <http://www.abs.gov.au/AUSSTATS%5Cabs@.nsf/0/632CDC28637CF57ECA256F1F0080EBCC?Opendocument> accessed 21 May 2016.

The Seventh Day Adventists in colonial Australia were also experienced political campaigners who had launched various campaigns aimed at the repeal of Sunday observance laws. In order to further their campaigns, the Seventh Day Adventists began the publication of a quarterly magazine called the *Australian Sentinel & Herald of Religious Liberty* (from 1895 the *Southern Sentinel & Herald of Religious Liberty*), targeted at the general population.[5] In the words of one Adventist writer at the time, it

> was issued for the sole purpose of educating public opinion upon the important question of true civil liberty, which at that era of Australian history was being seriously jeopardised by the militancy of such religio-political associations as the Christian Electors' Association [which had been established by the New South Wales Council of Churches to support Christian candidates for parliamentary elections] and other kindred bodies.[6]

The Seventh Day Adventists had their own religio-political official, styled Field Secretary for Religious Liberty, whose role was to lead political campaigns.

'Petitions seem to be much the order of the day just now, especially petitions from religious bodies to state officers and legislative bodies', the *Bible Echo* remarked in March 1897.[7] 'The Council of Churches, both of Sydney and Melbourne, is petitioning the Federal Convention to embody religious measures in the constitution for the proposed Australian commonwealth.' 'It is the old effort over again, to unite church and state, and have religion by law', the *Bible Echo* told its readers. A week later, the *Bible Echo* announced that the Seventh Day Adventists would join the fray of petitions.

The Seventh Day Adventist campaign against constitutional recognition of God

In a front page spread in the *Bible Echo* on 29 March 1897, the Seventh Day Adventists announced their own petition campaign in response the New South Wales Council of Churches' campaign for constitutional recognition of God. Recognising God in the Constitution, the *Bible Echo* wrote, 'would place the Constitution upon a *religious basis*, and lay the foundation for *religious legislation*, the inevitable result of which, as the Dark Ages, the Spanish Inquisition, and all history attest, is to restrict liberty of conscience, prevent the full and free exercise of religious worship, and cause *religious persecution*.' The *Bible Echo* again warned its readers that the necessary consequence of constitutional recognition of God 'would [be to] unite religion and the state.'[8]

'[I]n the interests of religious liberty, in the interests of good government and of the rights of all men,' the *Bible Echo* announced, 'there is being circulated for the consideration and approval of the people of these colonies (New Zealand only excepted), the following . . .'

> We, the undersigned, adult residents of ________ believing that religion and the State should be kept entirely separate, that religious legislation is subversive of good

5 A W Anderson, *Religious Liberty in Australasia: The Attitude of Seventh Day Adventists to Religious Legislation and to Military Service* (Signs Publishing Co, 1917) 8.

6 Ibid 10.

7 'Petitions', *Bible Echo* (Melbourne), 22 March 1897, 96.

8 'Religious Legislation or Religious Liberty: Which Shall it Be?', *Bible Echo* (Melbourne) 29 March 1897, 97.

> government, contrary to the principles of sound religion, and can result only in religious persecution, hereby humbly, but most earnestly, petition your honorable body not to insert any religious clause or measure in the Constitution of the Australian Commonwealth which might be taken as a basis for such legislation; but that a declaration be made in the Constitution stating that neither the Federal Government nor any State Parliament shall make any law respecting religion, or prohibiting the free exercise thereof.

A week later on 6 April 1897, the Federal Convention received the first petition organised by the Seventh Day Adventists. [9] On 7, 12 and 20 April 1897, the Convention received more Seventh Day Adventist petitions.

The Seventh Day Adventist petition was drafted by an American, A G Daniells, who was at the time editor of the *Southern Sentinel & Herald of Liberty.*[10] Daniells was also the president of the Australasian Union Conference, the denomination's governing body. A number of other senior Adventist leaders in Australia had considerable experience in conducting political campaigns in the United States for the Seventh Day Adventists there, particularly in relation to Sunday closing laws.[11]

Unlike the Council of Churches' petitions, the Seventh Day Adventists' petitions did not reveal in their text who was organising them. The historian J A La Nauze, in his classic *The Making of the Australian Constitution*, seems not to have known who organised those petitions.[12] He wrote that the signatories to the counter petitions 'were, after all, merely "adult citizens", not members of organized bodies.' La Nauze did not mention the Seventh Day Adventists. At the time of the petition, however, it did not take long for the identity of the organisers to become public knowledge. A Protestant newspaper, the *Southern Cross*, said of the petitions opposing those from the Councils of Churches: 'It is curious to learn that this petition, that God and religion may be 'ignored', is largely signed by Seventh-day Adventists. This is a new proof that this remarkable body is made up of cranks.'[13]

Unlike the Councils of Churches' methodology for soliciting signatures, the Seventh Day Adventists' methodology avoided any situational coercion. Given their small numbers, the Seventh Day Adventists had little opportunity to attempt situational coercion on a scale that would result in any influential number of signatories to their petitions. The *Bible Echo* invited Seventh Day Adventists to '[s]end for [petition] blanks and get your neighbours and friends to sign it.'[14] This is exactly what happened.

'We trust that most Seventh-day Adventists have the good sense to sign it' the *Bible Echo* explained in an article entitled 'Hard Names v Logic', [15] 'but it has been signed by over 7,000 persons, and there are not as yet 2,000 Seventh-day Adventists in all Australasia.' Refuting the claim of the *Southern Cross* that it was largely Seventh Day Adventists signing the petition, the *Bible Echo* continued: 'The very first signature we obtained to

9 *Official Report of the National Australasian Convention Debates*, Sydney, 6 April 1897, 405.

10 Milton Frederick Krause, *The Seventh Day Adventist Church in Australia: 1885–1900* (MA Thesis, The University of Sydney, 1969) 251; Anderson, above n 5, 12.

11 Ely, above n 3, 28.

12 J A La Nauze, *The Making of the Australian Constitution* (Melbourne University Press, 1972), 225.

13 Quoted in 'Hard Names v Logic', *Bible Echo* (Melbourne), 19 April 1897, 123.

14 'Religious Legislation or Religious Liberty: Which Shall it Be?', *Bible Echo* (Melbourne), 29 March 1897, 97.

15 'Hard Names v Logic', *Bible Echo* (Melbourne), 19 April 1897, 123.

the petition was that of a good Wesleyan brother.' 'The same petition contained the names of Wesleyans, Church of England, Presbyterians, Lutherans, Baptists, and Roman Catholics. Scores and hundreds of nearly all denominations have signed these petitions,' the *Bible Echo* pointed out. 'Are all these 'cranks'?'

Familiar harpings from America

The campaign for constitutional recognition of God seemed familiar to the Seventh Day Adventists. The New South Wales Council of Churches' resolution to pursue constitutional recognition of God 'sounds like the familiar harpings of the National Reform Association and other like organisations in America', said the *Bible Echo* of 22 February 1897.[16] Those organisations, readers were told, 'for the last thirty years and more, have been working with might and main to get 'God in the Constitution', as they call it.' The Seventh Day Adventists in Australia believed that the campaign for constitutional recognition of God was not only inspired by the American God in the Constitution campaign but had similar motivations.

It is not difficult to understand why the Seventh Day Adventists came to that conclusion. The National Reform Association's organisational constitution stated that the Association's purpose was

> To secure such an amendment to the *Constitution of the United States* as will declare the nation's allegiance to Jesus Christ, and its acceptance of the moral laws of the Christian religion, and so indicate that this is a Christian nation, and place all the Christian laws, institutions and usages of our government on an undeniable legal basis in the fundamental law of the land.[17]

'In other words,' the *Bible Echo* explained,[18] 'they wish God recognised in the Constitution that there may a 'legal basis' for 'all the Christian laws, institutions, and usages' in the country.' 'This means, about as plainly words can put it,' the *Bible Echo* continued, 'a foundation for ecclesiastical laws. This is what a religious clause in the Constitution of the United States would mean, and this is what the same thing would mean in the Federal Constitution of Australia.'

The National Reform Association began in the early 1860s with a meeting in Allegheny, Pennsylvania of ministers from eleven denominations. It had originally been called the 'National Association to Secure the Religious Amendment of the United States Constitution' and was sometimes referred to as the Christian Amendment Movement since what they were advocating was popularly called a 'Christian amendment' to the *United States Constitution.*[19] The Association's first petition called for the preamble to the *United States*

16 'The Council of Churches', *Bible Echo* (Melbourne), 22 February 1897, 60.

17 Robert T Handy, *Undermined Establishment: Church-State Relations in America, 1880–1920* (Princeton University Press, first published 1991, 2014 ed) 25–6.

18 'What Religion in the Constitution Means', *Bible Echo* (Melbourne), 26 July 1897, 233.

19 Steven Keith Green, *The National Reform Association and the Religious Amendments to the Constitution, 1864–1876*, (MA Thesis, University of North Carolina at Chapel Hill, 1987); Russell L Hanson, 'Secularizing the American State, 1876–1905', Paper Presented at Indiana University Department of Political Science Political Theory Luncheon, 4–7, http://polisci.indiana.edu/about/news/Hanson_TheoryLuncheon.pdf.

Constitution to be amended to include the words 'humbly acknowledging Almighty God as the source of all authority and power in civil government, the lord Jesus Christ as the Ruler among nations, his revealed will as the supreme law of the land.'[20] The Association was also a strong campaigner for Sabbath observance laws. The Seventh Day Adventists in America were ardent opponents of the Association.

It is not clear whether the New South Wales Council of Churches was aware of National Reform Association's Christian amendment campaigns. The decision to pursue constitutional recognition of God was made before the Council of Churches formed a subcommittee to inquire into American practice, whose report made no mention of such matters. Equally, reports in mainstream newspapers, not just in the *Bible Echo*, at the time of the Australian recognition of God debate showed that Australians knew about attempts to secure a Christian amendment to the *United States Constitution*.[21]

Whatever the Council of Churches knew about the American movement, it is not difficult to understand why the Seventh Day Adventists thought the Council of Churches was inspired by the American events. The Seventh Day Adventists obviously knew about the American situation. Indeed, before coming to Australia A G Daniells, who drafted the Australian petition opposing constitutional recognition, was personally involved in lobbying the United States Congress not to enact laws concerning religion.[22]

What the Adventists feared most was any power on the part of the Commonwealth to enact and enforce Sunday observance laws. They believed that this was the chief motive of the Council of Churches' recognition campaign. On 19 July 1897, the *Bible Echo* told its readers that '[t]his week we have additional evidence that the Council of Churches is a religio-political organisation whose chief aim is to unite church and state and enforce religious dogmas, chiefly the Sunday institution, on the people by law.'[23] The *Bible Echo* then extracted a report from the *Sydney Morning Herald* which reported that following a meeting between the New South Wales Colonial Secretary and the Council of Churches, the Inspector-General of Police issued instructions to the police that the existing Sunday laws were 'to be rigidly enforced.' 'Here is proof of what the church leaders are after in the vociferous clamours for what they are pleased to call a 'recognition of God in the Constitution',' the *Bible Echo* exclaimed. 'They simply want a constitutional basis for enforcing religious observances on the people by law.'[24]

The Seventh Day Adventists' legal reasoning

The Seventh Day Adventists engaged in amateur legal reasoning to reach the conclusion that a constitutional recognition of God would lead to a power to pass laws concerning religion. Although amateur in nature, the reasoning was not without some foundation.

20 T P Stephenson, 'History of the Movement to Secure the Religious Amendment of the Constitution of the United States' in *Proceedings of the National Convention to Secure the Religious Amendment of the Constitution of the United States* (James B Rodgers Co, 1872) vii–viii.

21 E.g., 'Is God to be Confessed in the Constitution?', *South Australian Register* (Adelaide), 17 April 1897, 6; 'Recognition of God', *Sydney Morning Herald* (Sydney), 3 August 1897, 5.

22 E.g. William Addison Blackley (ed), *American State Papers Bearing on Sunday Legislation* (Religious Liberty Association, 1911) 380–9.

23 'Enforcing the Sunday Law', *Bible Echo* (Melbourne), 19 July 1897, 232.

24 Ibid.

'The Constitution is the foundation of the government, the basis of its laws', the *Bible Echo* explained. 'The subjects treated in the Constitution are subjects for legislation. A declaration of religious belief in the Constitution, therefore, lays the foundation for religious legislation. This is as logical as anything can be.'[25] The *Bible Echo* also gave an example of this legal analysis in practice. It referred to a decision of the United States Supreme Court, which the article did not name, declaring that the United States was a Christian nation. The *Bible Echo* claimed that 'the religious leaders of the country . . . by making use of the decision of the Supreme Court . . . succeeded in influencing the Congress of the United States to pass a religious law – a law for the closing of the World's Fair on Sunday.' 'This', the *Bible Echo* concluded, 'demonstrates as clear as the beaming sun, that a religious clause in a Constitution *does* lay a foundation for religious or ecclesiastical laws.[26]

The Supreme Court decision to which the *Bible Echo* referred but which it did not name was the 1892 decision of *Church of the Holy Trinity v United States*.[27] The case concerned the *Alien Contract Labor Law 1885* (US),[28] which prohibited the importation into the United States of any foreigner 'to perform labor or service of any kind in the United States.' The Church of the Holy Trinity in New York had imported a minister from England. The United States Supreme Court held that the Church was not in breach of the statute. The Supreme Court gave two reasons to explain why there had been no breach. The first reason was that because 'the intent of Congress was simply to stay the influx of . . . cheap unskilled labor',[29] which Congress had deemed detrimental to the interests of American workers, the statute 'reaches only to the work of the manual laborer, as distinguished from that of the professional man.'[30]

The second reason given by the Supreme Court is what caused concerned for the Seventh Day Adventists. The Supreme Court said that various historical and official documents 'affirm and reaffirm that this is a religious nation'[31] and that 'this is a Christian nation.'[32] As a separate ground for its decision, the Supreme Court held that 'no purpose of action against religion can be imputed to any legislation, state or national.'[33] In other words, the Christian character of the nation gave rise to a rule of statutory interpretation that it was presumed that a statute was not intended to hinder religion. For this reason, the *Alien Contract Labor Law* could not apply to clergymen.

One of the historical and official documents the Supreme Court relied upon for holding that the United States was a Christian country was the preamble to the *Illinois Constitution* of 1870. Its opening words were: 'We, the people of the State of Illinois, grateful to Almighty God . . .'[34] To the Seventh Day Adventists, a recognition of God in a constitutional preamble looked like it had led to a judicial declaration that the nation was Christian in character.

25 'What Religion in the Constitution Means', *Bible Echo* (Melbourne), 26 July 1897, 233. This analysis was repeated in several editions of the *Bible Echo*. See, e.g., 'Religious Legislation or Religious Liberty: Which Shall it Be?', *Bible Echo* (Melbourne) 29 March 1897, 97.

26 'What Religion in the Constitution Means', *Bible Echo* (Melbourne), 26 July 1897, 233.

27 *Church of Holy Trinity v United States*, 143 US 457 (1892).

28 23 Stat 332, c 164.

29 *Church of Holy Trinity v United States*, 143 US 457, 465 (1892).

30 Ibid 463.

31 Ibid 470.

32 Ibid 471.

33 Ibid 465.

34 Ibid 468.

The Seventh Day Adventists relied on this case to make the point that the religious character of a constitution could give rise to an implied power to legislate on the subject of religion. At most, *Church of the Holy Trinity* provides a basis for fears that religious words in the *Australian Constitution* might give rise to two things: a holding that Australia has a religious character and a rule of statutory interpretation. However, the United States Supreme Court did not say that the Christian character of the nation gave rise to any power to pass laws concerning religion.

Nevertheless, the Seventh Day Adventists in America read the decision otherwise. In an 1893 document entitled *Appeal from the US Supreme Court Decision Making this "A Christian Nation"*, Alonzo T Jones writing on behalf of the International Religious Liberty Association (a lobby group set up by the Seventh Day Adventists) wrote:

> In this part of the decision [ie *Church of the Holy Trinity*] the court cites "historical" evidence by which it establishes the Christian religion as the national religion; justifies the use of the civil power to maintain the discipline of the churches; a religious test oath as a qualification for office; general taxation for the support of "public Protestant teachers of piety, religion, and morality;" the governmental requirement of a belief in the doctrine of the Trinity and the inspiration of the Scriptures of the Old and New Testaments . . .[35]

Jones also wrote that *Church of the Holy Trinity* authorised the enactment of federal Sunday closing laws:

> By this, therefore, the Supreme Court has decided that the civil power, even of the United States government, can rightly be employed to maintain the discipline of the churches. And this, as we know, and have shown over and over again, is exactly what the churches are aiming to bring about by the national enforcement of Sunday laws. This is precisely what is done by the enforcement of Sunday laws, either State or national. And this the decision of the Supreme Court fully sanctions and justifies by its decision, and its (mis)interpretation of the national Constitution.[36]

A version of that document had been published the previous year in pamphlet form under the title *The Union of Church and State in the United States.*[37] The passages extracted above appear in that pamphlet.[38]

'And one of the very first uses that was ever made of the decision [ie *Church of the Holy Trinity*]', Alonzo T Jones wrote, 'was when, in the month of April, 1892, the president of the American Sabbath Union took it in his hand and went before committees of the United

35 Alonzo T Jones, Appeal from the US Supreme Court Decision Making this "A Christian Nation" Review of the United States Supreme Court Decision in Case No.143–October Terms, 1891. The Rector, Church Wardens, and Vestrymen of the Church of the Holy Trinity, Plaintiffs in Error vs. the United States [February 29, 1892]. And also certain Acts of Congress for the closing of the World's Columbian Exposition on Sunday (International Religious Liberty Association, 1893) 17–8. The document is available online at http://www.adventaudio.org/ebooks/files/pdf/Jones%20-%20Appeal%20from%20the%20U.%20S.%20Supreme%20Court%20Decision%20Making%20this%20-A%20Christian%20Nation-.pdf.

36 Ibid 25.

37 See n 35.

38 Ibid 20, 28.

States Senate and House of Representatives, recited its "argument" and demanded the closing of the World's Fair on Sunday, by Congress, "because this is a Christian nation."'[39]

In 1893, Chicago hosted the World's Fair, a trade fair sometimes called the Chicago Exhibition. In the lead up to the Exhibition, a nation-wide campaign of petitions was undertaken.[40] Eighty-eight percent of members of the United States House of Representatives received petitions seeking that the Exhibition be closed on Sundays. Most of the petitions received came from the Members' own districts, suggesting that supporters of the measure could be found throughout the country.[41] Three-quarters of the petitions were identified as being from religiously affiliated groups.[42] The groups behind the campaign also sent lobbyists to Washington to aid the cause.[43]

The petition campaign was effective. Congress passed a law to provide financial assistance to the organisers of the Exhibition. However, the statute imposed a condition for the financial assistance. The organisers could have the money on condition that the Exhibition was not open on Sundays. [44]

The *Congressional Record* that reports the 1892 debate on the Bill imposing the Sunday closing condition indicates that several members of Congress advanced religious arguments in favour of the condition. One Senator argued in favour of the Sunday closing condition on the ground that the United States 'is profoundly a Christian state.'[45] One scholar of the influence of Christian lobbying on legislation in the United States writes, '[t]he petitions Congress had received did come up during the debate, and lawmakers clearly seemed influenced by them.'[46]

This statute does not prove the legal point the Seventh Day Adventists were trying to make. The reality is that the proposition that the United States had a religious character did not authorise the enactment of the Sunday closing condition but encouraged its enactment. The United States Congress may only legislate in respect of certain enumerated subject matters. Religion is not on the list of subject matters. However, one of those subject matters is 'Commerce with foreign Nations, and among the several States'.[47] A law granting financial assistance to a trade fair, with exhibitors from around the country and the world, is a law on the subject matter of international and interstate commerce.

39 Jones, Appeal from the US Supreme Court Decision Making this "A Christian Nation", above n 35, 40.

40 Gaines M Foster, *Moral Reconstruction: Christian Lobbyists and the Federal Legislation of Morality, 1865–1920* (University of North Carolina Press, 2002) 101.

41 Ibid 101–2.

42 Ibid 102.

43 Ibid.

44 Act of 5 August 1892, 52 Cong Ch 381, 27 Stat 389, § 4:

> That it is hereby declared that all appropriations herein made for, or pertaining to, the World's Columbian Exposition are made upon the condition that the said Exposition shall not be opened to the public on the first day of the week, commonly called Sunday; and if the said appropriations be accepted by the corporation of the State of Illinois, known as the World's Columbian Exposition, upon that condition, it shall be, and it is hereby, made the duty of the World's Columbian Commission, created by the act of Congress of April twenty fifth, eighteen hundred and ninety, to make such rules or modification of the rules of said corporation as shall require the closing of the Exposition on the said first day of the week commonly called Sunday.

45 See, 23 *Congressional Record* 5999 (Joseph Hawley) (1892, Senate).

46 Foster, above n 40, 105.

47 *United States Constitution* art 1 § 8 cl 3 'The Congress shall have power . . . To regulate Commerce with foreign Nations, and among the several States, and with the Indian Tribes.'

The legislative powers of the Federal Parliament established by the *Australian Constitution* were to be granted in the same way as the powers of the United States Congress. The Federal Parliament was to have power to enact laws only in respect of certain enumerated subject matters. Religion was not such a subject matter, and nor did anyone advocate putting religion in the list of enumerated powers.

The Australian Seventh Day Adventists' legal reasoning was misconceived. The Seventh Day Adventists had not demonstrated that the religious words of the preamble would give rise to implied power to pass laws on the subject of religion. What they had demonstrated was how laws on the subject of religion could fall within a seemingly non-religious subject matter of legislative power. This still, of course, demonstrates a need for a provision denying power on the subject matter of religion to the Federal Parliament, for which the Seventh Day Adventists also campaigned.

The Seventh Day Adventists' theological reasoning

The Seventh Day Adventists did not just rely on amateur legal reasoning. They also relied on theological reasoning. Another American who had been involved in Seventh Day Adventist political campaigns in America was W A Colcord. In the late 1890s, Colcord was the editor of the *Bible Echo* and the Field Secretary for Religious Liberty. Colcord wrote a pamphlet setting out the Seventh Day Adventists' concerns in syllogistic form and had it reprinted in the *Bible Echo*. The pamphlet explained:

> [W]e cannot approve of the proposal to make a formal recognition of God in the Constitution of any civil government. The whole idea is wrong, and the consequences must be disastrous.

In proof of this we submit the following, simply undeniable facts:–

> The recognition of God is an act of faith. Heb. 11:6.
> A statement of that recognition is a declaration of faith. Matt. 16:15, 16.
> To incorporate in the Constitution of a civil government a recognition of God, or a declaration of faith, is to insert a religious clause.
> To insert a religious clause in the Constitution is to give the government a religious basis.
> A religious basis confers power for religious legislation.
> Power to legislate in matters of religion implies power to execute religious laws.
> Power to execute religious laws means compulsion in matters of religion.
> To compel the conscience in religious matters is to invade the rights of men.
> To *invade* the rights of men is to subvert good government, whose primary object is to *protect* those rights.

Thus it is proved that–

> To insert a religious clause or a declaration of religious belief in the Constitution of a civil government lays the foundation for the subversion of that government.[48]

48 'Governmental Recognition of God: What Does it Mean?', *Bible Echo* (Melbourne), 12 June 1897, 220 (emphasis in original).

This argument reveals that the Adventists had something in common with the Councils of Churches. They were seeking to have the *Constitution* reflect their own religious views. The *Bible Echo* stated that any constitutional recognition of God 'is contrary to the Spirit of the gospel.'[49] The Adventists' demand for a constitutional denial of power in respect of religion was, the *Bible Echo*, explained 'in the interests of good religion [because] no religion that is the result of force is good religion . . . Any religion or religious service to be acceptable to God must be voluntary.'[50]

The Seventh Day Adventists' theological reasoning led to a conclusion forming a major premise of their legal argument. They used theological reasoning to argue that religious words in the preamble give a religious character or flavour to the *Australian Constitution*. They also used theological reasoning to argue that such a situation was wrong.

The first premise of Colcord's syllogism is that 'recognition of God is an act of faith' and Colcord cites a verse from Hebrews. The verse, in the King James Version of the Bible,[51] reads: 'But without faith it is impossible to please him: for he that cometh to God must believe that he is, and that he is a rewarder of them that diligently seek him.' The verse is part of a chapter dealing with the nature of faith generally. The chapter opens with: 'Now faith is the substance of things hoped for, the evidence of things not seen.' Belief or recognition of God, therefore, is not a matter of knowledge through the senses or other factual enquiry but a matter of faith.

The second premise of Colcord's syllogism is the proposition that any statement of belief or recognition of God is a declaration of faith. This proposition seems to follow logically from the first premise without the need for any further citation to authority to prove it. However, Colcord provides an additional citation to scripture to strengthen his claim. The cited verses read: 'He saith unto them, But whom say ye that I am? / And Simon Peter answered and said, Thou art the Christ, the Son of the living God.' These verses are from a conversation Jesus has about himself with a number of his disciples, in effect catechising his disciples. After enquiring of his disciples who others think he really is, Jesus in the first verse cited by Colcord asks his disciples who they think he is. The answer, in the second verse cited by Colcord, is in effect a confession or declaration of the Christian faith, here about the identity and nature of Jesus. Colcord's citation to scripture therefore supports his proposition that any statement of belief or recognition of God is a declaration of faith.

The Seventh Day Adventists were not the only ones who reached the conclusion that constitutional recognition of God amounted to a declaration of faith. So did the then Tasmanian Attorney-General, Andrew Inglis Clark. As the previous chapter explained, Clark observed that it was theologically inconsistent for Protestants, such as the colonial Councils of Churches who dominated the recognition campaign, to pursue constitutional recognition of God because it involved a corporate confession of religious faith and corporate confessions of faith are Roman Catholic in nature. Clark's analysis shows how the major premise reached by Colcord using scripture could be arrived at in other more general, albeit still theological, ways. There is no reason to suppose that Colcord would have had any substantive objections to Clark's reasoning.

49 'Religion and the Federal Constitution', *Bible Echo* (Melbourne), 19 July 1897, 225.

50 'Our Petition', *Bible Echo* (Melbourne), 19 April 1897, 128.

51 See <https://www.biblegateway.com/verse/en/Hebrews%2011:6> for the passage in 54 other English translations.

After explaining that constitutional recognition of God would lead to laws concerning religion and that this would be 'an invasion of the dearest rights of man', the front page of the *Bible Echo* announcing the Seventh Day Adventists' petition campaign continued:

> It is subversive of good government, and contrary to the gospel of Jesus Christ, which says: 'Render unto Caesar the things that are Caesar's, and unto God the things that are God's.' 'If any man hear My word and believe not, I judge him not;' 'Whosoever will, let him take of the water of life freely;' 'Faith cometh by hearing, and hearing by the word of God;' 'Whosoever is not of faith is sin;' 'Hast thou faith? have it to thyself before God;' 'Who art thou that judgest another man's servant? to his own master he standeth or falleth;' 'So then every one of us shall give account of himself to God.'[52]

The first verse Colcord quotes is a phrase attributed to Jesus in the gospels of Matthew,[53] Mark[54] and Luke.[55] The comment is Jesus' answer to the question of whether it is appropriate for Jews to pay taxes to Caesar. Seventh Day Adventists interpret the phrase to require a separation of church and state. The state is responsible for temporal matters and the church for spiritual matters. A G Daniells, the church elder who drafted the Seventh Day Adventists' petition, explained this position to the general public in the first issue of the *Sentinel* in 1894:

> We believe that the Church and civil government are both of divine origin. We believe that the Church was established by God for man's spiritual welfare, and that civil government was ordained by the same Authority to protect men in the exercise of their rights . . . [W]e also hold that they are ordained for entirely different lines of work, and that each has its particular sphere, and that the realm of one is in no sense the realm of the other.[56]

In 1913, Colcord wrote a book titled *The Rights of Man, or, Religion and the State: An Exposition of the Province of Civil Government and Religion and a Plea for Civil and Religious Liberty*. He explained the different realms of church and state with respect to Sabbath observance:

> Keeping the Sabbath is a religious duty, not a civil duty. It is a duty which men owe to God, not one which they own to the state . . . [W]hen men by law require their fellowmen to observe any day as the Sabbath, they put themselves in the place of God, and require men to render to them what is due only to God. And this is idolatry.[57]

52 'Religious Legislation or Religious Liberty: Which Shall it Be?', *Bible Echo* (Melbourne) 29 March 1897, 97.
53 Matthew 21:22.
54 Mark 12:17.
55 Luke 20:25.
56 *Sentinel* (Melbourne), May 1894, 1.
57 W A Colcord, *The Rights of Man, Or Religion and the State: An Exposition of the Province of Civil Government and Religion, and a Plea for Civil and Religious Liberty* (Echo Publishing Co, 1913) 210.

The common theme of the other Bible verses[58] quoted by Colcord to justify the Seventh Day Adventists' position is the voluntariness of religious belief and practice. Compulsion in matters of religious practice is therefore contrary to scripture, as Colcord understands it.

Whilst Colcord argued that it would be both 'subversive of good government, and contrary to the gospel of Jesus Christ', the religious argument was in no way in a secondary argument. Seventh Day Adventism adheres to the principle of *sola scriptura*, the principle that the scriptures have supreme authority.[59] It follows then, for the Seventh Day Adventists, that giving any sort of religious character to the *Australian Constitution* would be profoundly wrong as a matter of scriptural principle.

The previous chapter explained how the Council of Churches' campaign for constitutional recognition of God can be seen as an example of civic Protestantism in practice. The Seventh Day Adventist counter-campaign can be seen as an instance of corporate Protestantism in practice. In contrast to civic Protestantism, corporate Protestantism 'look[s] inward, to the perceived needs of the Church.'[60] Civic Protestantism views the church as 'the ecclesiastical institutions of the godly commonwealth, or the godly commonwealth itself performing its divine (as distinct from worldly) tasks.'[61] Rather differently, corporate Protestantism views the church as 'inherently distinct' from the state and a 'supernatural society.'[62] The Seventh Day Adventists were energetic in their efforts to maintain the scripturally-mandated distinction.

Both the Council of Churches' campaign and the Seventh Day Adventists' campaign were religio-political campaigns. Their different objectives reflected the different theologies of the two groups. So what appears to be a campaign for a secular separation of religion and state constitutional provision has deep theological underpinnings. This fact, of course, does not give the *Australian Constitution* a religious flavour. Indeed, the role of the Seventh Day Adventists in the inclusion of section 116 in the *Australian Constitution* is just one part of the story: how the provision came to be adopted by the National Australasian Convention is another key part of the story.

58 John 12:47; Revelation 22:17; Romans 10:17; Romans 14:23; Romans 14:22; Romans 14:4; Romans 14:12.

59 Raoul Dederen (ed), *Handbook of Seventh Day Adventist Theology* (Review and Herald Publishing Association, 2000) 58.

60 Richard Ely, 'Protestantism in Australian History: An Interpretative Sketch' (1989) 5 *Lucas: An Evangelical History Review* 11, 18.

61 Ibid 12.

62 Ibid 12.

4 A constitutional recognition of God

Leaving prayer to its proper place

Adelaide has long been known as the city of churches. However, for the Councils of Churches it was the location of an important, albeit temporary, failure of their campaign to secure a constitutional recognition of God.

The Federal Convention convened in Adelaide in March 1897 for the first of its three sessions. The Convention received the first of the campaign petitions seeking constitutional recognition of God on 26 March 1897. The petition was worded as the New South Wales Council of Churches had suggested. More petitions to similar effect were forthcoming: eight were received on 29 March, four on 30 March, ten on 31 March, two on 1 April, one on 2 April, ten on 5 April, three on 6 April, one on 7 April, and one on 23 April. On 6 April 1897, the Convention received the first of the Seventh Day Adventists' counter-campaign petitions. Other counter-petitions were forthcoming: one each on 7, 12 and 20 April 1897.[1]

The Convention began its task of drafting a constitution with a working draft largely modelled on the Constitution Bill drafted by the earlier 1891 Constitutional Convention, which had been sitting idle since then due to a lack of political will by colonial governments to pursue Federation. That Bill included only one clause relating to religion: clause 109 prohibiting the States from making laws prohibiting the free exercise of religion.

The first discussion of constitutional recognition of God at Adelaide took place in the Convention's Constitutional Committee on 8 April 1897.[2] At that meeting, John Quick, a Victorian delegate who had been present at the Bathurst People's Convention and spoke in support of Gosman's motion there, moved that the words 'invoking Divine Providence' be inserted in the preamble of the Constitution Bill so that it would read: 'Whereas the people, invoking Divine Providence, have agreed . . .'[3] The Committee's minutes simply indicate that the motion was negatived.[4] The minutes do not record any debate.

The Committee's minutes may be silent, but the *Sydney Morning Herald* reported that one of the Committee members, Joseph Carruthers, a New South Wales delegate, told a gathering of church leaders that the issue 'was exhaustively dealt with' by the Committee.[5]

1 For an analysis of the petitions on the religion issue received at all sessions of the Convention, including their wording, number of signatures and organisations sending petitions, see: Anne Winckel, 'Almighty God in the Preamble' (1999) 4 *The New Federalist* 78.

2 Constitutional Committee, Minutes, 8 April 1897, National Archives of Australia, Series R213, 105.

3 Ibid.

4 Ibid.

5 'Deputations. The Federal Bill. Recognition of God. Deputation to the Minister for Lands', *The Sydney Morning Herald* (Sydney), 23 July 1897, 3.

Carruthers apparently voted in favour of recognition but indicated that other committee members, whom he did not name, had raised a number of arguments against recognising God. Those arguments included that recognition would have no practical benefit, that it would open Australians to a charge of irreverence if the Constitution invoking God were to break down, that God should not be associated with a necessarily flawed human creation, and that it would be putting words into the mouth of the Imperial Parliament in London since the preamble was to be the preamble to an Imperial statute, namely, the *Commonwealth of Australia Constitution Act 1900*.[6] Those arguments seemingly carried the day.

There is some doubt about the credibility of Carruthers' account. One historian points out that Carruthers offered his account to a gathering of Christian groups and so 'may have been tempted to tell the delegation what it wanted to hear.' None of the reasons offered for rejecting the proposal contradicted the churches' general sentiments about the importance and status of religion. Another reason to doubt Carruthers' account is the fact that he 'seriously misdescribed the words of Quick's [motion].'[7] Carruthers said that the Committee had rejected the words 'by the Grace of God' when the words actually before the Committee were 'invoking Divine Providence.'[8] Whether or not Carruthers' account of the debate is accurate, a debate did take place and a majority of the Committee decided against constitutional recognition of God.

Two weeks later in the Convention proper on 22 April 1897, the recognition issue was again raised. Patrick Glynn, a South Australian delegate, moved that 'invoking Divine Providence' be inserted into the preamble.[9] In speaking to his motion, Glynn said:

> [T]he supremacy of God should be recognised, and His blessing invoked, in the opening lines of our Constitution. It is from a belief that we should give expression to that desire in the Convention, and that a consensus upon the great central fact of faith and feeling, strengthens, rather than weakens, the security of liberty of thought, that I move this amendment.
>
> . . .
>
> [S]hould we not fix in our Constitution the elements of reverence and strength, by expressing our share of the universal sense, that a Divine idea animates all our higher objects, and that the guiding hand of Providence leads our wanderings towards the dawn?[10]

The next speaker, Ayde Douglas, a Tasmanian delegate who was a former Premier, was far from impressed by Glynn. Douglas criticised Glynn's speech as a 'sermon'[11] and argued that '[n]othing can make religion more ridiculous than to have the form without the substance.'[12] New South Wales delegate and Convention Leader Edmund Barton then

6 Ibid.
7 Richard Ely, *Unto God and Caesar: Religious Issues in the Emerging Commonwealth, 1891–1906* (Melbourne University Press, 1976) 32.
8 Ibid 32.
9 *Official Report of the National Australasian Convention Debates*, Adelaide, 22 April 1987, 1184 (Patrick Glynn).
10 Ibid 1184–6.
11 Ibid 1186 (Ayde Douglas).
12 Ibid.

spoke against the motion. To cheers from some delegates according to the Adelaide *Advertiser*,[13] Barton said that Glynn should withdraw the motion from consideration.[14] Barton pointed out that the Convention would not be able to attest to the motives of the electors in approving the Constitution and that it would be improper to enquire into their motives.[15]

Barton continued explaining that religion had nothing to do with constitutions and government, which should be entirely secular in character. He said:

> [T]he whole mode of government, the whole province of the State, is secular. The whole business that is transacted by any community – however deeply Christian, unless it has an established church, unless religion is interwoven expressly and professedly with all its actions – is secular business as distinguished from religious business. The whole duty is to render unto Caesar the things that are Caesar's, and unto God the things that are God's. That is the line of division maintained in every State in which there is not a predominant church government which dictates to all civil institutions. In these colonies, where State aid to religion has long been abolished, this line of demarcation is most definitely observed, and there is no justification for inserting into your secular documents of State provisions or expressions which refer to matters best dealt with by the churches, and which every righteous citizen will deal with in his church and at his time of worship, and not intrude into those matters which are themselves secular, and in themselves cannot be anything but secular . . . [S]ecular expressions should be left to secular matters while prayer should be left to its proper place.[16]

The influence of the Bathurst People's Convention was then felt when James Walker, a New South Wales delegate, quoted the motion adopted there 'acknowledging the government of this world by Divine Providence.'[17] Although Glynn contemplated withdrawing his motion, it was put to a vote and rejected by 17 votes to 11.[18]

Glynn had not been acting entirely on his own initiative in moving his motion. Glynn told the Convention that he had been approached to move the motion. He said:

> I have done my duty in having, at the request, reflected by these petitions, of a very large body outside this Convention, and of members of this Convention, some of whom have left the colony to-day to return to their homes, brought forward this resolution. I did not act on personal initiative in bringing this matter forward . . .[19]

13 'The Convention', *The Advertiser* (Adelaide), 23 April 1897, 5.
14 Ibid 1886–7 (Edmund Barton).
15 *Official Report of the National Australasian Convention Debates*, Adelaide, 22 April 1987, 1886–7 (Barton).
16 Ibid 1887–8.
17 Ibid 1888 (James Walker).
18 Ibid 1189.
19 Ibid 1888 (Patrick Glynn).

While Glynn supported constitutional recognition of God, the expression 'invoking Divine providence' was not his preferred form of words. He revealed this in a letter to the editor of the *South Australian Register*, the purpose of which was to take issue with comments by a Presbyterian leader, Professor John Rentoul, who had complained that the motion's failure was a 'mischief arising through a young Roman Catholic barrister being entrusted with the motion. [Glynn] had not gone about it in the proper way.' In his own defence, Glynn wrote: 'The words were not those I had in private chosen, but were suggested to me by several members of the Convention as those likely to secure the greatest amount of support.'[20] Glynn did not reveal what his preferred form of words was or which of his fellow delegates had privately discussed the matter with him.

At the end of the Adelaide session of the Convention the position was that God was not recognised in the preamble and clause 109 was retained prohibiting the States from making laws prohibiting the free exercise of religion.[21]

Time to bombard Parliament with petitions

'The Convention, by their refusal, have simply forced upon us, needlessly, the labour and expense of having this good thing effected through the respective colonial legislatures',[22] the Presbyterian leader Rentoul complained in a letter to Melbourne's *The Age* of 26 April 1897.

The process for drafting the Constitution required that the draft Constitution Bill, as it stood following the Adelaide session of the Convention, be considered by the colonial parliaments. The idea was to allow the colonial parliaments to recommend changes for subsequent consideration by the Convention.[23] It made sense then for Protestant leaders to turn their attention to the colonial legislatures.

A few days before his letter to *The Age* appeared, Rentoul had addressed the Victorian Presbyterian Assembly about the failure of the constitutional recognition of God motion at Adelaide. He declared:

> Let the churches unite to see that this great blunder was not perpetuated . . . [The churches] are not going to allow a little squad of Seventh-Day Adventists and other such people . . . or some little coterie, to run sectarianism into this great Australian commonwealth to be . . . Let them [ie the churches] bombard Parliament [with petitions] . . .[24]

The Presbyterian Assembly endorsed Rentoul's formal recommendation that the Presbyterians undertake

20 Patrick Glynn, Letter to the Editor, *South Australian Register* (Adelaide), 12 May 1897, 3.

21 Reproduced in John M Williams, *The Australian Constitution: A Documentary History* (Melbourne University Press, 2005) 583–611.

22 Ely, above n 7, 37.

23 *Australasian Federation Enabling Act 1895 (NSW)* ss 26, 27; *Australasian Federation Enabling Act 1896 (SA)* ss 26, 27; *Australasian Federation Enabling Act 1896 (Vic)* ss 26, 27; *Australasian Federation Enabling Act 1896 (Tas)* ss 26, 27; *Australasian Federation Enabling Act 1896 (WA)* ss 26, 27.

24 'A Blow to Religion. Professor Rentoul on Petty Coteries', *The Argus* (Melbourne), 7 May 1897, 6.

> all efforts to secure concerted action on the part of the various churches in the respective colonies of Australia and Tasmania, so that the various Parliaments shall be effectively moved to decide in favour of an amendment in the preamble of the constitution, giving effect to the people's wish that there should be recognition of God as Ruler of Nations and Source of Righteous law.[25]

Rentoul had also come to the view that some re-drafting of the form of words was required. He told the Victorian Presbyterian Assembly that the Convention delegates who voted against recognition at Adelaide had stated that they did so because of the form it took and that he would take those delegates at their word.[26] Rentoul also explained in a letter to the *Argus* that if the amendment introduced at Adelaide had been more 'satisfactorily' phrased, 'all this weary trouble of undoing a national wrong' would be avoided.[27]

The transcript record of the Convention does not reveal any delegate saying that he had voted against recognition of God because of the form the proposal took. In saying that the proposal failed because of the form of words, Rentoul was either making things up or he had been in contact with at least some Convention delegates about constitutional recognition of God, perhaps those unnamed delegates who had approached Glynn to move the motion.

The churches' campaign for constitutional recognition of God around the country took the form of further petitions, public meetings and direct lobbying of colonial politicians.[28] Among the petitions directed to the colonial parliaments, was a Presbyterian one that, unlike the New South Wales Council of Churches' original petition, suggested a form of words which was obviously thought to be more satisfactory by those behind the campaign for constitutional recognition of God. After asking for recognition, it continued:

> That this recognition could be easily and briefly effected by some such wording of the Preamble as the following: 'Whereas the people of New South Wales, Victoria, etc., in dependence upon Almighty God, have agreed to form one indissoluble Federal Commonwealth,' etc.[29]

The Seventh Day Adventists also targeted the colonial legislatures. They sent copies of the *Southern Sentinel* 'to all the Members of Parliament in Australia and Tasmania, and to about 600 leading newspapers in the Colonies.'[30] The Seventh Day Adventists were confident this was useful, later reporting that '[w]e have had evidence that the *Sentinel* has been read and highly appreciated by many of influence and standing.'[31]

25 Ibid.
26 Ibid.
27 Gerard O'Collins, *Patrick McMahon Glynn: A Founder of Australian Federation* (Melbourne University Press, 1965) 140.
28 Ely, above n 7, ch 5; O'Collins, above n 27,139–42; Walter Phillips, *Defending "A Christian Country": Churchman and Society in New South Wales in the 1880s and After* (University of Queensland Press, 1981) 258–9; J A La Nauze, *The Making of the Australian Constitution* (Melbourne University Press, 1972) 224–5.
29 'Petitions to Parliament: Which Shall We Sign?', *Bible Echo* (North Fitzroy), 12 July 1897, 221.
30 Australasian Union Conference Record, Volume 1, Nos 1 and 2, January and February 1898, 13.
31 Ibid.

There was also direct lobbying of Convention delegates and colonial politicians by the Adventists.[32] On 10 February 1898, the Adventists' religious liberty secretary and editor of the *Bible Echo*, W A Colcord, wrote to Victorian politician and Convention delegate Henry Bournes Higgins. Higgins would later take the lead at the Convention in pursuing what became section 116. In his letter, Colcord indicated that the Adventists had received assurances from several other, unnamed Convention delegates that their fears of religious legislation were unfounded. Colcord wrote:

> Heretofore some of the Federal delegates, have, in conversation with us, told us we need have no fear over a religious declaration of faith being inserted in the Preamble; that there was a clause in the porposed [sic] Constitution, Clause 109, which would prevent anything like religious legislation.[33]

Colcord's letter indicates that a number of Convention delegates would have been well aware of the Seventh Day Adventists' concerns regarding constitutional recognition of God.

The colonial parliaments endorse constitutional recognition of God

As Rentoul had hoped, the parliaments of the five participating colonies (Queensland chose not to participate in the Convention and did not pass enabling legislation) were all 'effectively moved to decide in favour of an amendment in the preamble of the constitution.'[34]

The Federal Convention's enabling legislation required it to accept for consideration recommendations made by a single House of Parliament or by both Houses.[35] In addition to the recommendations concerning recognition of God, the Tasmanian House of Assembly recommended an amendment to clause 109 and an unsuccessful attempt was made in the South Australian House of Assembly to recommend its removal.

1 New South Wales

On 4 August 1897, in the New South Wales Legislative Assembly a motion was put by William Lyne, who was also a Convention delegate, to insert the words 'acknowledging Almighty God as the Supreme Ruler of the universe' in the preamble.[36] Lyne argued that 'several powerful bodies' were in favour of such words, that God was recognised in other

32 Ely, above n 7, 44.

33 Letter from W A Colcord to HB Higgins, 10 February 1898, in National Library of Australia, Papers of Henry Higgins 1851–1929, MS 1057, Series 1, Item 23.

34 See n 25.

35 *Australasian Federation Enabling Act 1895 (NSW)* ss 26, 27; *Australasian Federation Enabling Act 1896 (SA)* ss 26, 27; *Australasian Federation Enabling Act 1896 (Vic)* ss 26, 27; *Australasian Federation Enabling Act 1896 (Tas)* ss 26, 27; *Australasian Federation Enabling Act 1896 (WA)* ss 26, 27.

36 New South Wales, *Parliamentary Debates*, Legislative Assembly, 4 August 1897, 2599.

contexts such as oaths and the words 'God save the Queen', and that support for the draft Constitution would be encouraged by the inclusion of a constitutional recognition of God.[37]

The parliamentary debate appears to have involved procedural manoeuvring. It seems from *Hansard*, which indicates that no tellers for the noes were available, that the Chairman of the Committee of the Whole put the question and declared it carried, ignoring several members who sought to gain his notice in order to speak on the motion. The *Sydney Morning Herald* reported the next day:

> It was expected that the recognition of God in the preamble would be the occasion of a great deal of oratory, but as it turned out the matter was quickly disposed of. The addition was proposed and at a convenient opportunity the Chairman put the amendment and declared it carried, greatly to the chagrin of three or four gentleman who it was understood, had prepared elaborate speeches on this matter. One of these, indeed, was so indignant that he fulminated against the Chairman, and asked what he could do bring this outrage on the rights of free speech before the House. But the Chairman had the support of members.[38]

In the Legislative Council on 26 August, the same motion was put and agreed to without a division.[39] Other than the mover who spoke for only one and a half sentences,[40] the only speaker on the motion argued that the words were 'clumsy and stupid' and that a better way should be devised of recognising God.[41]

2 Victoria

Similar arguments were presented in the Victorian Parliament. In the Legislative Assembly on 20 August 1897, Isaac Isaacs, who was Jewish and a Convention delegate, moved that the Constitution Bill be amended to include the words 'in reliance upon the blessing of Almighty God' in its preamble.[42] Isaacs did not speak to his motion, stating that it was unnecessary to do so.[43] The only person to speak on the motion said that he 'look[ed] upon the name of Almighty God in the preamble of this Bill as a blasphemy in the face of high heaven.'[44] The speaker had no objection to recognising God in secular legal documents but objected to associating God's name with 'bad laws', such as the proposed Constitution.[45] Nevertheless, the speaker indicated his intention to vote for the amendment. *Hansard* simply records that the amendment was agreed to.[46]

37 Ibid 2599–600 (William Lyne).
38 'Parliament', *Sydney Morning Herald*, 5 August 1897, 5.
39 New South Wales, *Parliamentary Debates*, Legislative Council, 26 August 1897, 3478.
40 Ibid (Sir Arthur Renwick): 'These words had been inserted by the Legislative Assembly. Though the whole of this country we had established various forms of Christianity –.'
41 Ibid 3478 (Henry C Dangar).
42 Victoria, *Parliamentary Debates*, Legislative Assembly, 20 August 1897, 1696.
43 Ibid.
44 Ibid 1696–7 (Francis Longmore).
45 Ibid 1697.
46 Ibid.

The Legislative Assembly did not necessarily view the petitions with which they had been bombarded, mostly from Presbyterian groups, with much seriousness. The *Argus* on 30 June 1897 reported:

> [M]embers extracted a considerable amount of amusement in the presentation of the petitions. Nearly every member of the House had a petition to present from some congregation, several had two, and some even three or more. There was keen competition for turns, and when at least half the members rose to their feet at the same moment, each with a long document dangling in front of him, the effect was striking, and a laugh was raised, which was renewed from time to time, until the spirit of frivolity pervaded what should from the nature of the case have been, at least, a grave proceeding.[47]

In the Legislative Council, *Hansard* simply reports that on 24 August a proposal for an amendment to insert 'in reliance upon the blessing of Almighty God' was moved and agreed to.[48]

3 Western Australia

In Western Australia on 24 August 1897, the Legislative Council considered a motion to propose that the words 'Acknowledging Almighty God as the Supreme Ruler of the Universe' be inserted in the preamble of the Constitution Bill.[49] The motion was a Government decision taken following two meetings with religious groups, which were agitating in favour of recognition.[50] Only two members spoke before the amendment was passed. The first indicated that it would be the only portion of the Constitution that he could 'heartily approve of' and that the suggestion by a 'small and undesirable' section of the public that such words should be left out had only induced him to vote for it.[51] The other speaker described the public arguments made against recognition as 'very far-fetched'; he could not see how it would enable Parliament to enact religious laws or that it could lead to intolerance.[52]

The next day in the Legislative Assembly, Walter James moved that the words 'Grateful to Almighty God for their freedom, and in order to secure and perpetuate his blessings' be inserted in the preamble.[53] James acknowledged that those people opposed to recognition were 'actuated by motives just as high minded, and just as reverent' as those in favour, but argued that clause 109 prohibiting the States from prohibiting the free exercise of religion was a 'sufficient guarantee' against recognition becoming 'a lever for future religious discord.'[54] He added that recognition of Almighty God 'was not confined to

47 Untitled Article, *Argus* (Melbourne), 30 June 1897, 4.
48 Victoria, *Parliamentary Debates*, Legislative Council, 24 August 1897, 1730.
49 Western Australia, *Parliamentary Debates*, Legislative Council, 24 August 1897, 246.
50 Ibid 246 (Edward Wittenoom).
51 Ibid (Richard Haynes).
52 Ibid 247 (George Randell).
53 Western Australia, *Parliamentary Debates*, Legislative Assembly, 25 August 1897, 299.
54 Ibid 299 (Walter James).

Christians.'[55] James was met with arguments that recognition was unnecessary given that God was recognised in phrases such as 'God save the Queen', that 'anything which tended to advertise religion was derogatory', and that there was genuine community disagreement about the idea.[56] Another member articulated his 'strenuous opposition' to the amendment saying that he considered it 'dangerous for a church, or for any combination of churches, to take part in political affairs.'[57] He considered that if the amendment was adopted, government could 'expect to be bothered with similar appeals' and that it 'would be setting a dangerous precedent which might be used by fanatics of every kind.' The proposed amendment was accepted by seventeen votes to six.[58]

4 South Australia

In the South Australian Legislative Council there seems to have been a change of mind about the preamble. On 17 August 1897, the Legislative Council agreed to the preamble in the Adelaide draft; that is, a preamble without any recognition of God.[59] Two days later, John Warren moved that 'acknowledging Almighty God as the Supreme Ruler of the Universe' be inserted in the preamble.[60] Warren did not give a long speech, saying he was confident of the House's support.[61] Nor did he explain why he did not move his amendment two days earlier. Quite possibly Warren was acting after having been approached by Protestant lobbyists who acted after discovering the preamble had been approved without any attempt to amend it to recognise God. The only other speaker stated that the amendment 'had no denominational significance, but simply provided for an acknowledgment of the Sovereign Ruler of the universe.'[62] The proposed amendment was carried without a vote.[63]

In the House of Assembly Patrick Glynn, who moved the motion for recognition of God in the preamble at the Federal Convention, attempted to have clause 109, preventing the States from prohibiting the free exercise of religion, 'eliminated.'[64] Chapter 7 discusses that attempt as part of the Chapter's examination of why section 116 takes the form it does.

On 25 August 1987, the House of Assembly dealt with a motion proposing to insert 'acknowledging Almighty God as the Supreme Ruler of the Universe.'[65] The mover, William Gilbert, said that the amendment was 'simply a recognition of the idea that there

55 Ibid 299.
56 Ibid 300 (Charles Moran).
57 Ibid 300 (Frederic Vosper).
58 Ibid 301.
59 South Australia, *Parliamentary Debates*, Legislative Council, 17 August 1897, 159.
60 South Australia, *Parliamentary Debates*, Legislative Council, 19 August 1897, 174 (John Warren). There appears to be a typographical error in Hansard. It reports that the motion used the word 'acknowledge' and the words were to appear after the word 'Constitution' in the Adelaide preamble. For reasons of grammar, the motion must have actually used the word 'acknowledging.'
61 Ibid 174.
62 Ibid 174 (James O'Loghlin)
63 Ibid 174.
64 South Australia, *Parliamentary Debates*, House of Assembly, 25 August 1897, 497.
65 Ibid., 522 (William Gilbert).

was a Supreme Being overruling all the nations of the world.'[66] The next speaker, Thomas Price, indicated his opposition, expressing his belief that 'in all things they should keep the State and religion clear from each other.'[67] Further, Price argued, devotion to God should manifest itself in actions rather than phrases in a Constitution.[68] Sir John Downer, a Convention delegate and former Premier, indicated that although he 'entirely agreed' with Price and had voted against recognition at the Convention, he would not oppose the motion if others wished 'from a sense of reverence' the words to be included.[69] In the end, the proposed amendment was carried without a division.[70]

5 *Tasmania*

On 18 August 1897, the Tasmanian House of Assembly considered a motion for a proposal that the words 'acknowledging Almighty God as the Supreme Ruler of the Universe and the source of all true government' be inserted in the preamble.[71] The Treasurer, Sir Philip Fysh, a Convention delegate and former Premier, announced his intention to vote in favour of the motion even though at the Convention he had voted against recognition. Fysh told the House that he decided to change his position 'out of respect to the opinions and conscientious scruples' of the large number of citizens agitating for recognition.[72] Fysh had seemingly been moved to change his position as a result of the churches' campaign.

The Attorney-General, Andrew Inglis Clark, who was not a delegate to the Convention but had been a delegate to the earlier 1891 Convention, responded to his fellow Cabinet minister that there were other citizens whose opinions and religious convictions were 'the other way', which should be respected equally. Clark argued that the best compromise would be no mention of God at all; that way those in favour of recognition would be in no worse position than they were already and those against recognition would be spared a 'standing grievance.'[73] Clark also suggested that some people would find the proposal 'irritating' since it would be forcing them to join in a collective act of worship. Other members argued variously that it was not for the House to legislate in respect of people's consciences,[74] and that it was astonishing that there should be any objection to recognising God in the preamble.[75] One argued that 'Turk, Jew, and Christian alike, and in fact the universal world' acknowledged a 'Supreme Almighty, ever good Being.'[76] In the result, the motion was carried seventeen votes to three.

66 Ibid 522.
67 Ibid (Thomas Price).
68 Ibid.
69 Ibid 522 (Sir John Downer).
70 Ibid 522.
71 Tasmania, *Debates on the Draft Constitution Bill, as adopted by the Convention at Adelaide, March-May 1897*, House of Assembly, 18 August 1897, 266.
72 Ibid 266 (Sir Philip Fysh).
73 Ibid 266 (Andrew Inglis Clark).
74 Ibid 268.
75 Ibid 267 (Edward Mulcahy and Daniel Burke).
76 Ibid 267 (Edward Mulcahy).

In the Legislative Council a few days later, however, a motion to insert those words was lost, four votes to five.[77] Ayde Douglas, who had spoken strongly against recognition at the Convention, again spoke strongly against the idea. He took objection to a suggestion that unless the proposal was adopted members would be indicating that they were not believers in God.[78] 'Some people had the name of God constantly in their mouths,' Douglas replied, 'and they were not the best people.'[79] One member noted that there were petitions on both sides of the issue.[80] A supporter of recognition responded that a 'great preponderance' of the petitions were in favour of recognition and concluded his speech, apparently confusing the Declaration of Independence with the *United States Constitution*, stating that 'In America, Mr Jefferson had not hesitated in inserting words of a much similar effect.'[81]

The Federal Convention acquiesces

Petitions calling for constitutional recognition of God continued to bombard the Federal Convention. The second session of the Convention in Sydney in 1897 was not scheduled to consider either the preamble or clause 109 but petitions kept coming. Two each were received on 3 and 4 September 1897 and one each on 15 and 16 September 1897. At the Convention's final session in Melbourne in 1898 further petitions seeking the recognition of God in the preamble were received. One petition was received on each of 25 January, 16 February and 18 February 1898.

It was at the Melbourne session that the churches' petition campaign that had commenced a year earlier finally achieved its aim. In the Convention on 2 March 1898, Glynn again sought to have God recognised in the preamble. He moved that the words 'humbly relying on the blessing of Almighty God' be inserted. He said:

> I wish to move the insertion of this form of words in the preamble, because I think that it embodies the spirit of the nine suggestions in regard to this matter made by the various Houses of Parliament which have considered the Draft Constitution. The words I wish to insert are simple and unsectarian. They are expressive of our ultimate hope of the final end of all our aspirations, of the great elemental truth upon which all our creeds are based, and towards which the lines of our faiths converge. They will, I think, recommend the Constitution to thousands to whom the rest of its provisions may forever be a sealed book.[82]

77 Tasmania, *Debates on the Draft Constitution Bill, as adopted by the Convention at Adelaide, March-May 1897*, Legislative Council, 20 August 1897, 290.
78 Ibid.
79 Ibid.
80 Ibid (Edmund Piesse).
81 Ibid 290 (William Watchorn). This appears to be a reference to the *Declaration of Independence*, which contains a number of religious references and which Jefferson had participated in drafting, rather than to the *United States Constitution*, which Jefferson did not participate in drafting and the preamble to which reads: 'We the people of the United States, in order to form a more perfect union, establish justice, insure domestic tranquility, provide for the common defense, promote the general welfare, and secure the blessings of liberty to ourselves and our posterity, do ordain and establish this Constitution for the United States of America.'
82 *Official Report of the National Australasian Convention Debates*, Melbourne, 2 March 1898, 1732.

Glynn continued his speech in a manner similar to his speech on the topic at Adelaide. Pre-empting objections that constitutional recognition of God might lead to religious intolerance, Glynn argued that recognition would have the opposite effect. He told the Convention:

> In an affirmation of pure reverence and submission such as this, the adherents of all creeds, sinking their differences of form and method, can join, and will find the spirit of toleration in them growing strong under a sense of their common aim. It will thus become the pledge of religious toleration.[83]

After the Chairman of the Committee of the Whole noted that Glynn's amendment was broadly in line with the parliamentary suggestions on the matter, Henry Higgins was the first to speak. He told the Convention that since the Constitution Bill contained 'no provision to obviate the bad effect which the insertion of these words will have' he would have to vote against the proposal. He informed the Convention that he would seek to insert a clause to provide 'a sufficient safeguard against the passing of religious laws by the Commonwealth.'[84] Higgins then offered an argument understood by the other delegates to be suggesting that the religious words of the preamble might imply a power on the part of the Commonwealth to enact religious laws just as the Seventh Day Adventists feared.

Quick doubted the persuasiveness of Higgins' argument and added that the words proposed 'could be subscribed to not only by Roman Catholics and Protestants, but also by Jews, Gentiles, and even by Mahomedans. The words are most universal, and are not necessarily applicable only to Christians.'[85] It followed, Quick explained, that it would not be possible to interpret constitutional recognition of God as establishing Australia as a Christian country.

Barton then spoke. He noted that Glynn had consulted the Drafting Committee, which had been established by the Convention to draft the Constitution Bill in accordance with the Convention's decisions, about the precise form of words to be inserted and that those proposed were the 'least objectionable which could be devised.' Glynn later wrote in his diary that 'the words were settled after consultation with the drafting committee and reference to several other members of the Convention.'[86] Barton, however, expressed his view that it would be 'a danger to insert words of this kind in the preamble' because of the potential implications a court might draw.[87]

Douglas again spoke strongly against Glynn's motion. He asked:

> What is the object of inserting these words? Is it to make the people believe that they will be more religious if the words are inserted? Shall we be more religious if we put them in? Will it have any effect whatever upon us? Why, it is all nonsense – a sham and a delusion . . .[88]

83 Ibid.
84 Ibid, 1734.
85 Ibid, 1736–7.
86 Ely, above n 7, 69; O'Collins, above n 27, 142 extracts the same quote but refers to the 'deputy Committee' rather than drafting committee.
87 *Official Report of the National Australasian Convention Debates*, Melbourne, 2 March 1898, 1737.
88 Ibid, 1740.

He was also not persuaded by the argument that the words were universal. Douglas said:

> Dr Quick says we all have some religious views, and even Hindoos and Mahomedans – although I presume there are very few Mahomedans here – even religious Hindoos and religious Mahomedans would not apply the words of this amendment in the same sense as we apply them, nor are they applied in the same sense by Christians of one character and Christians of another. And we know that there are at least about 120 different descriptions of Christians, and, it may be, many more. The insertion of these words would be a mockery . . .[89]

Glynn's amendment was agreed to on the voices, and the amended preamble agreed to. That evening Glynn wrote in his diary about achieving constitutional recognition of God:

> Today I succeed in getting the words 'humbly relying on the blessing of Almighty God' inserted in the preamble. It was chiefly intended to secure greater support from a large number of voters who believe in the efficacy for good of this formal act of reverence and faith.[90]

Glynn did not write of what his non-chief or secondary intentions were. If there were any secondary intentions, they did not include empowering the Commonwealth to legislate with respect to religion, even if this might have been a desire on the part of the churches. His actions speak clearly against that possibility. A few hours after succeeding in inserting the recognition clause in the preamble Glynn voted in favour of section 116 to limit the Commonwealth's power to legislate with respect to religion. Quick, however, voted against section 116.

Given the fervour of the churches' campaign for constitutional recognition of God and the fact that the Convention delegates were mostly politicians, it is not surprising that the Federal Convention eventually agreed to constitutional recognition of God. The historians have been blunt in their analysis. J A La Nauze wrote that 'in effect the Convention was being blackmailed into making a gesture that was none of its proper business.'[91] As Ely puts it, on the whole, the Convention agreed to the proposal 'merely from considerations of expediency.'[92] In Phillips' words, '[i]t was a political rather than a religious decision for most of the delegates, although some like Dr John Quick, the Victorian lawyer, were moved by religious feelings.'[93]

What do the religious words of the preamble mean?

History is not always written by winners. Sometimes losers write history. Quick's religious feelings about the constitutional recognition of God may have ongoing significance.

89 Ibid, 1740.
90 Ely, above n 7, 74; La Nauze, above n 28, 226.
91 La Nauze, above n 28, 225.
92 Ely, above n 7, 74.
93 Phillips, above n 28, 259.

In 1901, he published the *Annotated Constitution of the Commonwealth of Australia* with Robert Garran, who had served as secretary to the Federal Convention. Quick and Garran's book is among the most cited scholarly works by the High Court and is often used by the High Court to understand the drafting of the *Australian Constitution*.[94]

Referring to the religious words of the preamble, Quick and Garran wrote:

> This appeal to the Deity was inserted in the *Constitution* at the suggestion of most of the Colonial Legislative Chambers, and in response to numerous and largely signed petitions received from the people of every colony represented in the Federal Convention. When the expression was first formulated, towards the close of the session held in Adelaide, it was thought advisable to postpone the final determination of a proposition so delicate and significant until a later stage, in order to give time and opportunity for further consideration and for the additional manifestation of public opinion and sentiment.[95]

Quick and Garran's analysis is problematic. In the first place, it is contradictory. Quick and Garran start by attributing the religious words of the preamble to colonial parliamentary suggestions. They then go on to note that the question of religious words in the preamble was already under consideration in Adelaide, on one occasion as it happens at Quick's own instigation, before the colonial parliaments came to consider the matter. Perhaps Quick and Garran meant that the colonial parliamentary pressure was key in persuading convention delegates to finally agree to constitutional recognition of God.

The second aspect of Quick and Garran's analysis requiring comment is the description of recognition as constituting an 'appeal to the Deity.' It is worth noting that Quick and Garran are not clear as to who or what was appealing to God. The language of the preamble speaks against its being the people appealing to God. Appealing to God would suggest God being the object in consideration. This does not accord with the text, which is clear that God was not the object in mind. It states that in agreeing to Federation the people were humbly relying on God's blessing. The language does not state or even imply that the people were appealing to God. Equally, that language speaks against the *Constitution* itself appealing to God.

A possible explanation exists for this erroneous description. Describing the language as an 'appeal to the Deity' has strong overtones of, if not synonymity with, the language of 'invoking' God that the Federal Convention rejected multiple times. Since the language that was accepted was considered the 'least objectionable' form, it follows that the Convention considered that the idea of invoking God was 'objectionable.' The religious words of the preamble do not constitute an appeal to God in the sense of an invocation.

The language of invoking God could suggest that in agreeing to Federation the Australian people were engaged in not simply a political act but a religious one as well.[96] That language lost. However, Quick had supported the language of invocation twice: first at

94 Carl McCamish, 'The Use of Historical Materials in Interpreting the Commonwealth Constitution' (1996) 70(8) *Australian Law Journal* 638.

95 Quick and Garran, *Annotated Constitution of the Commonwealth of Australia* (Angus & Robertson, 1901) 187.

96 Ely, above n 7, 41.

the Bathurst People's Convention and then when he proposed it himself at the Adelaide session of the Federal Convention. This, combined with Quick's 'religious feelings' about the matter,[97] might be an explanation for how that idea made its way into Quick and Garran's *Annotated Constitution.*

Given that everyone at the time referred to the issue as 'recognition of God', it might be wondered why Quick and Garran did not simply commence their analysis with 'This recognition of God was inserted in the *Constitution* . . .' The fact they did not and used somewhat stronger language – 'appeal to the Deity' – appears to attribute more legal, or perhaps ongoing social and political, significance to the religious words of the preamble than their actual text would suggest.

Whatever Quick was thinking, the form the religious words of the preamble took was not to the point from the perspective of the churches. Their idea all along was for a 'recognition' of God, vague as that notion might be. The desire for a constitutional recognition of God was one particular manifestation of the Australian churches' much broader and longer-held desire for what Dale described in 1889 in *Impressions of Australia* as a 'formal and public recognition by the State of the authority of God.'[98]

There were various formulations in language along the way for how constitutional recognition of God might be achieved. For the churches, the language of the preamble did constitute a recognition of God by the Australian state. Some of their petitions even stated that words to the effect of those adopted would be suitable for 'effect[ing]' recognition.[99] The churches, then, were not concerned that the actual language of recognition should imply the undertaking of a religious act. That sort of specificity was not essential from their perspective.

Just as the churches and the Seventh Day Adventists did not articulate a clear conceptual underpinning for the religious words of the preamble, neither did the colonial legislatures. The discussions in the colonial legislatures were, on the whole, brief and marked by a lack of considered debate. With some notable exceptions, such as Clark in the Tasmanian Legislative Assembly, and perhaps the New South Wales politicians who had prepared 'elaborate speeches' but were prevented from speaking on the issue, there was no deep engagement with the possible implications of what was proposed. The legislatures were acceding to the churches' demands primarily for pragmatic political reasons. The conceptual implications of what was proposed either did not occur to most of the politicians or were considered unimportant in the context of the political situation.

Likewise, and more importantly, the Federal Convention as whole did not articulate a clear conceptual understanding of what constitutional recognition of God was about. The speeches on the matter were certainly more thoughtful than the public utterances of the churches and the Seventh Day Adventists. Barton and Glynn's speeches at Adelaide are evidence of this. The fact that the words adopted had been the subject of private discussion between Glynn and the Drafting Committee and were thought to be the 'least objectionable' form of words indicates that some Convention delegates probably gave a lot more thought in private to the question of phraseology than did the churches. But

97 Phillips, above n 28, 259.

98 R W Dale, *Impressions of Australia* (Hodder and Stoughton, 1889) 261–2.

99 'Petitions to Parliament: Which Shall We Sign?', *Bible Echo* (North Fitzroy), 12 July 1897, 221 reproducing the text of one of the churches' petitions.

the debate as a whole was not conducted at a very deep level of sophistication. This is not a criticism. The preamble was not a key issue and was for many delegates a distraction from more important matters. The Convention's decision to include religious words in the preamble was not a decision based on a well-thought out conceptual understanding of what was being done.

For the churches, and possibly Quick and Garran, constitutional recognition of God amounted in some way to an official acknowledgment of the authority of God. For the Seventh Day Adventists, constitutional recognition was both a violation of God's command that church and state be separate and a source of potential religious oppression. For the Federal Convention as a whole, constitutional recognition of God was simply pragmatic politics.

The Convention did not have a deep conceptual understanding of the nature of what they were doing by inserting religious words in the preamble; but they were alive to the possibility that those words might somehow be legally important. Barton explained at the conclusion of the Convention, in summarising the Constitution Bill that had been adopted

> While . . . a concession has been made to the popular opinion that some reverential expression should be embodied in the preamble, due care has been taken by the Convention that no reliance upon that provision, and no far-fetched arguments based upon it, shall lead to any infraction of religious liberty under the laws of the Commonwealth which we hope to create. [100]

The churches' campaign, however, was not the only campaign that was successful. After adopting religious words in the preamble, the Convention adopted an antidote or counterbalance in the form of section 116. The Seventh Day Adventists' campaign also achieved some success.

100 *Official Report of the National Australasian Convention Debates*, Melbourne, 17 March 1898, 2474.

5 A constitutional prohibition against religious laws

Higgins alleges ulterior motives

Henry Bournes Higgins, a Victorian delegate to the Federal Convention, had a history with the Victorian Council of Churches. He did not trust in their bona fides when it came to their involvement in political matters. Higgins was a Victorian politician and had been firmly opposed to the efforts of an organisation affiliated with the Victorian Council of Churches, the National Scripture Education League, to require Victorian public schools to teach religion.[1] In response, the League campaigned against Higgins being re-elected at the 1897 Victorian election. In the course of that political debate, Higgins accused the League of failing 'to be frank and out' with their objectives, which he understood as being aimed at 'break[ing] the extreme secularity of the education system.'[2]

As one historian explains, there was

> considerable and personalized hostility between Higgins and the League or ultimately, since the League was virtually a subcommittee of the Council of Churches, between Higgins and the Victorian Council of Churches. Higgins believed that a group of militant and resolute Protestant churchmen were engaged in a long-term campaign to Protestantize the state schools.[3]

So quite separately to the constitutional recognition of God issue, and before it arose in the Federal Convention, Higgins had expressed concerns about the general political objectives of the Council of Churches.

Higgins also held specific concerns about the campaign for constitutional recognition of God before raising them in the Convention. The *Geelong Advertiser* of 2 October 1897 reported Higgins accusing the Council of Churches of ulterior motives in pursuing constitutional recognition of God. He is reported to have said during an election campaign speech:

> a few men have taken up the [recognition question] with a defined object, and he [ie Higgins] would have preferred them to have had more candour. Their object was not

1 Richard Ely, *Unto God and Caesar: Religious Issues in the Emerging Commonwealth, 1981–1906* (Melbourne University Press, 1976) 56–9.

2 'The Parliamentary Elections. Mr H B Higgins at the Exhibition Theatre. An Enthusiastic Reception.' *Geelong Advertiser* (Victoria), 2 October 1897, 2, 3.

3 Ely, above n 1, 58.

> to have respect or reverence to the Almighty . . . [T]he object . . . was to bring about religious oppression, and he did not believe that the people of Victoria want to compel people to become religious.[4]

Between the Adelaide and Sydney sessions of the Federal Convention when the colonial Parliaments were considering the draft Constitution Bill, Higgins was in contact with the Seventh Day Adventists. In early July 1897, he had sought to present one of their petitions to the Victorian Legislative Assembly but was prevented from doing so because the petition was typed rather than hand-written as required by the Assembly's standing orders.[5] Higgins would also have received copies of the Seventh Day Adventists' *Southern Sentinel* publication, since copies had been provided to all colonial politicians.

It might be inferred that it was at this time that Higgins became aware of the Sunday closing of the Chicago exhibition and that he became aware of it from a Seventh Day Adventist source. Higgins would also have become aware that the Seventh Day Adventists were accusing the Councils of Churches of seeking to authorise religious legislation. All this, combined with Higgins' existing antipathy to the Council of Churches' political activities, probably explains why Higgins sought to expand clause 109 to have it limit the Commonwealth's powers in respect of religion and explains where his thinking on his debating points originated.

The agenda for the Melbourne session of the Federal Convention included the preamble as one of the last issues to be considered, but it was apparent by the time of the Melbourne session that constitutional recognition of God was likely. Therefore, when on 7 February 1898 Higgins first rose to propose an amendment to clause 109,[6] he was doing so in anticipation of constitutional recognition of God in the preamble.

Higgins declared that the existing clause, limiting only the power of the States to make laws prohibiting the free exercise of religion, did not go far enough and that the issue was 'all the more important because a strong effort has been made to have a reference to the Almighty inserted in the preamble of the Constitution.'[7] Higgins said that any such recognition would make it 'necessary to re-assure a large number of good people that their rights with respect to religion will not be interfered with.'[8] Higgins' amendment would expand clause 109 so that it would bind both the States and the Commonwealth: 'A State shall not, nor shall the Commonwealth, make any law prohibiting the free exercise of religion, or imposing any religious test or observance.'[9]

Higgins then explained his amendment, making a serious political allegation against those behind the constitutional recognition of God campaign in the process:

> [The amendment] has been circulated for several days, and is to the effect that neither a state nor the Commonwealth shall make any law prohibiting the free exercise of any religion or imposing any religious test or observance. Of course, we all know that a

4 'The Parliamentary Elections. Mr H B Higgins at the Exhibition Theatre. An Enthusiastic Reception.' *Geelong Advertiser* (Victoria), 2 October 1897, 2, 3.
5 Victoria, *Parliamentary Debates*, Legislative Assembly, 7 July 1897, 232.
6 *Official Report of the National Australasian Convention Debates*, Melbourne, 7 February 1898, 654.
7 Ibid.
8 Ibid.
9 Ibid 656.

> great effort has been made to have an acknowledgment of the Almighty inserted in the preamble. This is a very difficult subject to speak about in mixed assembly; but I must speak plainly, or not at all. This recognition of God was not proposed merely out of reverence; it was proposed for distinct political purposes under the influence of debates which have taken place in the United States of America.[10]

Higgins explained:

> And now, Sir, it will be observed that in the Constitution of the United States of America there was not any such recognition in the preamble, and it is proposed that there shall be in our preamble. I am very sorry that those who first propounded this addition to the preamble did not tell the people with what object it was to be put in. They, no doubt, were perfectly fair and honest in their object, but they had read more than most people as to what had happened in the state of America, and I think, in all frankness, the people ought to have been told that there was a direct object and purpose in view.[11]

To articulate that object and purpose, Higgins then explained the course of the American *Church of the Holy Trinity* case.[12] This decision was the same decision the *Bible Echo* had referred to some months earlier in seeking to explain how constitutional recognition of God would result in religious legislation. There was, Higgins explained, a New York statute prohibiting the importation of foreign workers and a church had imported a clergyman from England. At first instance, it was held that the statute had been violated. However, on appeal, the Supreme Court held that there was no breach of the statute because the legislature did not intend to interfere with the importation of clergy since the United States was a Christian country. 'And for the purposes of establishing that it was a Christian country all through the states of America', Higgins explained, 'they went into elaborate charters and documents to show that from the first it had been a Christian country, and of course they were able to show that most of the states had been founded by denominations for the sake of their own adherents.'[13]

The point Higgins was getting at was the same as the point made by the Adventists in the *Bible Echo*. '[A] number of corollaries will be deduced,' Higgins told the Convention, 'and . . . attempts will be made, from time to time, to pass legislation of a character which I do not think we intend to give the Federal Commonwealth power to pass.'[14]

The Seventh Day Adventists were, Higgins said, 'exceedingly troubled over the fact that through putting the words in question in the preamble there may be an attempt to enforce the observance of Sunday upon them, whereas they observe Saturday.'[15] Higgins explained that he would be willing to support 'appropriate words' for constitutional recognition of God in the preamble in order to gain popular support for the Constitution,

10 Ibid.
11 Ibid 655.
12 Ibid.
13 Ibid.
14 Ibid 656.
15 *Official Report of the National Australasian Convention Debates*, Melbourne, 7 February 1898, 656.

but that 'without a safeguard in the Constitution itself, we shall be very likely to alienate a large force against us.'[16]

The clock was ticking close to 5 o'clock and the debate was adjourned shortly after Higgins spoke.[17]

The first debate in the Federal Convention

The next day on 8 February 1898, Higgins moved an amendment that would have clause 109 read: 'A state shall not, nor shall the Commonwealth, make any law prohibiting the free exercise of any religion, or for the establishment of any religion, or imposing any religious observance.'[18]

Richard O'Connor, a New South Wales delegate, immediately interjected, insisting that the application of such a provision to the Commonwealth was unnecessary since the Commonwealth was not being granted power to do any of those things.[19] In response, Higgins pointed out that the First Amendment to the *United States Constitution* imposes a similar restriction on Congress, and does so in the absence of any express power on religious topics being granted to Congress.[20] Higgins then gave another exposition of the course of American law:

> [F]rom single expressions used in the Constitution there have been inferential powers deduced. In consequence, for instance, merely of a decision of the Supreme Court that that country was a Christian country, there was a law passed and carried into effect prohibiting the opening of the Chicago Exhibition on Sunday, so that there is no doubt this will provide against a real subsisting danger, and I am moving this amendment with the view of reassuring a number of honest people here who, having regard to the experience of America, are gravely objecting to the insertion of any words in the preamble of the Constitution.[21]

The next chapter considers Higgins' argument in favour of section 116 in detail.

New South Wales delegate John Cockburn then spoke. He expressed the view that the whole idea of such a clause was an 'anachronism' which should be left out of the Constitution.[22] Barton, who had voted against recognition at Adelaide, then explained that he was 'rather doubtful' about Higgins' amendment.[23] Barton could not accept that an Australian or British court would ever find that a recognition of God in the preamble implied a power on the part of the Commonwealth to legislate with respect to religion, notwithstanding the American case cited by Higgins.[24]

16 Ibid.
17 Ibid.
18 *Official Report of the National Australasian Convention Debates*, Melbourne, 8 February 1898, 658.
19 Ibid.
20 Ibid.
21 Ibid.
22 Ibid.
23 Ibid.
24 Ibid 660–1.

After some further discussion, Higgins said that he would be satisfied for the clause to apply only to the Commonwealth and again gave the example of the Chicago Exhibition in support.[25] After a speech by Sir Joseph Abbott of New South Wales criticising the stance of the Seventh Day Adventists in seeking to prevent Sunday observance laws, Higgins' amendment was negatived on the voices.[26] Consistently with the consensus position reached that the powers of the States regarding religion should not be touched, the entire clause was negatived.[27]

Two days later on 10 February 1898, W A Colcord, the Adventists' Religious Liberty Secretary, wrote to Higgins congratulating him for seeking to expand clause 109.[28] The tenor of the letter suggests that it was the first piece of correspondence between Colcord and Higgins and that they had never previously met. This might be taken as speaking against the historian Richard Ely's suggestion that 'Higgins had in some measure become the agent and ally in the Convention of the Adventists.'[29] It seems entirely possible that Higgins was sympathetic to the Adventists' secular aims and used some of their campaign material for a likeminded purpose on his own initiative. In this sense, Higgins may have been the Adventists' ally. However, it is far from clear that Higgins was in any sense acting as the agent of the Adventists. Higgins' own longstanding views about the bona fides of the Council of Churches and the fact, as a later chapter will discuss, that Higgins never proposed the wording suggested by the Seventh Day Adventists point against any conclusion that Higgins was acting otherwise than on his own initiative.

The second debate in the Federal Convention

On 2 March 1898, the Convention returned to the question of an express denial of power on the subject of religion. That morning Glynn succeeded in having God recognised in the preamble. In debate on Glynn's motion, Higgins told the Convention that since the Constitution contains 'no provision to obviate the bad effect which the insertion of these words will have' he would, regrettably, have to vote against the proposal.[30] In this, Higgins differed from the Adventists. The Adventists would not countenance religious words in the Constitution under any circumstances. Higgins clearly was prepared to, as he had told the Convention during the debate on his attempt to expand clause 109. Higgins informed the Convention that he would again seek to insert a clause to provide 'a sufficient safeguard against the passing of religious laws by the Commonwealth.'[31]

Higgins continued, again explaining to the Convention the American Supreme Court decision and the federal statute closing the Chicago exhibition on Sundays he had mentioned a month earlier.[32] Again also, he repeated his belief about the motives behind the

25 Ibid.
26 Ibid 664.
27 Ibid.
28 Letter from W A Colcord to H B Higgins, 10 February 1898, in National Library of Australia, Papers of Henry Higgins 1851–1929, MS 1057, Series 1, Item 23.
29 Ely, above n 1, 55.
30 *Official Report of the National Australasian Convention Debates*, Melbourne, 2 March 1898, 1734.
31 Ibid.
32 Ibid.

constitutional recognition of God petition campaign.[33] Higgins told the Convention that the States should retain all their powers on the subject of religion, 'but I want to make it clear that in inserting these religious words in the preamble of the Bill we are not by inference giving a power to impose on the Federation of Australia any religious laws.'[34]

In truth, Higgins' preferred position was to limit the powers of the States as well as the Commonwealth in respect of religion. Higgins replied to Colcord's letter of 10 February expressing this opinion. Higgins' letter to Colcord, so far as is known, no longer exists.[35] However, Colcord's subsequent reply to Higgins is contained in the Higgins Papers at the National Library of Australia. In his letter to Higgins, Colcord wrote: 'Your letter of some days ago was duly received . . . While, as you suggest, it would have been desirable to have included the States as well as the Commonwealth in the provision . . .'[36] This suggests Higgins' considered view was that the States should have been similarly restricted in their powers in respect of religion as well as the Commonwealth.

Higgins' concession in respect of the powers of the States was based on a pragmatic calculation. The consensus among other delegates was that the existing powers of the States should not be altered. Higgins plainly preferred a partial win, limiting only the powers of the Commonwealth in respect of religion, rather than no win at all.

Sir John Downer agreed with Higgins that a clause denying the Commonwealth power in respect of religion was necessary but offered a different reason. Downer asked whether it had 'occurred to honourable members that the Christian religion is a portion of the English Constitution without any decision on the subject at all?'[37] Downer continued: 'because the Commonwealth will be from its first stage a Christian Commonwealth, and, unless its powers are expressly limited, it may legislate on religious questions in a way that we now little dream of.'[38] Downer's contribution was ignored by other delegates, who continued to discuss Glynn's proposal for constitutional recognition of God.

Later on 2 March, after the Convention had adopted Glynn's motion for constitutional recognition of God, a motion from Higgins to insert a clause to replace the deleted clause 109 came on for consideration.[39] Higgins began his speech noting that the matter had come on for discussion sooner than he had expected and that since he spoke earlier that day on the general subject he would not make a long speech.[40] Before actually moving his clause, Higgins stated that he had gone 'too far' in his former amendment in seeking to limit the powers of the States.[41] He explained his revised purpose:

> I do not want to interfere with any right the state has. I merely want to make it clear that, having inserted in the preamble of the Constitution certain words which, according to United States precedents, would involve certain inferential powers, there is no

33 Ibid 1734, 1735.
34 Ibid 1735.
35 Ely, above n 1, 140 n 2.
36 Letter from W A Colcord to H B Higgins, 23 March 1898, in National Library of Australia, Papers of Henry Higgins 1851–1929, MS 1057, Series 1, Item 23C.
37 *Official Report of the National Australasian Convention Debates*, Melbourne, 2 March 1898, 1740–1 (Sir John Downer).
38 Ibid 1740–1.
39 Ibid 1769.
40 Ibid (Henry Higgins).
41 Ibid.

> intention on the part of the Convention to confer even inferentially these powers on the Federal Parliament.[42]

Higgins then moved the insertion of a clause that would read:

> The Commonwealth shall not make any law prohibiting the free exercise of any religion, or for the establishment of any religion, or imposing any religious observance, and no religious test shall be required as a qualification for any office or public trust under the Commonwealth.[43]

Higgins explained to the Convention that the free exercise, establishment and religious tests clauses were taken from the *United States Constitution*.[44] He then explained that the religious observances clause was 'rendered necessary' by the recognition of God in the preamble and the effect of the United States Supreme Court decision he had previously outlined.[45] Higgins did not explain why he thought those four clauses would achieve his purpose, although he obviously viewed the religious observances clause as effective to prevent federal Sabbath observance laws.

After George Reid, the New South Wales Premier, indicated that he would vote for the proposal only if Higgins could point to some clause in the Constitution empowering the Commonwealth to make such laws in the first place,[46] Barton was the first to make a substantial speech on the matter. Barton began by noting his 'hesitation' about the proposed clause.[47] He continued explaining that the original States-only clause 109 was struck out because it was decided not to 'interfere unnecessarily' with the powers of the States and on the 'more solid ground' that there was no likelihood of a State ever making a law interfering with the free exercise of religion.[48] Barton then asked why the same reasoning should not apply equally to the Commonwealth.[49] Fellow New South Wales delegate Bernhard Wise interjected saying: '[y]ou might say the same thing as to Congress.'[50]

Barton, perhaps influenced by Downer's comments earlier that morning about the Christian religion being part of English law, responded to Wise, arguing that the case Higgins had referred to about America being a Christian country was 'really' based on the fact that the institutions of England, under the common law, were Christian and were imported to the American colonies.[51] Barton now also considered that the same reasoning could apply in Australia.[52] He continued:

> I think that because we are a Christian community we ought to have advanced so much since the days of State aid and the days of making a law for the establishment

42 Ibid.
43 Ibid.
44 Ibid.
45 Ibid 1769–70.
46 Ibid 1770 (George Reid).
47 Ibid (Edmund Barton).
48 Ibid.
49 Ibid.
50 Ibid (Bernhard Wise).
51 Ibid (Edmund Barton).
52 Ibid.

> of a religion, since the days for imposing religious observances or exacting a religious test as a qualification for any office of the State, as to render any such dangers practically impossible, and we will be going a little too far if we attempt to load this Constitution with a provision for dangers which are practically nonexistent.[53]

'That is the question', Higgins replied, 'are those dangers non-existent?'[54] Barton now thought those dangers to be non-existent. 'I do not think the fact that we may be held by law to be a Christian community is any reason for us to anticipate that there will be any longer any fear of a reign of Christian persecution,' Barton answered.[55] 'The whole of the advancement in English-speaking communities, under English laws and English institutions, has shown a less and less inclination to pass laws for imposing religious tests, or exacting religious observances, or to maintain any religion.'[56]

Barton continued his speech, expressing concern that Higgins' proposal might prevent the Commonwealth regulating, under the immigration and races powers, any objectionable religious practices performed by people of 'alien races.'[57] For that reason Barton considered himself 'prevented from voting for the first part' of Higgins' proposal concerning prohibitions on the free exercise of religion.[58] On the second part, Barton found the idea that the Commonwealth would ever establish a religion as preposterous: 'and as to establishing any religion, that is so absolutely out of the question, so entirely not to be expected.'[59]

Barton said 'the matter upon which I have had the least doubt' was the religious tests clause.[60] He said: 'I do not think that any such test would be required, and the only question is whether it is possible. I have come to the conclusion that it is not possible. Therefore, my disposition is to vote against the whole clause.'[61] Barton did not specifically mention the religious observances clause, presumably resting his conclusion with respect to it on his general arguments.

In response to a question from Reid, Barton assured the Convention that no church could ever receive money from the Commonwealth: 'you have only two powers of spending money, and a church could not receive the funds of the Commonwealth under either of them.'[62]

Bernhard Wise gave the next speech and spoke in favour of Higgins' motion. He did not share Barton's optimism about the decline of religious intolerance and was concerned to ensure that there should be no doubt about the inability of the Commonwealth to legislate in respect of religion.[63] Wise also thought that since the Convention had agreed to recognition in the preamble to satisfy the 'scruples and feelings' of one class of the

53 Ibid 1771.
54 Ibid (Henry Higgins).
55 Ibid (Edmund Barton).
56 Ibid (Edmund Barton).
57 Ibid 1771–2.
58 Ibid 1772.
59 Ibid.
60 Ibid.
61 Ibid.
62 Ibid.
63 Ibid 1773 (Bernhard Wise).

community, the Convention should agree to Higgins' motion to allay the fears of another.[64] Wise concluded his speech saying:

> What I fear is that we have not yet any sufficient security against a revival of the feeling which has existed for centuries, but which has not been able to make itself felt during the last 50 or 60 years in British-speaking countries, but which I believe, still exists in the hearts of hundreds and thousands of men only waiting for an opportunity to assert itself. If we put in Mr Higgins' amendment we shall remove those fears and establish a sound principle, and, I believe, will commend the Constitution to a very large number of those who at present are doubtful as to its effects.[65]

The next speakers did not give long speeches. John Cockburn, a former South Australian premier, was concerned about the creation of 'an ambiguous area between the powers specifically vested in the Commonwealth and the powers forbidden.'[66] The Victorian Simon Fraser agreed with Barton that no danger existed and was concerned about the potential effect of the proposal: 'We are now a homogeneous people, and the safer plan is to leave us so.'[67] Fraser was also not impressed by Higgins' American argument:

> I hope that we are not going to be driven to accept all sorts of extraordinary proposals simply because of something that has taken place in the United States. We are able to take care of ourselves, and I think the clause would do more harm than good.[68]

Josiah Symon, a South Australian delegate, then sought to amend Higgins' proposed clause. Symon's amendment would have had the clause read: 'Nothing in this Constitution shall be held to empower the Commonwealth to require any religious test as a qualification for any office of public trust under the Commonwealth.'[69] Symon argued that the preamble might be construed as allowing the Commonwealth to impose religious tests and that, in any event, a clause such as his would serve a 'solatium' to those who held concerns about the possible effect of the preamble.[70] A Tasmanian delegate, Henry Dobson, asked whether the preamble might not also allow the Commonwealth to enact Sunday closing laws.[71] Symon said that the Constitution gave the Commonwealth no power to do that.[72] Moreover, Symon said he was 'satisfied that it is embodied in the Constitution as a part of the unwritten law that no church establishment shall prevail, and that religious freedom shall be observed.'[73] Symon did not explain how it was he was satisfied of this.

64 Ibid 1773–4.
65 Ibid 1774.
66 Ibid (John Cockburn).
67 Ibid 1775 (Simon Fraser).
68 Ibid.
69 Ibid 1775–6 (Josiah Symon).
70 Ibid 1776.
71 Ibid (Henry Dobson).
72 Ibid (Josiah Symon).
73 Ibid.

Charles Kingston, the South Australian premier, spoke next, in favour of Higgins' proposal. He thought that the Convention should 'make a declaration of this description [i.e. denying power in respect of religion] in the broadest possible terms, for the purpose of allaying any apprehension that might otherwise be entertained on the subject.'[74] Kingston was followed by New South Wales delegate William Lyne who thought that any possible danger should be counteracted and preferred Higgins' proposal to Symon's.[75] Lyne thought that Symon's proposal was no better than no clause at all since it did nothing to prohibit Sunday observance laws.[76]

Wise then suggested that Symon withdraw his motion so that Higgins' motion, based on the possibility of the American decision being replicated in Australia, could be decided.[77] O'Connor objected to that course. He thought that a prohibition on religious tests could be justified but there was no ground for thinking that the Commonwealth could legislate in respect of the other three matters addressed by Higgins' clause.[78] Higgins responding by asking O'Connor to explain the presence of the religion clauses of the First Amendment in the *United States Constitution*.[79] O'Connor's answer was that the *United States Constitution* did not create as definite a division of powers between the States and the Federal Government as the Australian Constitution proposed to do.[80] O'Connor did not explain further what he meant by this.

Kingston then pointed out to O'Connor that the Commonwealth might legislate in respect of religious practices under its power to make special laws for the people of any race.[81] O'Connor thought that was unproblematic and continued his speech by expressing concern that by expressly limiting the Commonwealth's power in respect of certain religious subjects an implication might arise that it was not so limited in respect of other religious subjects.[82]

Higgins concluded the debate making three points. First, '[y]ou have put in the preamble a religious recital which is not in the Constitution of the United States of America, but you have not put in the safeguard against religious intolerance which they have there.'[83] Secondly, the Convention ought to reassure those people who hold concerns about the effect of recognition of God in the preamble.[84] Higgins' third point was that the States would be able to do all things he was seeking to prohibit the Commonwealth from doing.[85]

74 Ibid 1776–7 (Charles Kingston).
75 Ibid 1777 (William Lyne).
76 Ibid.
77 Ibid (Bernhard Wise).
78 Ibid 1778 (Richard O'Connor).
79 Ibid (Henry Higgins).
80 Ibid (Richard O'Connor).
81 Ibid (Charles Kingston).
82 Ibid 1778–9 (Richard O'Connor).
83 Ibid 1779 (Henry Higgins).
84 Ibid.
85 Ibid.

The Federal Convention agrees to a constitutional prohibition on religious laws

The Convention first voted 22 to 19 to keep the amendment in Higgins' form, thus rejecting Symon's proposal.[86] The Convention then voted 25 to 16 to accept Higgins' clause.[87]

In agreeing to Higgins' clause, the Convention was acting on the basis of a number of arguments. Partly, the Convention was acting to assuage the fears of people like the Seventh Day Adventists about the Commonwealth having power to enact laws that interfere with religious freedom. The more substantive legal basis on which the Convention was acting in agreeing to Higgins' clause was Higgins' argument about the possibility that the Commonwealth would be able to legislate in respect of religion. The next chapter examines Higgins' argument in detail.

86 Ibid.
87 Ibid.

6 The argument for section 116

The standard account of Higgins' argument for section 116

Was Higgins really arguing that section 116 was needed to prevent an implied power to make laws concerning religion arising from the religious words of the preamble? That is certainly how everyone has understood Higgins' argument, until now.

What might be called the 'standard account' of Higgins' argument for section 116 tends to be presented as follows: The insertion of the words 'humbly relying on the blessing of Almighty God' in the preamble to the Commonwealth of Australia Constitution Bill (Imp) might give rise to an implication that, notwithstanding the absence of an express power to legislate with respect to religion, the Commonwealth was indeed empowered to legislate with respect to religion. A provision such as section 116 is therefore necessary to prevent any such implication being drawn or to counteract any such implication.

This is how Edmund Barton, the Leader of the Convention, seems to have understood Higgins' argument. At the close of the Federal Convention on 17 March 1898, Barton summarised the key parts of the Constitution Bill. Referring to the preamble and to section 116, he said:

> While . . . a concession has been made to the popular opinion that some reverential expression should be embodied in the preamble, due care has been taken by the Convention that no reliance upon that provision, and no far-fetched arguments based upon it, shall lead to any infraction of religious liberty under the laws of the Commonwealth which we hope to create.[1]

It is also the account presented by Quick and Garran in their *Annotated Constitution of the Commonwealth of Australia*:

> Referring to [the preamble], it was stated by Mr Higgins that, although the preamble to the *Constitution of the United States* contained no such words as these, it had been decided by the courts in the year 1892 that the people of the United States were a Christian people; and although the *Constitution* gave no power to Congress to make laws relating to Sunday observance, that decision was shortly afterwards followed by a Federal enactment declaring that the Chicago Exhibition should be closed on

1 *Official Report of the National Australasian Convention Debates*, Melbourne, 17 March 1898, 2474.

> Sundays. This law, he said, was passed simply on the ground that among Christian nations Christian observances should be enforced. If, then, such Federal legislation could be founded on a Constitution which contained no reference whatever to the Almighty, how much more likely was it that the Federal Parliament might, owing to the recital in the preamble, be held to possess power with respect to religion of which we have no conception. Consequently, argued Mr Higgins, the power to deal with religion in every shape and form should be clearly denied to the Federal Parliament.[2]

Later scholarly commentators have followed Quick and Garran's account.[3] In addition to scholars, members of the High Court have presented the 'standard' account of Higgins' argument. In the *DOGS case* in 1981, the High Court rejected a challenge to Commonwealth funding of non-government primary and secondary schools on the ground that funding extended to schools operated by religious groups and thereby violated section 116's proscription against laws establishing any religion. In giving his reasons, Mason J said: 'Mr H B Higgins thought that the reference to Almighty God in the preamble might have yielded by implication a power in the Commonwealth Parliament to legislate upon the topics mentioned in the section.'[4] In the same case, Wilson J said that the provision was adopted due to 'an anxiety lest an inference of power was to be drawn from the acknowledgment of Almighty God in the preamble to the *Commonwealth of Australia Constitution Act*.'[5]

Regarding the free exercise clause of section 116, a similar analysis of Higgins' argument was presented in *Kruger v Commonwealth* ('*Stolen Generations case*') in 1997. That case concerned a challenge to the laws allowing the removal of 'half-caste' Aboriginal children from their families, resulting in what is now known as the 'stolen generations.' The claim was that the removal of Aboriginal children from their families and communities prohibited the free exercise of religion. In that case, Dawson J said: 'ultimately the matter with which those responsible for [section 116's] drafting were concerned was the possibility that, because of the reference to "Almighty God" in the preamble to the

2 John Quick and Robert Garran, *The Annotated Constitution of the Commonwealth of Australia* (Angus & Robertson, 1901) 952.

3 Clifford Pannam, 'Travelling Section 116 with a US Road Map' (1963) 4 *Melbourne University Law Review* 41, 53; J A La Nauze, *The Making of the Australian Constitution* (Melbourne University Press, 1972) 229; Constitutional Commission, *Final Report of the Constitutional Commission* (Australian Government Publishing Service, 1988) vol 1, 610; Stephen McLeish, 'Making Sense of Religion and the Constitution: A Fresh Start for Section 116' (1992) 18 *Monash University Law Review* 207, 219; Joshua Puls, 'The Wall of Separation: Section 116, the First Amendment and Constitutional Religious Guarantees' (1998) 26 *Federal Law Review* 139, 140; George Williams, *Human Rights under the Australian Constitution* (Oxford University Press, 2002) 110; Reid Mortensen, 'Judicial (In)activism in Australia's Secular Commonwealth' in Christine Parker and Gordan Preece (eds), *Theology and Law: Partners or Protagonists* (ATF Press, 2005) 52, 55; Reid Mortensen, 'The Establishment Clause: A Quest for Meaning' (2014) 33 *University of Queensland Law Journal* 109, 111; Carolyn Evans, *Legal Protection of Religious Freedom in Australia* (Federation Press, 2012) 70; Nicholas Aroney, 'Freedom of Religion as an Associational Right' (2014) 33 *University of Queensland Law Journal* 153, 169.

4 *Attorney-General (Vic); ex rel Black v Commonwealth* ('*DOGS Case*') (1981) 146 CLR 559, 612.

5 Ibid 654.

Constitution, there might be a perception that the Commonwealth had the power to interfere in matters of religion.'[6]

This may be the standard account of Higgins' argument but it is far from a complete or accurate account. The repetition of the standard account by various scholars and judges is understandable. As will be seen, the way Higgins presented his argument certainly looks at least to some extent like the standard account. That scholars and judges have followed the interpretation of Higgins' argument offered by his contemporaries who heard it in person, namely Barton, Quick and Garran, is intellectually defensible.

What did Higgins say?

Higgins advanced the same general argument on four separate occasions in early 1898 as to why a clause such as his was necessary: on 7 February, on 8 February, in the morning of 2 March in debate on the preamble and in the afternoon of 2 March in debate on his clause.

As the previous chapter noted, Higgins told the Convention on 7 February that constitutional recognition of God in the preamble 'was not proposed merely out of reverence; it was proposed for distinct political purposes under the influence of debates which have taken place in the United States of America.'[7] Higgins noted that there was no religious reference in the preamble to the *United States Constitution*[8] and then gave an explanation of the course of a case that had come before the United States Supreme Court in 1892. Higgins did not identify the case by name, but it is clear he was referring to *Church of the Holy Trinity v United States.*[9]

As the previous chapter also noted, Higgins explained to the Convention that there was a New York statute prohibiting the importation of foreign workers, and a church in New York had hired a clergyman from England. When the matter first went to court, it was held that the statute had been violated. Ultimately, on appeal, however, the United States Supreme Court held that there was no breach of the statute because the legislature did not intend to interfere with the importation of clergy, since the United States was a Christian country. 'And for the purposes of establishing that it was a Christian country all through the states of America', Higgins said, 'they went into elaborate charters and documents to show that from the first it had been a Christian country, and of course they were able to show that most of the states had been founded by denominations for the sake of their own adherents.'[10]

Higgins said the decision had resulted in religious discord. There had been, he said, 'a lifting of banners of those who wish to impose, for instance, a compulsory sabbath (sic) all through, in, and upon every state, and a lifting of the banner of those who oppose

6 *Kruger v Commonwealth* ('*Stolen Generations Case*') (1997) 190 CLR 1, 60.

7 *Official Report of the National Australasian Convention Debates*, Melbourne, 7 February 1898, 654.

8 *United States Constitution*, preamble: 'We the people of the United States, in order to form a more perfect union, establish justice, insure domestic tranquility, provide for the common defense, promote the general welfare, and secure the blessings of liberty to ourselves and our posterity, do ordain and establish this Constitution for the United States of America.'

9 *Official Report of the National Australasian Convention Debates*, Melbourne, 7 February 1898, 655 referring to *Church of the Holy Trinity v United States*, 143 US 547 (1892).

10 *Official Report of the National Australasian Convention Debates*, Melbourne, 7 February 1898, 654.

that movement.'[11] Higgins told the Convention that the Seventh Day Adventists were 'exceedingly troubled over the fact that through putting the words in question in the preamble there may be an attempt to enforce the observance of Sunday upon them.'[12]

Higgins explained that his amendment was necessary because:

> there will be in the preamble of this Constitution a declaration of a religious character, from which, as experience shows, a number of corollaries will be deduced, and upon which attempts will be made, from time to time, to pass legislation of a character which I do not think we intend to give the Federal Commonwealth power to pass.'[13]

It was only the next day – 8 February – that Higgins gave any explanation to support his claim that legislation could be enacted in consequence of a nation's religious character. He told the Convention in reliance on the comment in *Church of the Holy Trinity* (which he never referred to by name in the Convention), that the United States was a Christian nation, the United States Congress had enacted a law prohibiting the Chicago Exhibition of 1893 from opening on Sundays.[14] Higgins said that his amendment would therefore 'provide against a real subsisting danger.'[15] He summarised his position in this way:

> It has been found in the United States that, even though there is no reference to the Almighty in the preamble, yet it has been held that it is a Christian country, and, therefore, there was a federal law which prevented the opening of the Chicago Exhibition on Sunday . . . it is not a question whether it is proper to open exhibitions on Sunday but that law was framed and enforced, and people were compelled to obey it on account of the dictum of the Supreme Court that it was a Christian country. Now, if you can enforce a good thing you can also enforce a bad thing made by the same power.[16]

Higgins told the Convention that 'in the face of the decisions given in the United States, it is not safe for us to assume that there may not be an inferential power in this preamble.'[17]

In the morning of 2 March, Higgins spoke against the motion to recognise God in the preamble.[18] He told the Convention that since the Constitution Bill contained 'no provision to obviate the bad effect which the insertion of these words will have' he would have to vote against the proposal.[19] He informed the Convention that he would again seek to insert a clause to provide 'a sufficient safeguard against the passing of religious laws by the Commonwealth.'[20]

11 Ibid.
12 Ibid 656.
13 Ibid 655–6.
14 *Official Report of the National Australasian Convention Debates*, Melbourne, 8 February 1898, 658.
15 Ibid.
16 Ibid 663.
17 Ibid.
18 *Official Report of the National Australasian Convention Debates*, Melbourne, 2 March 1898, 1732.
19 Ibid 1734.
20 Ibid.

Higgins continued, again explaining *Church of the Holy Trinity* (although not naming the case) to the Convention and the federal statute closing the Chicago Exhibition on Sundays he had mentioned a month earlier. Again also, he repeated his belief about the motives behind the petition campaign seeking to have God recognised in the preamble. Higgins told the Convention: 'I want to make it clear that in inserting these religious words in the preamble of the Bill we are not by inference giving a power to impose on the Federation of Australia any religious laws.'[21]

Later that day, after the proposal to recognise God in the preamble had been carried, the motion from Higgins to insert a clause limiting the Commonwealth's power in respect of religion came on for consideration. Higgins again explained his thinking:

> I merely want to make it clear that, having inserted in the preamble of the *Constitution* certain words which, according to United States precedents, would involve certain inferential powers, there is no intention on the part of the Convention to confer even inferentially these powers on the Federal Parliament.[22]

He explained to the Convention that 'most of this clause [the establishment, free exercise and religious tests clauses] . . . is already in the American Constitution.'[23] He then explained that the religious observances clause is 'rendered necessary' by the recognition of God in the preamble and the effect of *Church of the Holy Trinity*.[24]

Higgins' general line of argument appears clear and, on first inspection, certainly appears to accord with the 'standard account.' Recognition of God in the preamble might lead to a judicial interpretation that the *Constitution* created the Commonwealth of Australia as a Christian nation. The United States Supreme Court in *Church of the Holy Trinity* was able to reach such a conclusion without a religious preamble. The religious character of the nation might empower the Commonwealth to legislate with respect to religion. The Chicago Exhibition Sunday closing law was seemingly evidence of this. Such a power was not intended to be given and might be used improperly. Therefore, a provision to prevent a decision and legislation of this nature was necessary.

The form of Higgins' argument, with its focus on inferential powers derived from the preamble, does not properly illuminate Higgins' principal concern. In order to discover that concern, it is necessary to examine the American facts on which Higgins based his argument.

What was *Church of the Holy Trinity* really about?

Higgins was not the only delegate at the Convention who gave an explanation of *Church of the Holy Trinity*. Barton commented on the case in arguing against Higgins' proposed clause on the ground that it was unnecessary, since the Commonwealth was not being

21 Ibid 1735.

22 Ibid 1769.

23 Ibid referring to *United States Constitution* art VI cl 3 '. . . but no religious Test shall ever be required as a Qualification to any Office or public Trust under the United States' and amend I 'Congress shall make no law respecting an establishment of religion, or prohibiting the free exercise thereof . . .'

24 *Official Report of the National Australasian Convention Debates*, Melbourne, 2 March 1898, 1769–70.

granted any express power to legislate with respect to religion. Barton explained that the decision rested on the finding that the statute in question was directed at manual labourers so that the importation of workers other than manual labourers was not affected.[25] Barton said that the comments about America being a Christian nation were merely obiter dicta.[26]

Barton was right. In *Church of the Holy Trinity*, the statute in question prohibited the importation into the United States of any foreigner 'to perform labor or service of any kind in the United States.'[27] The Supreme Court acknowledged that these words could extend to clergymen.[28] However, the Supreme Court pointed to the title of the Act, which referred to the importation of workers 'to perform labor', and concluded that 'the thought expressed in this reaches only to the work of the manual laborer, as distinguished from that of the professional man.'[29] Moreover, the Court pointed out that the mischief prompting the statute's enactment was that American capitalists were increasingly importing cheap foreign labour to the detriment of American workers. The Supreme Court concluded 'the intent of Congress was simply to stay the influx of this cheap unskilled labor.'[30]

Higgins acknowledged this point. But, as Higgins emphasised to the Convention, the Court also held that the United States was a Christian country. The Court said that various historical and official documents 'affirm and reaffirm that this is a religious nation'[31] and that 'this is a Christian nation.'[32] As a separate ground for its decision, the Court held, 'no purpose of action against religion can be imputed to any legislation, state or national.'[33] In other words, the Christian character of the nation gave rise to a rule of statutory interpretation that it was presumed that a statute was not intended to hinder religion. Among the documents relied upon for this conclusion was the preamble to the *Illinois Constitution* of 1870 which began: 'We, the people of the State of Illinois, grateful to Almighty God . . .'[34] Given the similarity with the Australian expression 'humbly relying on the blessing of Almighty God', Higgins' fear that the Australian preamble might similarly result in a judicial finding that Australia was a religious nation might have had some basis.

However, the United States Supreme Court did not say, and there is no hint in the Court's opinion, that the Christian character of the nation gave rise to any legislative power. Yet, the Seventh Day Adventists in America read the Court's decision otherwise. In an 1893 document entitled *Appeal from the US Supreme Court Decision Making this "A Christian Nation"*, Alonzo T Jones writing on behalf of the International Religious Liberty Association (a lobby group set up by the Seventh Day Adventists) wrote:

> In this part of the decision [ie *Church of the Holy Trinity*] the court cites "historical" evidence by which it establishes the Christian religion as the national religion; justifies the use of the civil power to maintain the discipline of the churches; a religious test

25 *Official Report of the National Australasian Convention Debates*, Melbourne, 8 February 1898, 661.
26 Ibid.
27 *Church of the Holy Trinity v United States*, 143 US 457, 458 (1892) quoting 23 Stat 332, c 164, § 1.
28 Ibid.
29 Ibid 463.
30 Ibid 465.
31 Ibid 470.
32 Ibid 471.
33 Ibid 465.
34 Ibid 468.

> oath as a qualification for office; general taxation for the support of "public Protestant teachers of piety, religion, and morality;" the governmental requirement of a belief in the doctrine of the Trinity and the inspiration of the Scriptures of the Old and New Testaments . . .[35]

Jones also wrote that *Church of the Holy Trinity* authorised the enactment of federal Sunday closing laws:

> By this, therefore, the Supreme Court has decided that the civil power, even of the United States government, can rightly be employed to maintain the discipline of the churches. And this, as we know, and have shown over and over again, is exactly what the churches are aiming to bring about by the national enforcement of Sunday laws. This is precisely what is done by the enforcement of Sunday laws, either State or national. And this the decision of the Supreme Court fully sanctions and justifies by its decision, and its (mis)interpretation of the national Constitution.[36]

A version of that document had been published the previous year in pamphlet form under the title *The Union of Church and State in the United States*.[37] The passages extracted above appear in that pamphlet.[38]

There is no known evidence that Higgins had ever read either document or even that copies of them were present in Australia at the time. However, given that Higgins was in contact with them, it might be wondered whether it was the Seventh Day Adventist leaders in Australia who alerted Higgins to the existence of *Church of the Holy Trinity* and the Sunday closing law. This is a distinct possibility given that, as previous chapters noted, a number of the Seventh Day Adventist leaders in Australia at the time of the Federal Convention were Americans who had been involved in political campaigns in the United States including in relation to Sunday closing laws.[39] They might also have provided Higgins with a copy of one or other of the Jones texts.[40]

35 Alonzo T Jones, *Appeal from the US Supreme Court Decision Making this "A Christian Nation" Review of the United States Supreme Court Decision in Case No.143–October Terms, 1891. The Rector, Church Wardens, and Vestrymen of the Church of the Holy Trinity, Plaintiffs in Error vs. the United States [February 29, 1892.] And also certain Acts of Congress for the closing of the World's Columbian Exposition on Sunday* (International Religious Liberty Association, 1893) 17–8. The document is available online at http://www.adventaudio.org/ebooks/files/pdf/Jones%20-%20Appeal%20from%20the%20U.%20S.%20Supreme%20Court%20Decision%20Making%20this%20-A%20Christian%20Nation-.pdf.

36 Ibid 25.

37 Alonzo T Jones, *The Union of Church and State in the United States, a Protest: Review of the United States Supreme Court Decision in case no. 143, October term, 1891. The Rector, Church Wardens and Vestrymen of the Church of the Holy Trinity, Plaintiffs in error, vs. the United States. (February 29, 1892), and also certain Acts of Congress for the closing of the World's Columbian Exposition on Sunday* (Pacific Press Publishing Co, 1892). A copy of this document is available online at http://text.egwwritings.org.

38 Ibid 20, 28.

39 Richard Ely, *Unto God and Caesar: Religious Issues in the Emerging Commonwealth, 1981–1906* (Melbourne University Press, 1976) 28 n 22, 42.

40 The Higgins Papers, held in the National Library of Australia, do not contain any papers throwing any light on this issue.

The Sunday Closing statute

Higgins' comments in the Convention that in the United States there had been a lifting of banners by those seeking to have Sunday observance laws enacted throughout the country were accurate, although the banners were lifted long before *Church of the Holy Trinity* was decided.

There is a long history in the United States of agitation for Sunday observance laws, with various lobby groups pursuing the matter with varying degrees of vigour and success throughout the country.[41] Higgins' comments suggest that he had some knowledge of this history.

That history includes the success in 1876 of a campaign to persuade the Commission appointed by Congress to oversee the Philadelphia Exhibition of that year to close it on Sundays.[42] It also includes the introduction into Congress, following the receipt of 21,000 petitions in 1888, of a Bill that aimed to stop interstate commerce, postal services and military parades and drills on Sundays.[43] The Bill also sought to impose a general Sunday closing throughout the areas of the country under the exclusive jurisdiction of the United States, such as the territories and the District of Columbia.[44] The Bill did not pass. However, President Benjamin Harrison ordered that the military should no longer parade on Sundays and the Postmaster-General reduced the amount of work performed by the postal service on Sundays.[45]

The history of agitation for Sunday observance laws in America also includes, as Higgins told his fellow Convention delegates, Congress' attempt to close the Chicago Exhibition of 1893 on Sundays. In the lead up to the Exhibition, a nationwide campaign of petitions was undertaken.[46] Eighty-eight percent of members of the United States House of Representatives received petitions seeking that the Exhibition be closed on Sundays. Most of the petitions received came from the Members' own districts, suggesting that supporters of the measure could be found throughout the country.[47] Three-quarters of the petitions were identified as being from religiously affiliated groups.[48] The groups behind the campaign also sent lobbyists to Washington to aid the cause.[49]

That campaign prompted the Sunday closing condition that Higgins had described to the Convention. However, contrary to what Higgins suggested to the Convention, the statute in question did not simply provide that the Exhibition should not open on Sundays. The statute appropriated money for the operation of the Exhibition, granting it to the corporation organising the Exhibition on condition that the Exhibition not open on

41 Gaines M Foster, *Moral Reconstruction: Christian Lobbyists and the Federal Legislation of Morality, 1865–1920* (University of North Carolina Press, 2002) ch 5. See also David N Laband, Deborah Hendry Heinbuch, *Blue Laws: The History, Economics and Politics of Sunday-closing Laws* (Lexington Books, 1987).

42 Foster, above n 41, 96.

43 Ibid 97–100.

44 Ibid.

45 Ibid.

46 Ibid 101.

47 Ibid 101–2.

48 Ibid 102.

49 Ibid.

Sundays.[50] In their *Annotated Constitution of the Commonwealth of Australia*, Quick and Garran suggest that the statute was passed under the American foreign and interstate commerce power[51] rather than on the basis of some implied power derived from the religious words of the preamble.[52] This is a view confirmed by American text writers of the time.[53]

Quick and Garran also write that the debates in Congress for the legislation contain no references to religion or to *Church of the Holy Trinity*, and suggest that Higgins had no basis on which to claim that the religious words of the preamble might authorise laws with respect to religion.[54] It is true that *Church of the Holy Trinity* is not mentioned in the *Congressional Record* – the American version of Hansard – that reported the 1892 debate on the Bill including the Sunday closing condition. However, the *Congressional Record* indicates that several members of Congress advanced religious arguments in favour of the condition. One Senator argued in favour of the Sunday closing condition on the ground that the United States 'is profoundly a Christian state.'[55] Moreover, as one scholar of the influence of Christian lobbying on legislation in the United States writes, '[t]he petitions Congress had received did come up during the debate, and lawmakers clearly seemed influenced by them.'[56]

The Seventh Day Adventists in America, who were involved in the political debates on the issue, also thought that the law was influenced by those behind the petitions. Alonzo T Jones wrote:

> And one of the very first uses that was ever made of the decision [ie *Church of the Holy Trinity*] was when, in the month of April, 1892, the president of the American Sabbath Union [one of the bodies behind the petitions] took it in his hand and went before committees of the United States Senate and House of Representatives, recited its "argument" and demanded the closing of the World's Fair on Sunday, by Congress, "because this is a Christian nation."[57]

50 Act of 5 August 1892, 52 Cong Ch 381, 27 Stat 389, § 4:

> That it is hereby declared that all appropriations herein made for, or pertaining to, the World's Columbian Exposition are made upon the condition that the said Exposition shall not be opened to the public on the first day of the week, commonly called Sunday; and if the said appropriations be accepted by the corporation of the State of Illinois, known as the World's Columbian Exposition, upon that condition, it shall be, and it is hereby, made the duty of the World's Columbian Commission, created by the act of Congress of April twenty fifth, eighteen hundred and ninety, to make such rules or modification of the rules of said corporation as shall require the closing of the Exposition on the said first day of the week commonly called Sunday.

51 *United States Constitution* art 1 § 8 cl 3 'The Congress shall have power . . . To regulate Commerce with foreign Nations, and among the several States, and with the Indian Tribes.'

52 Quick and Garran, above n 2, 290.

53 Ezra Parmalee Prentice, *The Commerce Clause of the Federal Constitution* (Callaghan and Co, 1898) 304; Henry Campbell Black, *Handbook of American Constitutional Law* (West Publishing Co, 1895) 297.

54 Quick and Garran, above n 2, 290.

55 See, 23 *Congressional Record* 5999 (Joseph Hawley) (1892, Senate).

56 Foster, above n 41, 105.

57 Jones, *Appeal from the US Supreme Court Decision Making this "A Christian Nation"*, above n 35, 40.

It would appear from this that the notion the United States had a religious character did not so much *authorise* as *encourage* the enactment of the Sunday closing condition Higgins referred to.

In addition, Higgins was wrong to tell the Convention that people were forced to obey the Sunday closing condition. In fact, the operators of the Chicago Exhibition chose to ignore the Sunday closing condition and opened the Exhibition on Sundays.[58] An attempt by the United States Government to obtain an injunction to restrain the Exhibition's opening on Sundays was refused by the Seventh Circuit Court of Appeals.[59] The Court held that the equitable remedy of injunction was not warranted in the circumstances of the case and that the United States Government should be left to seek a legal remedy if it wished to pursue the matter.

Although not mentioned in the judgment, it had been argued by the Exhibition organisers before the Court that the Sunday closing condition violated the religion clauses of the First Amendment.[60] A Senator had also suggested this in the Congressional debate on the Bill granting funds to the Exhibition on condition it not open on Sundays.[61] An academic note of the case in the 1893 edition of the *American Law Review* commented that the argument was 'plainly fallacious' and that '[t]o suppose that to attach such a condition to a grant of money amounts to a law respecting the establishment of religion or prohibiting the free exercise thereof, is an argument which does not rise to a very exalted level. It requires no answer.'[62]

Higgins' thinking

Higgins had a good knowledge of the statute he explained to the Convention. There is evidence that in preparation for the debate, Higgins visited the State Library of Victoria and looked at its copy of the *Congressional Record* that reported the debate on the Sunday closing condition in Congress. His reading of the *Congressional Record* was careful. He marked certain pages with torn-off pieces of an envelope and even underlined various passages. The envelope fragments remained in the book until removed by Richard Ely who discovered them when researching his 1976 book *Unto God and Caesar: Religious Issues in the Emerging Commonwealth, 1891–1906*. Ely outlines the evidence for supposing Higgins had read the *Congressional Record*:

> The slips of paper used to mark off these places were parts of an envelope, and about half of the postmark remained. 'FIT . . . . . . TH VIC' and 'JA . . . . . . 20 . . . 98' is fairly clearly 'Fitzroy North, Victoria, January 20, 1898. 251 St Georges Road, North Fitzroy, was at this time the address of the Australasian Tract Society and the Echo Publishing Company. It was also the Victorian headquarters of the Adventists.

58 Foster, above n 41, 105–6; David F Burg, *Chicago's White City of 1893* (University Press of Kentucky, 1976) 91.

59 *World's Columbian Exposition v United States*, 56 F 654 (7th Cir, 1893). See further Burg, above n 69, 91.

60 Note, 'Enjoining the Sunday Opening of the World's Fair' (1893) 27 *American Law Review* 571.

61 23 *Congressional Record* 6003–4 (John Morgan) (1982, Senate).

62 Note, 'Enjoining the Sunday Opening of the World's Fair' (1893) 27 *American Law Review* 571, 572.

> Therefore one reasonably can surmise that the letter to the reader of the *Congressional Records* came *from* the Adventists. We know that around this time Colcord, the Adventist's religious liberty secretary, was corresponding with Higgins. We know that at this time Higgins lived in the suburb of Malvern, *not* Fitzroy . . . We know from what Higgins said on 7 and 8 February, and 2 March, that he was closely familiar with the events relating to the closing of the 1893 Chicago Exhibition on Sunday. The probability therefore is that the vigorously underlining reader was none other than Higgins himself.[63]

Higgins must have known the statute was not simply a Sunday closing statute, as he intimated at the Convention, but rather a statute granting funds on condition. Higgins most likely also knew that *Church of the Holy Trinity* was not mentioned in the debate in Congress about the statute. But it seems Higgins sincerely believed, and he even managed to convince Barton, that the dictum that the United States was a Christian country had indeed been acted upon.

When Barton concluded his explanation of *Church of the Holy Trinity* to the Convention stating that '[t]he latter part of the decision was what lawyers call an obiter dictum', Higgins interjected saying 'But that decision has been acted upon.'[64] Barton replied:

> Yes, since then, *as is pointed out in a little handbook which my honourable [sic] friend lent me*. But the question for us to consider is whether a court like the Federal High Court or the Privy Council would ever come to such a conclusion. One would think it highly improbable.[65]

Higgins then indicated to the Convention that he and Barton had had a private conversation about *Church of the Holy Trinity* on the afternoon of 7 February 1898.[66] He gave no details about that conversation. It is likely that it was at that point Higgins lent Barton the 'little handbook' and persuaded him that the dictum had been acted upon. Neither Barton nor Higgins identified this book by title or author.

It is possible to investigate the book's identity. The book, which discusses *Church of the Holy Trinity,* must have been published sometime after 29 February 1892, which is the date the case was decided. And, it must have been published sometime before February 1898, when Barton referred to it. Given what was said at the Convention, it also appears that the book states or gives reason to infer that the *Church of the Holy Trinity* dicta that the United States is a Christian country had been acted upon.

The 'Making of Modern Law' database allows users to make full text searches of American legal treatises published between 1800 and 1926.[67] A full text search for the expression 'Church of the Holy Trinity' within the subject 'Constitutional law – United States' for works published between 1892 and 1898 retrieves three results: the first and second

63 Ely, above n 39, 142–3 (original emphasis).

64 *Official Report of the National Australasian Convention Debates*, Melbourne, 8 February 1898, 661.

65 Ibid (emphasis added).

66 Ibid 658.

67 See Gale Cengage Learning, Fact Sheet, 'Making of Modern Law: Legal Treatises, 1800–1926' <http://www.gale.cengage.com/pdf/facts/momlTreaties.pdf>.

editions of Henry Campbell Black's *Handbook of American Constitutional Law*[68] and Ezra Parmalee Prentice's *The Commerce Clause of the Federal Constitution*.[69] Prentice's work was published in 1898 and *Church of the Holy Trinity* is mentioned in three places: in the table of cases and in two other places; first, as authority for the proposition that Congress might prohibit the entry into the country of certain classes of person[70] and, secondly, for the proposition that it was prohibited to assist the immigration of aliens under contracts for their service or labour.[71] This is clearly not the book Barton referred to.

Black's work presents as a promising possibility: it even has the word 'handbook' in its title. The first edition was published in 1895 and the second edition in 1897. Neither edition is particularly 'little': the first is 651 pages and the second 765 pages in length. (Barton may well have been being ironic in describing it as such.) The preface to the second edition is dated June 1897, which probably gives enough time for a copy of the book to have found its way to Australia by February 1898. In the first edition, *Church of the Holy Trinity* is mentioned twice: in the table of cases and as authority for the proposition that the commerce power authorises legislation prohibiting the importation of foreign labourers.[72] It is the same in the second edition.[73]

Whilst that is the extent of the case's appearance in Black, both editions contain a discussion of Sunday closing laws. In the first edition, Black writes that Sunday closing laws 'are universally in force in the States'[74] and that their constitutional validity 'is sustained by the decisions of the courts.'[75] Black does not mention federal Sunday closing laws. Black does, however, write:

> The fact is that the great majority of the American people are Christians, and the laws are made with reference to this fact. And although others may be put to inconvenience by laws of this kind, it is but an application of the principle that the wishes and preferences of the majority must govern.[76]

In the second edition, Black is clearer on the question of federal Sunday laws. He writes that the religion clauses of the *United States Constitution* do not prevent the enactment of such laws.[77] Black also repeats his earlier comments about the validity of State Sunday laws,[78] and he repeats the passage quoted above.[79]

Is this passage the proof Higgins had presented to Barton? The passage does not say that the fact the American people are Christian gives rise to any legislative power, which

68 Henry Campbell Black, *Handbook of American Constitutional Law* (West Publishing Co, 1895); Henry Campbell Black, *Handbook of American Constitutional Law* (West Publishing Co, 2nd ed, 1897).
69 Prentice, above n 53.
70 Ibid 304.
71 Ibid 337.
72 Black, *Handbook of American Constitutional Law* (West Publishing Co, 1895) 297.
73 Black, *Handbook of American Constitutional Law* (West Publishing Co, 2nd ed, 1897) 341.
74 Black, *Handbook of American Constitutional Law* (West Publishing Co, 1895) 392.
75 Ibid 393.
76 Ibid 393.
77 Black, *Handbook of American Constitutional Law* (West Publishing Co, 2nd ed, 1897) 447.
78 Ibid 451.
79 Ibid 452.

is the proposition Higgins repeatedly advanced at the Convention. The passage only says that this fact is context in which laws are made. That might well have amounted to acting upon the fact in the minds of Higgins and Barton. And certainly, the Congressional debate on the Sunday closing condition for the Chicago Exhibition appears to have had this context in mind.

However, the Jones texts noted above also present as possible candidates for the 'little handbook.' They, unlike Black's tome, are indeed little: both are fewer than 100 pages in length. And they both claim that *Church of the Holy Trinity* authorises the enactment of Sunday closing laws. Higgins' interactions with the Australian Seventh Day Adventists, some of whom were Americans, also suggests a means by which such obscure works might have come into his possession. Indeed, Jones himself has a link to the Australian debate over constitutional recognition of God: the Adventist leaders in Australia had unsuccessfully approached Jones to come to Australia to assist them with their campaign against recognition of the God in the *Constitution*.[80]

The evidence is, of course, inconclusive and a confident identification of the 'little handbook' is therefore not possible. Reasons can be marshalled in favour of suspecting that it was to Black that Higgins and Barton were referring, and an additional reason in favour will emerge during subsequent discussion. Reasons can also be marshalled in favour of suspecting that it was to Jones they were referring. Ultimately, the identity of the 'little handbook' is not essential to the challenge this Chapter presents to the 'standard account' of Higgins' argument for section 116. What Barton's reference to the book indicates is that Higgins was able to persuade sceptical delegates to the Convention that there was indeed a possibility that the Commonwealth would somehow possess power to make laws with respect to religion.

To understand Higgins' explanation of the validity of the Sunday closing condition, it is necessary to bear in mind his thinking as to how constitutional grants of legislative power should be interpreted. Higgins was appointed to the High Court of Australia in 1906. Justice Higgins' judgment in the 1909 case of *Huddart, Parker & Co v Moorehead*[81] is instructive. That case concerned the scope of the Commonwealth's power to make laws with respect to '[f]oreign corporations, and trading or financial corporations formed within the limits of the Commonwealth.'[82] The question for the Court was whether legislation making it an offence for corporations to enter into contracts in restraint of trade was a valid exercise of that power.

Justice Higgins stated that the words 'with respect to' in section 51 of the *Constitution* meant 'on the subject of', such that for a law to be with respect to corporations it must be a law on the subject of corporations.[83] Justice Higgins concluded that the provisions in question were not laws on the subject of corporations but rather laws on the subject of trade and thus beyond the Commonwealth's power.[84]

80 Milton Frederick Krause, *The Seventh Day Adventist Church in Australia, 1895–1900* (MA Thesis, The University of Sydney, 1968) 238.

81 (1909) 8 CLR 330.

82 *Constitution* s 51(xx).

83 (1909) 8 CLR 330, 409.

84 Ibid 410.

Justice Higgins refused to accept that it was enough if the law applied to corporations.[85] He said that if that was the case 'the results are certainly extraordinary, big with confusion.'[86] He then set out what was later described as a list of 'horribles.'[87] Higgins suggested in his list that such an interpretation would authorise, among other things, libel laws applicable to newspapers owned by corporations, minimum wage laws covering employees of corporations, and alcohol licensing regimes for venues operated by corporations.[88] He also offered an example more directly relevant to section 116: '[i]f [the argument that a law will be valid as with respect to corporations simply if it refers to corporations] is right, the Federal Parliament can enact that no officer of a corporation shall be an Atheist or a Baptist, or that all must be teetotallers.'[89]

Justice Higgins summarised his thinking in this way:

> Those who support a federal law must show affirmatively that it is made 'with respect to' some federal subject; and the mere fact that aliens, or corporations, or something else named in the list of federal subjects, are mentioned in the law, and are affected by the law, is not enough. In short, the thirty-nine articles contained in s 51 are subjects for legislation, not pegs on which the Federal Parliament may hang legislation on any subject that it likes.[90]

Higgins had also expressed similar views about the nature of grants of legislative power at the Convention. These views were not exceptional but they cast light on the substance of Higgins' argument.

Higgins' argument reconsidered

During debate in the Convention, Higgins faced demands from other delegates for him to identify a source of power that would enable the Commonwealth to legislate with respect to religion.[91] The consensus view was that no such power existed. That consensus was noted by Quick and Garran in commenting on section 116:

> The Federal Parliament is a legislative body capable only of exercising enumerated powers. Its powers are determined and limited by actual grants to be found within the Constitution. Anything not granted to it is denied to it. If it is not granted the power to deal with religion, it cannot legislate concerning religion. It is superfluous to deny to it what is not granted—what it does not possess. The force of this reasoning, based on recognized canons of federal construction, was generally conceded.[92]

85 Ibid.
86 Ibid 409.
87 P H Lane, *The Australian Federal System* (Lawbook Co, 1979) 160.
88 (1909) 8 CLR 330, 409–10.
89 Ibid 410.
90 Ibid 415.
91 E.g., *Official Report of the National Australasian Convention Debates*, Melbourne, 2 March 1898, 1770.
92 Quick and Garran, above n 2, 952.

That consensus also reflected Higgins' preferred mode of thinking, as he later demonstrated by his judgment in *Huddart Parker*. But given the events in America, Higgins realised the world did not necessarily work that way, although he did not properly understand why. He told the Convention: 'although I should have thought in the absence of express powers that the Commonwealth could not legislate on this subject, still I cannot but see, having regard to the decisions in the United States Court, that there is danger in an implied power.'[93]

Referring to the American Sunday closing condition, Higgins told the Convention:

> There is nothing in the *Constitution of the United States of America*, even indirectly, suggesting a law of this sort . . . [T]here was nothing in the *Constitution* enabling the Congress to pass a law for the closing of the Exhibition on Sunday . . . I understand though that there has been no dispute among the legal men in that country as to its being constitutional. Honourable members will hardly realize how far the inferential powers have been extended in America. I should have thought it obvious . . . that the Congress had no power to pass a law of that sort . . . I should have thought that it was not in the scope of Congress to pass a law, no matter how righteous, to close the Exhibition on Sunday, but I find, on looking to a number of decisions in the United States, that it has been held again and again that, because of certain expressions, words, and phrases used in the *Constitution*, inferential powers are conferred upon the Congress that go beyond any dreams we have at present.[94]

Higgins knew that Congress could only legislate in accordance with the powers granted to it by the *United States Constitution*. This, as the framers of the *Australian Constitution* intended, was also to be the case in respect of the Commonwealth Parliament. But Congress had enacted a Sunday closing law and that law was apparently perfectly valid. Higgins simply could not identify a head of power that could support it: it was, in Higgins' mind, an entirely religious law. If that was possible in America, it might also be possible in Australia.

Higgins' principal concern – although he could not articulate it properly, as he himself recognised – was that, although none of Congress' powers looked like a religious power, they could nevertheless extend to authorising religious measures such as the Sunday closing condition. Higgins seems to have believed that thinking like that expressed in *Church of the Holy Trinity* worked to enable such an extension.

Black's comment that '[t]he fact is that the great majority of the American people are Christians, and the laws are made with reference to this fact' may, if Higgins had read it, have worked to encourage Higgins in such thinking. This would, of course, be a misinterpretation of Black's comment. Black was not suggesting that the religiosity of the American people works to expand the scope of Congress' enumerated legislative powers. Black was simply making the political observation that laws are enacted with reference to the preferences of majorities. But, given his thinking about how constitutional grants of power should be interpreted, how else could Higgins explain in his own mind the validity

93 *Official Report of the National Australasian Convention Debates*, Melbourne, 8 February 1898, 663.
94 *Official Report of the National Australasian Convention Debates*, Melbourne, 2 March 1898, 1734–5.

of the Sunday closing condition? This might be taken as an additional reason in favour of suspecting that Black's work is the mysterious 'little handbook.'

Higgins gave a convoluted explanation of this thinking to the Convention. After quoting the preamble to the *United States Constitution* which states that the American people united, among other things, to 'promote the general welfare', Higgins said:

> Under the head of 'general welfare', coupled with the statutory powers, they [ie the American courts] have extended the power of the Commonwealth [ie the United States] hugely. If you are going to confer absolute power to promote the general welfare you do not know how far that will extend. First of all, the plea was to promote the general welfare; then there is power to make all laws which are necessary and proper for carrying into execution the foregoing powers, and all other powers vested by the Constitution in the Government or proper officers of the states. Then, if you have coupled with that a declaration by the Supreme Court that this is a Christian nation, there is power to enforce Christian observances.[95]

This is the only occasion on which Higgins suggested that the American Sunday closing condition's validity was sourced from the United States constitutional preamble.[96] This is noteworthy because the reasoning in this explanation was not applicable to Australia. There is nothing in the Australian preamble that would serve the purpose Higgins claimed that the 'general welfare' had served in America. Moreover, it is not an accurate statement of American constitutional law. In 1905, Harlan J for the Supreme Court wrote that the preamble to the *United States Constitution* 'has never been regarded as the source of any substantive power conferred on the Government of the United States.'[97] These defects aside, Higgins' explanation to the Convention clearly indicates his concern about seemingly non-religious legislative powers extending to authorising religious measures.

Given Higgins' reasoning, his argument about the preamble potentially giving rise to a similar chain of constitutional reasoning in Australia is not so fanciful as it might at first seem. It is not difficult, in light of Higgins' understanding of the American example, to see how the preamble might suggest some sort of religious character to the Commonwealth.

95 *Official Report of the National Australasian Convention Debates*, Melbourne, 8 February 1898, 663.

96 It is possible that Higgins might have been mistaken or confused in his reference to the 'general welfare.' That expression appears not only in the preamble but also in art 1 § 8 of the *United States Constitution* granting Congress power to 'To lay and collect Taxes, Duties, Imposts and Excises, to pay the Debts and provide for the common Defence and general Welfare of the United States.' Even if the preamble provides a source of power, it is not a power that is conferred; it would be an inferred power. The general welfare clause of art 1 § 8 has been given a broad interpretation by the Supreme Court allowing a wide power to tax and spend: *United States v Butler*, 297 US 1 (1936); *Helvering v Davis*, 301 US 619 (1937); see also *National Federation of Independent Business v Sebelius*, 567 US 519 (2012).

97 *Jacobson v Commonwealth of Massachusetts*, 197 US 11, 22 (1905). However, Dan Himmelfarb, 'The Preamble in Constitutional Interpretation' (1991) 2 *Seton Hall Constitutional Law Journal* 127, 207 n 314 has identified *Hepburn v Griswold*, 75 US (8 Wall) 603 (1870) as a case where the Supreme Court 'effectively derived federal right from preamble's "establish justice" language' and *Mahon v Justice*, 127 US 700 (1888) as a case in which a single justice in dissent 'effectively derived limitation on power of state government from preamble's "insure domestic tranquillity" language.'

In Higgins' mind, that conclusion would be sufficient to enable the High Court to read the Commonwealth's enumerated powers in such a way that they would extend to authorising religious laws like the American statute. This was a 'horrible' and needed to be guarded against.

Higgins knew that section 116 was not superfluous and the American Sunday closing condition proved that section 116 was not superfluous. He just could not explain properly the constitutional basis for it not being superfluous. Higgins was not alone in this. Quick and Garran should also have realised that section 116 was not superfluous. After all, they correctly identified that the statute pointed to by Higgins was enacted by the United States Congress under its commerce power and they knew it involved a Sunday closing requirement.[98] But they seem to have believed that the Australian Commonwealth could not enact a similar statute even though the Commonwealth possessed a similar commerce power. They wrote that, apart from the religious tests clause, section 116 was 'superfluous'; it was, Quick and Garran wrote, unnecessary 'to deny to [the Commonwealth] what is not granted.'[99]

There is a straightforward reason for Higgins' poorly articulated explanation of the validity of the Sunday closing condition and Quick and Garran's failure to put two and two together. As noted above, legal thinking in Australia about the interpretation of constitutional grants of legislative power at the time was generally consistent with the consensus referred to by Quick and Garran; namely, that absent an express power in respect of religion Parliament would be unable to legislate in respect of religion. The now prevailing view as to the constitutional validity of a law that can be characterised as one with respect to multiple subject matters[100] would almost certainly not have occurred to Higgins (or others at the time) as being plausible. That view would be inconsistent with Higgins' thinking as expressed in the Convention and in his later judgment in *Huddart Parker*. Moreover, it is a view that did not really gain any serious acceptance until the 1960s.[101] Higgins' thinking about the interpretation of grants of legislative power prevented him from realising that although the American Sunday closing condition was indeed on the subject of religion it was nonetheless also on the subject of foreign and interstate commerce and constitutionally valid for that reason.

What Higgins labelled an exercise of 'inferential powers' is better understood as an instance of what would now be described as a law with multiple characterisations.

Section 116 as an exception to express powers

Higgins was seeking to do more than simply have the Constitution operate as if God had not been recognised in the preamble. He also wanted to ensure that the Commonwealth could not make religious laws at all, at least those of the kind mentioned in section 116, including pursuant to any of its express powers.

98 Quick and Garran, above n 2, 290.

99 Ibid 952.

100 On the technique of characterisation see, e.g., Leslie Zines, *The High Court and the Constitution* (Federation Press, 5th ed, 2008) chs 2 and 3.

101 See *Herald & Weekly Times Ltd v Commonwealth* (1966) 115 CLR 418. See also *Murphyores Incorporated Pty Ltd v Commonwealth* (1976) 136 CLR 1; Zines, above n 111, 39–41.

The challenge presented here to the 'standard account' of Higgins' argument for section 116 is more than just a matter of correcting the historical record. There is reason to suppose the Federal Convention as a whole misunderstood what Higgins was getting at. As the previous chapter explained, in the denouement of the debate on Higgins' provision, Wise asked that Symon withdraw an amendment to Higgins' provision that would have limited the prohibition to only religious tests.[102] Wise said:

> Unless the amendment of the honorable member (Mr Higgins) were carried, the Commonwealth authority might, under the ruling of the Supreme Court of the Commonwealth, have this implied power. For this reason, I appeal to the honorable and learned member (Mr Symon) to withdraw his amendment, so that we may take a vote upon the clause as it stands.[103]

Symon did not withdraw his amendment, but the Convention rejected it nevertheless. Immediately after the vote on Symon's amendment, the question was put to adopt Higgins' provision and the Convention voted to adopt that provision.[104] Delegates were clearly casting their votes on the basis that what was in issue was the danger that there might be an implied religious power.

The conclusion that the Convention misunderstood what Higgins was proposing is more than just of historical interest. If correct, it reveals that there is something not fully coherent about section 116. This is not to say that the provision is itself incoherent or that the conclusion reached about the Convention's understanding of Higgins' argument means that the Convention did not know what Higgins was asking it to do. Indeed, it was clear to all present at the Convention that Higgins was seeking to deny power to the Commonwealth to legislate in respect of religion. There was, and could be, no misunderstanding about that matter.

The misunderstanding was subtle. The misunderstanding does not relate to *what* Higgins was seeking to do. It relates to *why* it was thought necessary to do that. The Convention seems to have been under the impression that the reason why it was necessary to insert this denial of power was because of the possibility an implied power to legislate in respect of religion might arise from constitutional recognition of God in the preamble. In reality, the source of the power to legislate in respect of religion identified by Higgins was the various express powers granted to the Commonwealth. What Higgins labelled an exercise of inferential powers was really an instance of what would now be understood as a law that can be characterised as one with respect to multiple subjects.

Explaining Higgins' reasoning in this way exposes something of an incoherency between his purpose and his reasoning. Those framing the *Constitution* realised that a number of the Commonwealth's express powers might be able to deal with issues that a contemporary constitutional analysis might describe as touching religion. For example, there were instances when Convention delegates suggested that the 'races power' might support laws interfering with the exercise of religion by 'alien races.' Higgins' argument that the Commonwealth

102 The evolution of the language of the provision is traced in the next chapter.
103 *Official Report of the National Australasian Convention Debates*, Melbourne, 2 March 1898, 1777.
104 Ibid 1778.

should not have power to make, in his words, 'any religious laws' is inconsistent with this thinking. Such laws would today be characterised as being with respect to religion.

This suggests that Higgins' aim was not a complete and total denial to the Commonwealth of power concerning religion. It suggests that his aim was a denial to the Commonwealth of power to make laws 'on the subject of' religion, as Higgins understood that concept. The language adopted as section 116 is rather more limited and focused in its terms than a simple denial of power in respect of religion. The next chapter seeks to understand why the language of section 116 was chosen.

7 The language of section 116

Language matters

The heading to section 116 reads: 'Commonwealth not to legislate in respect of religion.' This is entirely consistent with what Higgins told the Convention he was trying to do. Higgins was determined, he told his fellow Convention delegates, to see included in the *Constitution* 'a sufficient safeguard against the passing of religious laws by the Commonwealth'[1] and that his clause, or one like it, would 'provide this safeguard.'[2] As Quick and Garran summarised the position in their *Annotated Constitution of the Commonwealth of Australia*, Higgins argued that 'the power to deal with religion in every shape and form should be clearly denied to the Federal Parliament. These arguments were allowed to prevail, and the provisions of section 116 became part of the *Constitution*.'[3]

Yet the language of section 116 is not consistent with the heading to the section or with what Higgins said he was trying to do. Section 116 restricts the Commonwealth's power in respect of religion in only four stated ways. If denying the Commonwealth power 'on the subject of' religion was the general purpose of section 116, why, then, was the language of section 116 chosen?

The High Court believes that the language of section 116 was carefully chosen. In *Attorney-General (Vic); ex rel Black v Commonwealth* ('*DOGS case*'),[4] concerning a challenge to federal funding of religious schools under the establishment clause of section 116, members of the High Court asserted that the Federal Convention made a deliberate decision to modify the language of the religion clauses of the *United States Constitution* for the purposes of adopting the modified language as section 116. The High Court emphasised the use of the word 'for' in section 116 as opposed to 'respecting' in the First Amendment ('Congress shall make no law respecting an establishment of religion or prohibiting the free exercise thereof'), the suggestion being that the Australian terminology indicates a purposive requirement.[5] The High Court also distinguished between section 116's

1 *Official Report of the National Australasian Convention Debates*, Melbourne, 2 March 1898, 1734 (Higgins).

2 Ibid.

3 John Quick and Robert Garran, *The Annotated Constitution of the Commonwealth of Australia* (Angus & Robertson, 1901) 952.

4 *Attorney-General (Vic); Ex Rel Black v Commonwealth* ('*DOGS case*') (1981) 146 CLR 559.

5 Ibid 579 (Barwick CJ), 599 (Gibbs J), 609 (Stephen J), 615–6 (Mason J), 653 (Wilson J).

'establishing *any* religion' and the First Amendment's 'an establishment of religion', the suggestion being that the First Amendment was concerned with religion generally whereas section 116 is concerned with particular religions.[6] Is the language of section 116 really the result of a careful and deliberate drafting choice?

Andrew Inglis Clark's draft Constitution

In preparation for the National Australasian Convention of 1891, the Tasmanian Attorney-General Andrew Inglis Clark prepared a draft Constitution Bill[7] as a starting point for discussions. Clark described his Bill as 'embodying a Federal Constitution upon the lines which I believe would be most acceptable and most beneficial to the people of the several colonies.'[8] Clark provided copies to his fellow Tasmanian delegates to the Convention as well as to selected delegates from other colonies. Clark's draft is important. As J M Neasy has commented, '[O]f Clark's ninety-six sections, all but eight found their way into the Draft Bill [that was agreed to by the 1891 Convention] in similar or reworked form, and only ten failed to find a recognizable counterpart in the *Constitution*.[9]

Clark's draft included two provisions relating to religion:

> 46. The Federal Parliament shall not make any Law for the establishment or support of any religion, or for the purpose of giving any preferential recognition to any religion, or for prohibiting the free exercise of any religion.
> 81. No Province shall make any law prohibiting the free exercise of any religion.

Clark's clause 81 was included in the Constitution Bill produced by the 1891 Convention. From there it was carried over into the working draft used at the Federal Convention of 1897–8 and was the provision, at the time numbered clause 109, that Higgins initially sought to amend.

Clark's general motivation for including these provisions in his draft can be gleaned from his political writings. In his 1885[10] essay 'Denominational Education', arguing for secular public education, Clark wrote that the 'inviolability of the human conscience' is one of the 'fundamental principles of true political freedom.'[11] In another essay, 'Why I am a Democrat', written during the 1890s,[12] Clark wrote that he believed in the 'natural

6 Ibid 599 (Gibbs J), 612–3, 615 (Mason J).

7 Reproduced in John M Williams, *The Australian Constitution: A Documentary History* (Melbourne University Press, 2005) 80–93.

8 Reproduced in ibid 65–9.

9 J M Neasy, 'Andrew Inglis Clark Senior and Australian Federation' (1969) 15(2) *Australian Journal of Politics and History* 1, 7–8.

10 This is the date suggested in Richard Ely, 'Andrew Inglis Clark and Church-State Separation' (1975) 8 *Journal of Religious History* 271, 271–2, 274–6.

11 Andrew Inglis Clark, 'Denominational Education' in Richard Ely (ed), *A Living Force: Andrew Inglis Clark and the Ideal of Commonwealth* (Centre for Tasmanian Historical Studies, 2001) 145, 146.

12 This is the dating suggested in Richard Ely, 'Clark's "Why I am a Democrat"' in Richard Ely (ed), *A Living Force: Andrew Inglis Clark and the Ideal of Commonwealth* (Centre for Tasmanian Historical Studies, 2001) 27, 27–8.

and fundamental rights of the individual.'[13] In that essay, Clark also wrote that 'fundamental laws for the protection of natural rights of the individual beyond the reach of the majority of the hour' are an important feature of a genuine democracy.[14] It seems reasonable to conclude that clauses 46 and 81 were, for Clark, instances of such fundamental laws.

The historians F M Neasy and L J Neasy have described Clark's two clauses as 'curiously inconsistent' given the more comprehensive restriction Clark's clauses would have placed on the Federal Parliament.[15] Clark had strong views about the separation of church and state, and was firmly opposed to proposals about granting state aid to Catholic schools. Indeed, 'Denominational Education' was written as part of Tasmanian political debates about that issue,[16] and in that essay Clark argued that such aid would amount to 'state endowment of particular forms of religion.'[17] From Clark's perspective then it seems that clause 46 had some potential to prohibit state aid. The same cannot be said of clause 81, given public funding of one religion does not amount to prohibiting the free exercise of other religions. The Memorandum[18] in which Clark provided a commentary on his Draft Constitution offers no explanation as to why Clark used the language that he did or why he sought to limit the powers of the Federal and Provincial (i.e. State) Parliaments in different ways.

Clark's religion provisions are curious for reasons beyond simply the differing restrictions they would have imposed. Clark was deeply familiar with the *United States Constitution* including its prohibition in the First Amendment that 'Congress shall make no law respecting an establishment of religion, or prohibiting the free exercise thereof.' This familiarity, or as one commentator has called it, Clark's 'American sympathies',[19] probably explains the inclusion of prohibitions against religious establishment and interference with the free exercise of religion. It probably also explains Clark's choice of the verb 'prohibiting.' The *United States Constitution* also contains a prohibition on the imposition of religious tests for public office and yet Clark's draft does not include a similar prohibition.[20] No explanation for this absence is apparent.

It is also unclear whether Clark's clause 46 is intended to be broader in its coverage than the First Amendment or whether Clark's expanded language is more for the avoidance of any doubt that 'support' and 'preferential recognition' were prohibited under the rubric of establishment. In his *The Making of the Australian Constitution*, J A La Nauze takes the view that Clark's clause 46 was broader in scope than the First Amendment, writing that 'Clark was bound to appropriate or adapt such an admirable provision and

13 Andrew Inglis Clark, 'Why I am A Democrat' in Marcus Haward and James Warden (eds), *An Australian Democrat: The Life, Work, and Consequences of Andrew Inglis Clark* (Centre for Tasmanian Historical Studies, 1995) 200, 204.

14 Ibid.

15 F M Neasy and L J Neasy, *Andrew Inglis Clark* (University of Tasmania Law Press, 2001) 146.

16 See Richard Ely, 'Protecting Commonwealth from Church: Clark's "Denominational Education", and Beyond' in Richard Ely (ed), *A Living Force: Andrew Inglis Clark and the Ideal of Commonwealth* (Centre for Tasmanian Historical Studies, 2001) 140.

17 Clark, 'Denominational Education', above n 11, 148.

18 Reproduced in Williams, above n 7, 65–79.

19 John Reynolds, 'A I Clark's American Sympathies and his Influence on Australian Federation' (1958) 32(3) *Australian Law Journal* 62.

20 *United States Constitution* art VI cl 3.

indeed he went further, to make sure that neither believers nor nonbelievers should have power to enforce their views on others.'[21] However, La Nauze offers no further explanation for his conclusion, which presumably rests on the fact of additional language being included in the clause.

Of particular interest for section 116 jurisprudence, is Clark's use of the expression 'for the purpose of' in connection to only one of the matters prohibited by his clause 46. Why Clark chose to include a purposive element is not clear and nor is it clear whether this suggests that the word 'for' used in connection with the other matters prohibited in clause 46 was intended to mean something broader than 'for the purpose of.' It is also puzzling that the word 'for' features in clause 46's prohibition against laws prohibiting the free exercise of religion but not in the same prohibition in clause 81 directed to the States. It is far from clear if Clark intended this to have any significance or whether he thought his clauses imposed the same restriction on the Commonwealth and the States. Much, jurisprudentially, has been made of section 116's use of the word 'for' and there is authority that it introduces a purposive element to the prohibitions contained in that provision.[22] Whether that is an accurate historical analysis of section 116's language, and the significance of the language of Clark's clauses to that question, will be examined in detail in the next chapter.

Ultimately, it seems that Clark's religion clauses were, as Neasy and Neasy put it, 'poorly thought out.'[23] Clark's later actions in 1897 in seeking to expand the prohibition during the interval between the Adelaide and Sydney sessions of the Federal Convention in which the colonial parliaments were suggesting amendments to the draft constitution would seem to support Neasy and Neasy's view. Those actions also speak against any possibility that the narrower prohibition directed to the States was a matter of deference to States' rights.

Clark's provisions at the 1891 Convention

In the event, Clark's clause 81 was included in the draft Constitution Bill produced by the 1891 Convention but a version of clause 46 was not.[24] What was then clause 16 of Chapter V, 'The States', read: 'A State shall not make any law prohibiting the free exercise of any religion.' How that provision made its way into the draft is not entirely clear since the Convention did not debate either of Clark's clauses or the ideas embodied in those clauses. Indeed, in their *Annotated Constitution of the Commonwealth of Australia*, Quick and Garran write: 'How such a clause crept into the Bill of 1891 it is difficult to conjecture.'[25] However, it is possible to assemble some clues.

On 18 March 1891, the Convention resolved to establish three committees: one to examine provisions relating to finance, taxation and trade regulation, one to consider the

21 J A La Nauze, *The Making of the Australian Constitution* (Melbourne University Press, 1972) 228.

22 *Attorney-General (Vic); Ex Rel Black v Commonwealth* (*'DOGS case'*) (1981) 146 CLR 559, 583 (Barwick CJ), 599 (Gibbs J), 609 (Stephen J), 616 (Mason J), 653 (Wilson J); *Kruger v Commonwealth* (*'Stolen Generations case'*) (1997) 190 CLR 1, 40 (Brennan J), 86 (Toohey J), 124, 132–3 (Gaudron J), 160 (Gummow J).

23 Neasy and Neasy, above n 15, 147.

24 The Draft Bill is printed as an appendix to *Official Report of the National Australasian Convention Debates*, Sydney, 1891.

25 Quick and Garran, above n 3, 953.

establishment of a federal judiciary, and one for the consideration of constitutional machinery and the distribution of functions and powers.[26] In addition to its own duties, the latter committee, known as the Constitutional Committee, would receive reports from the other two committees and put together a draft Bill for the consideration of the whole Convention.

The Constitutional Committee consisted of 14 members, two from each of the colonies participating in the Convention. Clark was one of its members. The Committee met between 18 and 30 March 1891 with Sir Samuel Griffith, the Premier of Queensland, as its chairman.

In Griffith's *Successive Stages of the Constitution of the Commonwealth of Australia*[27] – a collection of various of Griffith's papers relating to the drafting of the *Constitution* – is reproduced a 'List of matters submitted to the Constitutional Committee for decision preparatory to drawing Constitution.'[28] The list is dated 19 March 1891. It is typed, with some additional points handwritten to the side. There is no mention of religion. However, to the side of the list of matters under the heading 'States' is written 'Limitation of powers.' Immediately following that list in Griffith's volume is a typed document entitled 'Memorandum of Decisions of Constitutional Committee' and marked 'confidential.'[29] There is no mention in that document of religion and under the heading 'States' there is nothing about limiting the powers of the States.

Nevertheless, the Committee produced a draft Constitution Bill including a clause limiting the power of the States to make laws prohibiting the free exercise of religion.[30] Indeed, such a clause is found in every one of the working drafts produced by the Committee.[31] Moreover, the Committee commenced its work with such a clause. Griffith had prepared a draft that was put before the Committee as a starting point for its work that included a clause prohibiting States from making laws prohibiting the free exercise of religion.[32] None of the drafts included a provision limiting the Commonwealth's power to legislate on religious matters.

The Committee's minutes say nothing about Clark's clause 46.[33] In relation to clause 16 of Chapter V, the official, and slightly rephrased, version of Clark's clause 81, the minutes reveal that the clause was agreed to by a vote of seven to five.[34] The minutes do not indicate how individual Committee members voted and do not note the point or

26 *Proceedings of the National Australasian Convention Debates*, Sydney, 18 March 1891, 509.
27 Sir Samuel Griffith, *Successive Stages of the Constitution of the Commonwealth of Australia*, held in the State Library of New South Wales call number DLMSQ 198.
28 Also reproduced in Williams, above n 7, 56.
29 Also reproduced in Ibid 58–60.
30 The draft is reproduced in Ibid 293–337.
31 See the various reproductions in Ibid 135ff.
32 Reproduced in Ibid 136–60.
33 Constitutional Committee, Minutes of the Proceedings of the Committee on the Constitution Bill, National Archives of Australia, series R26. In *The Making of the Australian Constitution* (Melbourne University Press, 1972), 46 J A La Nauze writes that 'no minutes [of the Committee's meetings] are available beyond the confidential record of decisions.' After La Nauze wrote, the minutes of the Constitutional Committee's meetings were discovered and have been made available in the National Archives of Australia.
34 Constitutional Committee, Minutes of the Proceedings of the Committee on the Constitution Bill, National Archives of Australia, series R26, 69.

points of disagreement. Significantly, the inclusion of that clause appears contrary to the instructions provided to the Committee by the Convention in the form of resolutions embodying guiding principles. The first of those resolutions required the preservation of the powers of the States except as was 'necessary and incidental to the power and authority of the National Federal Government.'[35] It is difficult to conclude that a clause prohibiting the States from interfering with the free exercise of religion fits this description. It seems likely that Clark brought sufficient influence to bear to ensure that the clause was included.

There is some evidence to suggest that Clark's clause 46, or at least a prohibition directed to the Commonwealth, may have been contemplated by delegates in 1891. In 1898, Edmund Barton, who had been a member of the 1891 Constitutional Committee, told the Melbourne session of the Australasian Federal Convention of 1897–8 that

> the reason why the prohibition in the first draft of the Bill which was prepared in 1891 was confined to the states was that it could not, by any possibility, be concluded that it was necessary to extend such a provision to the Commonwealth, because no power was given to the Commonwealth to deal with the matter of religion.[36]

There are, however, no official records from 1891 indicating any discussion of Clark's clause 46 or the possibility of a prohibition directed to the Commonwealth. Indeed, Barton's comment in 1898 appears to be the only record.

Referring to Barton's comment and Clark's provisions, La Nauze writes:

> The provisions concerning the federal Parliament were . . . removed before Griffith's official draft came to the Convention, for the simple reason (if Barton's recollection was correct) that since there was no specific Commonwealth power to legislate on religion, there was no point in forbidding something that could not be done anyhow.[37]

La Nauze is mistaken in his use of the word 'removed.' A prohibition directed to the Commonwealth was never included in any draft prepared by the Constitutional Committee and indeed the initial draft Griffith had prepared for the Committee did not include a prohibition directed to the Commonwealth.[38] For whatever reason, Griffith adopted Clark's clause 81 but not Clark's clause 46. It was therefore not possible for it to have been 'removed.'

35 *Proceedings of the National Australasian Convention*, Sydney, 18 March 1891, 499. It should also be noted that on 3 March 1891 Clark wrote to Griffith enclosing draft resolutions that included one to similar effect:

> All the powers now possessed by the respective Parliaments of the colonies shall continue to be possessed and to be exercisable by such Parliaments after Federation excepting only such of the powers aforesaid as the Federal Parliament shall require to possess for the purpose of performing the functions specifically delegated to it.

The letter is reproduced in Ely, *A Living Force*, above n 12, 343–5.

36 *Official Report of the National Australasian Convention Debates*, Melbourne, 8 February 1898, 661 (Edmund Barton).

37 La Nauze, above n 33, 228 (citation omitted).

38 Reproduced in Williams, above n 7, 136–60.

On 31 March 1891, Griffith submitted to the Convention the report of the Constitutional Committee, which included a draft Bill as an appendix.[39] The Convention did not discuss clause 16 of Chapter V, which remained untouched in the Constitution Bill adopted by the Convention on 9 April 1891.[40] Whilst Quick and Garran may have found it difficult to conjecture as to why a clause prohibiting the States from prohibiting the free exercise of religion was included in the 1891 draft Constitution Bill, it seems likely that the influence of Andrew Inglis Clark was key.

The Seventh Day Adventists' petitions

The Seventh Day Adventists' campaign sought that no religious references be included in the *Constitution* and that an explicit denial of power in respect of religion to both the Commonwealth and the States be included. Their petitions included suggested wording.

The petitions send to the Federal Convention by the Seventh Day Adventists and drafted by the American A G Daniells who was editor of the *Southern Sentinel & Herald of Liberty*[41] asked that not only should there be no constitutional recognition of God 'but that a declaration be made in the Constitution stating that neither the Federal Government nor any State Parliament shall make any law respecting religion, or prohibiting the free exercise thereof.'[42]

The language suggested by the Seventh Day Adventists is significant. On first glance, it appears to be a paraphrase of the religion clauses of the First Amendment to the *United States Constitution*, which state 'Congress shall make law respecting an establishment of religion, or prohibiting the free exercise thereof.' The slight change to the language in the form of deleting 'an establishment of' was significant.

The Seventh Day Adventist language was comprehensive; indeed it was complete. It appears to prohibit the Commonwealth, as well as the States, from dealing with religion in every shape and form: the prohibition is against 'any law respecting religion.' That language would have had serious legal consequences. For example, a law authorising ministers of religion to solemnise marriages might be characterised as law respecting religion and therefore be invalid. The additional words 'or prohibiting the free exercise thereof' appear redundant: a law prohibiting the free exercise of religion would be a law respecting religion. Unlike the actual language of section 116, the Seventh Day Adventist language meets the description 'Commonwealth not to legislate in respect of religion' provided in the heading to section 116.

The modification of the language of the First Amendment may well have been deliberate. The First Amendment, adopted in 1791, seemingly did nothing to assist the Seventh Day Adventists on the issue of Sabbath observance laws in America. In America the Seventh Day Adventists had also been 'enthusiastic pamphleteers, lobbyists, and petitioners' against

39 The draft is reproduced in Ibid 293–337.

40 The Draft Bill is printed as an appendix to *Proceedings of the National Australasian Convention Debates*, Sydney, 1891.

41 Milton Frederick Krause, *The Seventh Day Adventist Church in Australia: 1885–1900* (MA Thesis, The University of Sydney, 1969) 251; A W Anderson, *Religious Liberty in Australasia: The Attitude of Seventh Day Adventists to Religious Legislation and to Military Service* (Signs Publishing Co, 1917) 12.

42 *Official Report of the National Australasian Convention Debates*, Adelaide, 6 April 1897, 405.

various proposals for religiously-inspired plans to amend the *United States Constitution* to expressly recognise God, introduce temperance laws, and introduce Sunday observance laws where they did not exist in the period from the adoption of the First Amendment to the 1890s and afterwards.[43]

The Seventh Day Adventists in Australia knew that the language of the First Amendment was not necessarily sufficient to ensure that a new Australian parliament would not be able to enact laws concerning religion, and particularly to ensure that Sunday observance laws would be invalid. The 'little handbook' Higgins lent to Barton at the Convention was potentially a pamphlet published by the Seventh Day Adventists criticising the United States Supreme Court decision in *Church of the Holy Trinity* and arguing that the decision authorised the enactment of federal Sunday observance laws even in the face of the First Amendment.

A G Daniells who drafted the Seventh Day Adventists' petition to the Federal Convention was a prominent player in the Adventists' campaigns in America.[44] For this reason, it might be surmised that the comprehensive language suggested by the Seventh Day Adventists was a deliberate departure from the language of the First Amendment. The inclusion of the redundant words 'or prohibiting the free exercise thereof' might be explained as non-lawyers acting out of an abundance of caution.

There is also evidence against the idea that modifying the language of the First Amendment was a deliberate decision. Following the Adelaide session of the Convention, the draft Constitution Bill did not mention God in the preamble and contained a clause prohibiting the States from making laws prohibiting the free exercise of religion. Daniells, it seems, was happy with this situation. In response to lobbying organised by the Councils of Churches directed to the parliaments of the colonies participating in the Convention seeking the recognition of God in the constitutional preamble, Daniells drafted another petition to be sent to the colonial parliaments asking them not to recommend:

> any measure or amendment for the insertion of any religious clause or declaration of religious belief in the Constitution of the Australian Commonwealth which might be taken as a basis for such legislation, but that, in this respect, it be allowed to remain framed and adopted by the delegates to the Adelaide Federal Convention.[45]

In the *Sentinel*, Daniells editorialised:

> The Constitution of the Australian Commonwealth, framed and adopted by the delegates to the Adelaide Federal Convention, takes its place with the noblest political documents ever produced, so far as it pertains to the question of Church and State. By withholding from the Federal Government the power to touch religious matters, and prohibiting the States from religious legislation, it recognises the total separation of religion and civil government, and thus guarantees full religious liberty to all it citizens.[46]

43 Richard Ely, *Unto God and Caesar: Religious Issues in the Emerging Commonwealth, 1891–1906* (Melbourne University Press, 1976), 27.

44 Ibid 28, n 22.

45 Anderson, above n 41, 16.

46 Ibid 14.

This is a quite different view to that expressed in the original Seventh Day Adventist petitions. Those original petitions sought not only the absence of any mention of God but also an express prohibition directed to the Commonwealth as well as the States. The original position was not satisfied simply with the absence of an express federal religion power, as the latter position seems to have been. Daniells may have subscribed to the general view of the time that a lack of any express power over religion meant the Commonwealth could not legislate in respect of religion and, given the Adelaide draft Constitution Bill had no religious references, he might well have been satisfied that an express prohibition was unnecessary.

Whatever the thinking underlying the original Seventh Day Adventist language and Daniells' analysis of the Adelaide position, Higgins did not propose the Convention adopt that language, which would almost certainly have constituted more than 'a sufficient safeguard against the passing of religious laws by the Commonwealth', which was his expressed aim. At no point during the Federal Convention did Higgins propose language that would have gone as far as the Seventh Day Adventist language.

The Federal Convention's Adelaide language

On the second day of the Federal Convention, three committees were established.[47] As in 1891, there was a Constitutional Committee, a Finance Committee and a Judiciary Committee, and the Constitutional Committee was tasked with preparing a draft Constitution Bill for consideration by the whole Convention.

The Constitutional Committee presented its report to the Convention on 12 April 1897, and included a draft Constitution Bill drawn up by a drafting sub-committee consisting of Edmund Barton, Sir John Downer and Richard O'Connor.[48] The Committee's draft included the religion clause from the 1891 Bill: 'A State shall not make any law prohibiting the free exercise of any religion.'[49] The Committee's minutes do not reveal any discussion about this provision,[50] nor was the provision debated by the Convention at Adelaide.

Unlike in 1891, inclusion of the clause in the first draft of the Constitution Bill was not necessarily contrary to the instructions issued to the Committee by the Convention. The Convention's resolutions required preserving the powers of the States 'except in respect of such surrenders as may be agreed upon to secure uniformity of law and administration in matters of common concern.'[51] It is possible that the free exercise of religion was considered to be a matter of common concern. The Constitutional Committee might also have thought that it was a matter about which agreement could be reached, with the *Constitution* itself providing the uniformity of law.

It is also possible that the clause was included, without any real thought given to the matter, simply because the clause appeared in the 1891 Constitution Bill. Given the silence

47 *Official Report of the National Australasian Convention Debates*, Adelaide, 23 March 1897, 19.

48 Reproduced in Williams, above n 7, 499–525.

49 Ibid 522 (clause 108).

50 National Archives of Australia, Series R213.

51 *Official Report of the National Australasian Convention Debates*, Adelaide, 23 March 1897, 17.

of the Committee's minutes on this matter and the absence of other records it is impossible to know. At the close of the Adelaide session, the prohibition directed to the States was numbered as clause 109.

The draft produced at Adelaide then fell for consideration by the colonial Parliaments. Motions were moved in the South Australian and Tasmanian parliaments to amend clause 109.

In the South Australian House of Assembly, Patrick Glynn, who later moved the motion for recognition of God in the preamble at the Federal Convention, sought to have clause 109, in his word, 'eliminated.'[52] He argued that the clause had nothing to do with Federation and so the power of the States on the matter should remain untouched. Glynn also argued that, in any case, there was 'practically absolute [religious] tolerance in Australia' making the clause simply unnecessary. Clause 109 was, Glynn said, '[n]othing more than an insult to the State[s].' Sir John Downer argued to the contrary that clause 109 was a 'most proper provision' and served a useful purpose as a guarantee against religious intolerance ever arising.[53] The next speaker, Clement Giles, who was not a Convention delegate, made an argument that would later be made at subsequent sessions of the Convention. He also asked: 'so long as they did not recognise a religion or a God as far as the State was concerned why should they have the clause?[54] The next speaker echoed Glynn's position[55] and another thought that the clause would reflect poorly on the States.[56] In the end, clause 109 was accepted without a vote.[57]

In contrast, in the Tasmanian House of Assembly there was a successful attempt to recommend expansion of clause 109. Andrew Inglis Clark, at the time Tasmanian Attorney-General but not a delegate to the Federal Convention, moved that it be recommended that the words 'nor appropriate any portion of its revenues or property for the propagation or support of any religion' be added to clause 109.[58] This motion seems to confirm the suggestion that Clark's original religion clauses were not properly thought out. After all, clause 109 was Clark's own clause 81. Clark only stated that the words were necessary because the clause as it stood did not deal with the issue of funding religion.[59] Interestingly, whilst Clark's draft Constitution Bill included a clause binding on the Commonwealth, Clark did not seek to extend clause 109 to bind the Commonwealth. The only other speaker on the motion was the former Premier and current Treasurer and Convention delegate, Philip Fysh, who noted that the effect of the motion would be to deny to Tasmania a power it currently possessed and which was not being surrendered to the Commonwealth.[60] Clark's motion was agreed to without a vote.[61] Clark provided further

52 South Australia, *Parliamentary Debates*, House of Assembly, 25 August 1897, 497.
53 Ibid 497.
54 Ibid 497.
55 Ibid 498 (Egerton Batchelor).
56 Ibid 498 (Frederick Coneybeer).
57 Ibid 498.
58 Tasmania, *Debates on the Draft Commonwealth Bill, as adopted by the Convention at Adelaide, March–May, 1897*, House of Assembly, 18 August 1897, 257.
59 Ibid.
60 Ibid.
61 Ibid.

explanation of his amendment in a memorandum he sent to Convention delegates. He wrote:

> In its present form section 109 secures religious equality for all the citizens of a State, so far as it prevents the State from placing the adherents of any form of religion under any disadvantage or restriction in the exercise of it in comparison with adherents of other forms of religion; but it does not secure perfect religious equality to all the citizens so far as the granting of any special privileges or favours or endowments to particular forms of religion are concerned. And the object of the proposed amendment is to secure perfect religious equality in both directions, by preventing any particular benefit or support being given by the State to any form of religion.[62]

The Tasmanian Legislative Council voted against Clark's additional words by a vote of five to six, but the Tasmanian *Hansard* does not record any debate on the question.[63]

The Federal Convention's February language

The Sydney session of the Convention did not consider clause 109 which, accordingly, remained unchanged in the draft carried forward to the Melbourne session.[64] However, it appears to have been at the Sydney session that Higgins placed on the notice paper a proposed amendment to clause 109.[65] The Higgins amendment would have read: 'A State shall not, nor shall the Commonwealth, make any law prohibiting the free exercise of religion, or imposing any religious test or observance.'

In terms of form, Higgins had simply added additional words to the existing 'A State shall not make any law prohibiting the free exercise of any religion.' In terms of substance, Higgins' amendment did not reflect a considered view as to the most appropriate form of words for such a provision.

At the Melbourne session of the Convention on 7 February 1898 Higgins introduced, but did not formally move, his amendment to clause 109.[66] Higgins said:

> An amendment of this clause, which has hitherto been passed without discussion, has been standing in my name for some time. I do not think the clause goes far enough . . . In the American Constitution they have gone further, and the first amendment of that Constitution contains these words: -
>
> > Congress shall make no law respecting the establishment of a religion [sic], or prohibiting the free exercise thereof.

62 The memorandum is reproduced in Williams, above n 7, 705–10.

63 Tasmania, *Debates on the Draft Commonwealth Bill, as adopted by the Convention at Adelaide, March–May, 1897*, 20 August 1897, 278.

64 See *Official Report of the National Australasian Convention Debates*, Sydney.

65 Ely, *Unto God and Caesar*, above n 43, 55.

66 *Official Report of the National Australasian Convention Debates*, Melbourne, 7 February 1898, 654.

> Some people will think that it is idle at this time of day to pass a law to prevent the prohibition [or][67] the establishment of a religion; but it is not idle in the eyes of a number of people whose votes we should like to secure for the Constitution . . .
>
> [The amendment] has been circulated for several days, and is to the effect that neither a state nor the Commonwealth shall make any law prohibiting the free exercise of any religion or imposing any religious test or observance.[68]

Given Higgins' reference to the *United States Constitution*, it is curious that he chose not to include a prohibition concerning religious establishment. Whether this is an indication that the Seventh Day Adventists' language had some sort of influence on Higgins' thinking, given that the Seventh Day Adventists' suggested wording did not refer to the concept of establishment either, is not clear.

After speaking on the subject of why a provision limiting the Commonwealth's power in respect of religion was necessary, Higgins concluded his remarks for that day in this way:

> There is . . . I am bound to admit, a defect in the amendment I have suggested. My amendment, as printed, is as follows: -
>
> > After word "not" insert "nor shall the Commonwealth"; and after word "religion" insert "or imposing any religious test or observance."
>
> I think we must qualify that in some way, because it has been said that it would void our imposing of the ordinary oaths in the courts and elsewhere.[69]

Higgins did not indicate where it had been said or by whom that ordinary oaths might be affected by his additional words or whether it was the prohibition on religious tests, religious observances or both that was the potential problem. Presumably, the concern arose sometime after Higgins had placed his amendment on the notice paper.

After Higgins finished his introductory remarks, the Tasmanian Premier and delegate, Sir Edward Braddon, indicated that he would seek to move the Tasmanian House of Assembly's amendment to clause 109 as well as an amendment of his own. Braddon's own amendment would insert 'some such words' as '[b]ut shall prevent the performance of any such religious rites, as are of a cruel or demoralizing character or contrary to the law of the Commonwealth.'[70] Braddon's announcement concluded the day's discussion of clause 109.

The next morning – 8 February 1898 – Higgins formally moved that clause 109 be amended. He began his remarks:

> I spoke on this clause yesterday evening. I now want to say that, after careful deliberation, I think the wording of my amendment ought to be rectified before it is submitted to the Convention. The existing clause is-
>
> > A state shall not make any law prohibiting the free exercise of any religion.

67 The transcript has the word 'of.' This appears to be a typographical error.
68 *Official Report of the National Australasian Convention Debates*, Melbourne, 7 February 1898, 654.
69 *Official Record of the Debates of the Australasian Federal Convention*, Melbourne, 7 February 1898, 656–7.
70 Ibid 657.

There is no application to the Federal Parliament at all in the clause as it stands. I intend to propose amendments which, if adopted, will make the clause read as follows:

> A state shall not, nor shall the Commonwealth, make any law prohibiting the free exercise of any religion, or for the establishment of any religion, or imposing any religious observance.[71]

Higgins said:

> If you look at the First Amendment of the [United States] Constitution you will find that there is no prohibition on a state doing this thing, but there is a prohibition on Congress against either making a law prohibiting the free exercise of any religion, or for the establishment of a religion. I add, here, "or imposing any religious observance."[72]

So between the adjournment in the evening of 7 February and the commencement of proceedings on 8 February, Higgins had rethought his desired clause. He now wished to include a prohibition against establishment such that each of the two religious prohibitions in the First Amendment of the *United States Constitution* would find a counterpart in the *Australian Constitution*, in addition to the uniquely Australian express prohibition against the imposition of religious observances.

It is noteworthy that in his proposed clause Higgins uses the word 'for' only in connection to one of his prohibitions. What meaning or significance, if any, Higgins thought 'for' had is not apparent from looking to the text of his provision and nor did he comment on the word in the Convention. The next chapter of this book examines what the Convention might have understood the word 'for' to mean in more detail as part of a broader discussion of the Convention's understanding of the meaning of section 116's terms. For the purposes of this chapter, the significance of this point is that Higgins did not seem to believe the word 'for' amounted to a substantive change to the meaning of the First Amendment's language, given that he described the First Amendment as including a prohibition against laws 'for the establishment of a religion.'

After some discussion as to why a religious prohibition was necessary at all, the former South Australian Attorney-General and delegate, Josiah Symon, asked 'whether it would not be better to do away with this clause altogether, and limit the prohibition to the imposition of any religious test?'[73] Higgins immediately replied that 'observance' might be a better word because '"[t]est" might include oaths administered in our courts and elsewhere.'[74] In this, Higgins was expressing the same concern about oaths that he had expressed the previous afternoon.

Higgins' 'careful deliberation' overnight, which sought to 'rectif[y]' the clause in order to address the concern about religious tests, seems not to have been particularly careful at all. The *United States Constitution* also has a provision prohibiting religious tests. Article VI

71 *Official Record of the Debates of the Australasian Federal Convention*, Melbourne, 8 February 1898, 658.

72 Ibid. The religion clauses of the First Amendment later came to be binding on the States by reason of the 'incorporation doctrine' of the Fourteenth Amendment: *Cantwell v Connecticut*, 310 US 296 (1940); *Everson v Board of Education of Ewing*, 330 US 1 (1947).

73 *Official Record of the Debates of the Australasian Federal Convention*, Melbourne, 8 February 1898, 660.

74 Ibid.

provides in part that 'no religious test shall ever be required as a qualification to any office or public trust under the United States.' Presumably, it is from this American provision that Higgins got the idea in the first place to include a prohibition against religious tests in the provision that was discussed on 7 February.

It seems inconsistent that overnight Higgins decided to add the American concept of establishment but also delete the American concept of religious tests. After all, Higgins justified the inclusion of a prohibition against religious establishment on the basis that it was in the First Amendment. Consistency in reasoning might have demanded that any other American religion provision should also be proposed for inclusion in the *Australian Constitution*. Indeed, after Higgins expressed concern about oaths, Symon pointed to the American provision.[75] Had Higgins adopted the phraseology of the American religious tests provision, as Symon had suggested in asking Higgins whether a prohibition only against religious tests might be better, his concern about the effect of a prohibition against religious tests would most probably have been alleviated, since the American provision limits the prohibition to offices and public trusts.

Higgins' deliberation over the new wording of his clause was plainly not careful and it may not have been very long either. Higgins was facing an uphill battle to persuade other delegates that some sort of religious prohibition was necessary in the first place and devoting his time and intellectual energies to that matter may have been more pressing than the precise language of his clause. Indeed, it was in the afternoon or evening of 7 February that Higgins had a private conversation with Barton about that very matter. That conversation included a discussion of the effects of the United States Supreme Court's decision in *Church of the Holy Trinity*. It is also likely that it was during that conversation that Higgins lent Barton a copy of the mysterious 'little handbook.' Higgins may well have been too busy with lobbying activity to engage in much intellectual deliberation at all about the most appropriate form of words. This might provide an explanation for his inconsistent approach in deciding to adopt the American prohibition against religious establishment but not the American prohibition against religious tests.

Whatever the case, discussion continued in the Convention and it became apparent to Higgins that there was little support for any prohibition directed to the States. Recognising the general consensus on this issue, Higgins stated: 'I am willing that the prohibition should extend only to the Commonwealth.'[76] Symon put it to Higgins that it might be better if the whole clause was struck out and replaced with 'a declaration of this sort:- "No religious test shall be imposed as a qualification for any public office or trust in the Commonwealth or in a state."'[77] Symon's language has some resemblance to the religious tests clause of the *United States Constitution* in that it limits its operation to public positions thereby avoiding issues about oaths in court.

Braddon then indicated that he had changed his mind about his own amendment, fearing that even with a qualification such as he had suggested, it might prevent the law from dealing with unacceptable practices.[78] Braddon indicated that he would prefer the clause be struck out altogether.

75 Ibid.
76 Ibid 662.
77 Ibid.
78 Ibid.

Ignoring Symon and Braddon's specific comments, Higgins continued:

> I am very glad that I have called attention to this clause. I thoroughly agree that as it stands it is an anomaly, and that there should not be a prohibition upon the states. All I said was that if you prohibited the states from making laws respecting religious observance, and if you inserted in the preamble a recognition of the Almighty, it was fit that you should extend a similar prohibition to the Commonwealth. It would answer my purpose absolutely if the clause only enacted that the Commonwealth should be prohibited from passing a law of this kind. A number of honest people will have a great deal of difficulty about voting aye for the Constitution if there is no prohibition against the making of laws affecting religion by the Parliament of the Commonwealth. What they ask is: "Why cannot we follow the example of the United States of America?"[79]

Higgins was indicating that it was the text of the *United States Constitution* that provided a useful model to emulate for the purposes of adopting language for his clause. However, following the example of the United States would surely involve including a prohibition against religious tests. Higgins' general thinking, as he outlined it, was not fully reflected in the language of his proposed provision. The form of Higgins' provision seems not to have been well thought out.

After further discussion as to why a provision limiting the Commonwealth's power in respect of religion might be necessary, Higgins' clause was negatived on the voices without a vote.[80] The Tasmanian House of Assembly's proposed amendment was also negatived without any specific discussion of it.[81]

The Federal Convention's March language

The Convention considered the question of including an express denial of power in respect of religion again on 2 March. That morning during debate on what was ultimately a successful motion to include the words 'humbly relying on the blessing of Almighty God' in the constitutional preamble, Higgins indicated he would again try to insert a religious prohibition in the *Constitution* to serve as 'a sufficient safeguard against the passing of religious laws by the Commonwealth.'[82] He explained he had prepared a 'clause modified to meet some criticisms which have been made on the point' in February.[83]

That afternoon, Higgins' new clause to replace the deleted clause 109 came on for discussion.[84] In introducing his motion, Higgins said:

> My idea is to make it clear beyond doubt that the powers which the states individually have of making such laws as they like with regard to religion shall remain undisturbed

79 Ibid 662–3.
80 Ibid 664.
81 Ibid.
82 *Official Record of the Debates of the Australasian Federal Convention*, Melbourne, 2 March 1898, 1734.
83 Ibid.
84 Ibid 1769.

> and unbroken, and to make it clear that in framing this Constitution there is no intention whatever to give to the Federal Parliament the power to interfere in these matters . . .
>
> I beg to move the insertion of the following new clause to replace clause 109 already struck out: -
>
> > The Commonwealth shall not make any law prohibiting the free exercise of any religion, or for the establishment of any religion, or imposing any religious observance, and no religious test shall be required as a qualification for any office or public trust under the Commonwealth.[85]

Higgins explained to the Convention that 'most of this clause, with regard to the making of laws, is already in the American Constitution, either in the original Constitution or by way of an amendment of the Convention.'[86] He said:

> In the Constitution of the United States there is a provision that the Federal Parliament is not to make any law prohibiting the free exercise of any religion, and there is also a clause, the very first amendment of the Constitution, that the Federal Parliament is not to make any law for the establishment of any religion. In the original Constitution you will find also a clause to the effect that there is to be no religious test required as a qualification for any post or office. The only difficulty, therefore, is in respect of these words about imposing religious observances, and that part, as I have already indicated this morning, is rendered necessary by the inclusion in the preamble of our Constitution of words which they have not got in the American Constitution.[87]

Higgins' new clause, like his earlier February one, was not necessarily the result of careful deliberation. Contrary to the suggestion in his comments, Higgins' prohibition against religious tests is not 'with regard to the making of laws.' The grammatical structure of Higgins' clause has that prohibition disconnected from the command 'The Commonwealth shall not make any law.' That command forms part of only the first three clauses of the provision. Higgins, it appears, simply copied the American religious tests clause, which prohibits religious tests for offices or public trusts under the United States and is not expressed as a denial of legislative power. It is also worth noting that Higgins seems to have decided that a prohibition against religious tests phrased similarly to the *United States Constitution* would not be problematic after all.

More significantly, Higgins' comments appear to suggest that he believed that by roughly copying the three religion clauses of the *United States Constitution* and adding an additional prohibition against the imposition of religious observances the Commonwealth would have no power to make laws 'on the subject of' religion. However, Higgins' language is not a complete denial of power to the Commonwealth in respect of religion in the manner that the Seventh Day Adventists' language might well have been. Higgins' language prohibits four things and no more.

85 Ibid.
86 Ibid.
87 Ibid.

No explanation suggests itself as to why Higgins believed his language would be a comprehensive denial of power to make laws 'on the subject of' religion. It is unlikely that Higgins was under the impression that the only way the United States Congress could interfere with religion was in respect of religious observances. Higgins knew that the religion clauses of the *United States Constitution* did not constitute a complete denial of power over religion to the United States Congress. After all, it was Higgins who told the Convention repeatedly about how Congress had imposed a religious observance in the form of the Sunday close condition on its funding of the Chicago Exhibition. If Congress could impose a religious observance notwithstanding the religion clauses in the *United States Constitution* then Higgins may well have wondered whether Congress might be able to legislate in respect of religion in other ways too.

Why then did Higgins believe that the *United States Constitution* provided a useful model to emulate? Given that Higgins was facing some difficulty in persuading delegates that any clause denying power to the Commonwealth to legislate in respect of religion was necessary in the first place, there appears to be a degree of pragmatism in emulating the *United States Constitution* with an added prohibition against religious observances. When sceptical delegates put it to Higgins that a clause prohibiting laws concerning religion was unnecessary because the Commonwealth was not being granted any express power to legislate in respect of religion, Higgins was able to respond with: 'Will you explain why they have these words in the First Amendment of the American Constitution?'[88] Higgins' approach was thus to point out that neither the *United States Constitution* nor the draft *Australian Constitution* conferred an express federal power to legislate in respect of religion and yet the *United States Constitution* provided an express religious prohibition. Accordingly, Higgins argued, Australia should do likewise. As Higgins said, 'most of this clause . . . is already in the American Constitution . . . The only difficulty, therefore, is in respect of these words about imposing religious observances.' What Higgins appears to have been suggesting was that the Americans had already done the thinking about the utility of the other clauses. This may have served to allay fears that the free exercise clause might have the unintended effect of preventing legislation against obnoxious practices done in the name of religion.

In respect of the religious observances clause, Higgins was obviously under the impression that a prohibition against prohibiting the free exercise of religion would not invalidate legislative efforts to impose religious observances. But why did Higgins think that? It is at least arguable that the imposition of a religious observance is an interference with the free exercise of religion. Higgins had provided an explanation of sorts as to the source of the power possessed, he believed, by Congress to impose a religious observance by closing the Chicago Exhibition on Sundays but he did not provide an explanation to the Convention of why that law was not invalid by reason of the First Amendment. In the Convention, after Higgins had given one of his explanations of the Sunday closing law, Bernhard Wise asked: '[w]as that held to be constitutional?'[89] The question was posed in terms of the law being unsupported by a head of power. Barton replied that the law 'has not been challenged yet.'[90] Higgins commented: 'I will say frankly that I am not aware that it has

88 Ibid 1778.
89 Ibid 1734.
90 Ibid.

been held to be constitutional. I understand though that there has been no dispute among the legal men in that country as to its being constitutional.'[91]

Barton was not quite right that there had been no challenge to the Sunday closing law, but Higgins may have been right about the consensus view of American lawyers. The United States Government took legal action seeking to compel the operators of the Chicago Exhibition to comply with the Sunday closing requirement. The Exhibition operators had argued before the Seventh Circuit Court of Appeals that the Sunday closing condition violated the religion clauses of the First Amendment.[92] A Senator had also suggested this in the Congressional debate on the law.[93] The matter was not discussed in the judgment since the United States Government failed on other grounds. However, Black's *Handbook of American Constitutional Law* stated that Sunday closing laws were constitutionally valid.[94] A contemporaneous academic note of the case commented that the argument was 'plainly fallacious' and that '[t]o suppose that to attach such a condition to a grant of money amounts to a law respecting the establishment of religion or prohibiting the free exercise thereof, is an argument which does not rise to a very exalted level. It requires no answer.'[95] Whether or not aware of this case note, Higgins' comment above suggests that he was aware of this thinking. This thinking seems to provide an explanation as to why Higgins thought that a religious observances clause was necessary in the *Australian Constitution* in addition to the clauses he borrowed from the *United States Constitution*. Of course, Higgins knew that the Sunday closing law had been enacted notwithstanding the First Amendment and this would have given him sufficient reason to suppose that the religion clauses of the First Amendment were not sufficient to prohibit the imposition of religious observances.

After further discussion about whether there was any need for a religion clause, Symon sought to amend Higgins' proposed clause so it would read: 'Nothing in this Constitution shall be held to empower the Commonwealth to require any religious test as a qualification for any office of public trust under the Commonwealth.'[96]

Symon was plainly following up on his suggestion as to the proper scope of a religious prohibition that he had first expressed on 8 February. There are two textual features of Symon's religious tests clause that should be highlighted. The first is that Symon uses the expression 'office *of* public trust' whereas Higgins, as with the *United States Constitution*, uses the expression 'office *or* public trust.' Higgins' clause was plainly broader than Symon's in this respect. Symon's suggested amendment on 8 February used the word 'or', suggesting that Symon was not particularly careful in the selection of his proposed language. (Alternatively, there may be a transcription error). The second textual difference concerns the entity to which the prohibition is directed. Symon's clause prohibits only the

91 Ibid 1735.

92 *World's Columbian Exposition v United States*, 56 F 654 (7th Cir, 1893).

93 23 *Congressional Record* 6003 (John Morgan) (1982, Senate):

This proposed law, Mr President, in one sense prohibits the free exercise of religion. If the majority of the gentlemen who compose the World's Fair Commission were Israelites or Seventh-Day Baptists they would consider this Act of Congress as being very obnoxious, because it controls the freedom of religion.

94 Henry Campbell Black, *Handbook of American Constitutional Law* (West Publishing Co, 1895) 392–3.

95 Note, 'Enjoining the Sunday Opening of the World's Fair' (1893) 27 *American Law Review* 571, 572.

96 *Official Record of the Debates of the Australasian Federal Convention*, Melbourne, 2 March 1898, 1775–6.

Commonwealth from requiring a religious test for the positions identified. Higgins' clause, like the *United States Constitution*, prohibits religious tests for the positions identified without limiting the prohibition to religious tests imposed only by the federal government for those positions. Higgins' clause would prevent the States from imposing religious tests for federal offices whereas Symon's would not. Neither of these textual features was the subject of any comment in the Convention. This tends to reinforce the general theme that the precise language of section 116 did not receive close attention by the Convention.

The Drafting Committee's final language

The clause proposed by Higgins and accepted by the Convention is not the clause that is now section 116 of the *Constitution*. The Convention's Drafting Committee made potentially significant alterations to its phrasing. Higgins' clause, as accepted by the Convention, stated:

> The Commonwealth shall not make any law prohibiting the free exercise of any religion, or for the establishment of any religion, or imposing any religious observance, and no religious test shall be required as a qualification for any office or public trust under the Commonwealth.

The clause as modified by the Drafting Committee and now found as section 116 states:

> The Commonwealth shall not make any law for establishing any religion, or for imposing any religious observance, or for prohibiting the free exercise of any religion, and no religious test shall be required as a qualification for any office or public trust under the Commonwealth.

There are two key differences. The Drafting Committee rearranged the order of the clauses and inserted the word 'for' in the observances and free exercise clauses. Barton, who chaired the Drafting Committee, explained to the Convention that, with one presently irrelevant exception, the Committee had 'endeavoured to faithfully interpret the wishes' of the Convention in putting together a Constitution Bill.[97] The Bill, including the modified clause, was adopted by the Convention on 16 March 1898.[98] It would seem, therefore, that the framers of the *Constitution* saw no substantive difference between the two textual formulations.

Rearranging the order of clauses appears to be trivial and of no potential legal consequence, reflecting simply a drafting style choice. However, in the *DOGS case*, Mason J states, without further analysis or elaboration, that '[t]he position of the establishment provision as the first clause in s 116 evidences the importance which was attached to it.'[99] Justice Mason was plainly wrong.

The Drafting Committee's second change – inserting the word 'for' in the observances and free exercise clauses – is not trivial and had potential legal consequences. The High

97 *Official Report of the National Australasian Convention Debates*, Melbourne, 12 March 1898, 2440.
98 Ibid 2523–44.
99 *Attorney-General (Vic); ex rel Black v Commonwealth* ('*DOGS Case*') (1981) 146 CLR 559, 617.

Court has latched onto 'for' as indicating that the first three clauses of section 116 prevent only the enactment of laws that have the purpose of establishing a religion, imposing a religious observance or prohibiting the free exercise of a religion. Laws that in fact impose religious observances, for example, but which do so in the pursuit of some other purpose are perfectly valid according to this theory.

The one thing that the Drafting Committee did not change, but which it ought to have changed, is the location of the provision in Chapter V titled 'The States.' The reason for the provision's original placement in that chapter is clear from the drafting history. In its earlier forms, the provision was a prohibition directed to the States. While it is not clear why the provision was not relocated, La Nauze suggests that 'Barton must have noticed it during his final revision, but perhaps he was too fed up to care.'[100]

The discordance between section 116's purpose and language

This chapter began by noting that there is a discordance between the expressed general purpose of section 116 to deny the Commonwealth power to make laws 'on the subject of' religion and the language of the provision. The four matters proscribed by the terms of section 116 do not amount to a complete denial to the Commonwealth of power in respect of religion. In part, this discordance is a result of the pragmatic political need on Higgins' part to persuade Convention delegates that a clause such as section 116 was necessary in the first place.

Another part of the explanation for the discordance lies in the fact that the precise language of section 116 was not the result of a careful drafting choice. Indeed, neither Clark nor Higgins were particularly thoughtful in their choice of language, and neither the 1891 Australasian Convention nor the 1897–8 Federal Convention carefully considered and debated the precise language of the provision. The language used in section 116 is rather haphazard.

100 La Nauze, above n 33, 229.

8 The original understanding of section 116

If the choice of language for section 116 was not the result of a careful drafting decision, what, if anything in particular, did the delegates to the Federal Convention understand the words they adopted as section 116 to mean?

The word 'for'

The previous chapter showed how the High Court is wrong to believe that the framers of the *Australian Constitution* made a careful decision to use the word 'for' rather than the word 'respecting' like the First Amendment does. What, if anything, did the framers understand 'for' to mean?

The starting point for an analysis of the word 'for' is the draft Constitution Bill prepared by the Tasmanian Attorney-General Andrew Inglis Clark before the 1891 National Australasian Convention. Those clauses provided:

> 46. The Federal Parliament shall not make any Law for the establishment or support of any religion, or for the purpose of giving any preferential recognition to any religion, or for prohibiting the free exercise of any religion.
> 81. No Province shall make any law prohibiting the free exercise of any religion.[1]

The previous chapter showed that it is not clear whether the language of clause 46 was intended to indicate that 'for' and 'for the purpose of' had different meanings, with only the second expression being purposive in character. The previous chapter also noted that it is not clear whether the two free exercise prohibitions were intended to have a different substantive content. The prohibition directed to the Commonwealth uses 'for' and the free exercise prohibition directed to the States does not use 'for.'

What is significant from Clark's clauses is the fact that the delegates to the 1897–8 Federal Convention would have been aware of language that was unambiguously purposive ('for the purpose of') and language that was not unambiguously purposive ('for'). It is possible, of course, that the Convention might not have recognised any substantive difference in the language. In the end, the Convention did not choose language that was unambiguously purposive.

The previous chapter showed that the religion clauses of the First Amendment, which use the word 'respecting', were relied upon heavily in developing the language of section 116. It is far from clear, however, that the delegates understood the Australian phraseology

1 Reproduced in John M Williams, *The Australian Constitution: A Documentary History* (Melbourne University Press, 2005) 80–93.

('for') to be substantively different to the American phraseology ('respecting') that they paraphrased. Henry Higgins, for instance, said in the Convention on 8 February 1898: 'If you look at the First Amendment of the [*United States*] *Constitution* . . . there is a prohibition on Congress . . . *for* the establishment of a religion.'[2] Again on 2 March 1898, Higgins said: 'In the *Constitution of the United States* . . . there is also a clause, the very first amendment of the *Constitution*, that the Federal Parliament [i.e. Congress] is not to make any law *for* the establishment of any religion.'[3] Higgins also said of his proposed clause that 'most of this clause . . . is already in the *American Constitution*.'[4] Higgins seems to have thought that 'for' and 'respecting' were synonymous. It was in this manner that he explained his proposed provision to the Convention. At the very least, it seems it did not occur to Higgins to reflect on the nuances of the language being used.

Indeed, as the previous chapter explained, in the clause (that became section 116) ultimately moved by Higgins and adopted by the Convention, the word 'for' appeared only once. The word 'for' appeared in the establishment clause but not in any of the other clauses. It was added to the free exercise and religious observances clauses by the Drafting Committee. Higgins did not explain his drafting choice, suggesting that the word 'for' was not significant.

Edmund Barton, who chaired the Drafting Committee, explained to the Convention that in putting together a Constitution Bill, the Drafting Committee had made one substantive amendment to a provision relating to disqualification from parliament on the ground of criminal conviction and that '[i]n everything else . . . the Drafting Committee has, in all instances, endeavoured to faithfully interpret the wishes of honorable members.'[5] When the Convention voted to adopt the final Constitution Bill, including with the 'for' added to the free exercise and religious observances clauses of section 116, the Convention did so thinking the word 'for' had no significance.

An early High Court decision confirms that the Convention did not think that the word 'for' was significant or had any particular meaning. The *Defence Act 1903* (Cth) required boys aged between 14 and 18 years to undertake 64 hours of military training each year. In 1912, Edgar Krygger was prosecuted at the Ballarat Court of Petty Sessions along with 115 other boys for failing to attend military training. Krygger was a Jehovah's Witness and told the magistrate that his religion prohibited his involvement in any military matters. He was convicted but challenged the legislation in the High Court arguing that it prohibited the free exercise of his religion. Chief Justice Samuel Griffith and Justice Edmund Barton heard the case. Both judges held that the legislation did not in fact prohibit the free exercise of Krygger's religion because he remained free to practise his religion as he saw fit even though he was compelled to do something his religion prohibited.[6]

If the word 'for' was intended to mean 'for the purpose of' then *Krygger's Case* would have been decided differently. Instead of deciding the case on the ground that the legislation did not in fact prohibit the free exercise of religion, The High Court would have decided the case on the ground that the legislation did not have the purpose of prohibiting the free exercise of religion. Justice Barton was, after all, earlier in his career Leader of the Federal Convention and chairman of its Drafting Committee. He would have known exactly what

2 *Official Record of the Debates of the Australasian Federal Convention*, Melbourne, 8 February 1898, 658 (emphasis added).
3 *Official Record of the Debates of the Australasian Federal Convention*, Melbourne, 2 March 1898, 1769.
4 Ibid.
5 *Official Report of the National Australasian Convention Debates*, Melbourne, 16 March 1898, 2440.
6 *Krygger v Williams* (1912) 15 CLR 366, 369, 372–3.

the Convention's general view was and what significance, if any, the textual difference between section 116 and the First Amendment had. The word 'for' was not significant.

Establishment

The High Court has expressed beliefs about what the framers of the *Australian Constitution* thought about the expression 'establishing any religion' that have no basis in historical fact. In the *DOGS case*, Mason J said: 'The text of s 116 more obviously reflects a concern with the establishment of one religion as against others than the language of the First Amendment which speaks of the "establishment of religion", not the "establishment of any religion."'[7] Justice Mason's comment suggests that the Convention was concerned about the possibility of the establishment of one religion as against others. However, the Convention gave almost no attention to the meaning of this expression.

Higgins did not offer any direct comments in the Convention as to what he understood the concept of establishment to mean or why he included the determiner 'any' in his language. However, he did make some indirect comments and those appear to speak against what would later be Mason J's suggestion.

Higgins said on 8 February 1898 that the First Amendment of the *United States Constitution* includes a prohibition 'for the establishment of a religion',[8] and on 2 March 1898 he said the First Amendment prevented the making of 'any law for the establishment of any religion.'[9] Higgins, it seems, did not contemplate a distinction between 'religion' and 'any religion' as a linguistic matter. Higgins treated the expressions as synonymous. Indeed, the 'little handbook' on which Higgins may have relied to persuade Barton that the *Church of the Holy Trinity* dicta had been acted upon – Henry Campbell Black's *Handbook of American Constitutional Law* – described the establishment clause of the First Amendment as providing a 'guarantee against the establishment of *a* church or religion.'[10] Even if Black's book is not the 'little handbook', it was nevertheless a respected contemporary treatise on American constitutional law and shows that what Mason J thought the American establishment clause meant is not what the Americans thought it meant.

There is simply no evidence that Higgins viewed the distinction in phraseology identified by Mason J as in any way meaningful. The reality is that during the course of debate Higgins did not express any concern such as identified by Mason J. It may simply be that Higgins did not turn his mind to the precise question. Either way, there is nothing in section 116's drafting history to support Mason J's comment.

What, more generally, did the Convention say about the concept of establishing a religion? At the Convention, on 2 March 1898, in suggesting that Higgins' provision might be unnecessary, Barton said:

> The whole of the advancement in English-speaking communities, under English laws and English institutions, has shown a less and less inclination to pass laws for imposing religious tests, or exacting religious observances, or to maintain any religion. We have not done that in Australia. We have abolished state religion in all these colonies.[11]

7 (1981) 146 CLR 559, 615.

8 *Official Record of the Debates of the Australasian Federal Convention*, Melbourne, 8 February 1898, 658.

9 *Official Record of the Debates of the Australasian Federal Convention*, Melbourne, 2 March 1898, 1769.

10 Henry Campbell Black, *Handbook of American Constitutional Law* (West Publishing Co, 2nd ed, 1897) 453 (emphasis added); see also at 449: 'establish a religion.'

11 *Official Record of the Debates of the Australasian Federal Convention*, Melbourne, 2 March 1898, 1771.

These comments seem to suggest an overlap between the concepts 'establishing any religion' and 'maintaining any religion.' This overlap, however, is useful for determining what the framers of the *Constitution* might have understood the establishment clause to mean only insofar as any explanation or understanding of 'maintaining any religion' is apparent. Barton offered no such explanation in the Convention beyond his cryptic comment that the Australian colonies had abolished state religion. That comment requires an understanding of what is meant by state religion and what process abolished it. The fact that Barton did not pause to explain more precisely what he meant, and the fact that none of the delegates asked Barton what he meant, may also be taken as evidence that the Convention was not overly concerned with the precise meaning of the language of section 116. This is unsurprising given that the initial general mood of the Convention was that a provision such as section 116 was unnecessary in the first place.

Another ambiguous comment involving Barton and the notion of establishment was made in the Convention on 2 March 1898. During Barton's speech, South Australian delegate Josiah Symon interjected saying that '[i]t is part of the unwritten law of the Constitution that a religion shall not be established.'[12] Barton immediately responded: 'It [i.e. establishment] is so foreign to the whole idea of the Constitution that we have no right to expect it.'[13] Later on that day, Symon again said: 'I am satisfied that it is embodied in the Constitution as a part of the unwritten law that no church establishment shall prevail, and that religious freedom shall be observed.'[14] These comments are noteworthy. The comments suggest that these speakers had in mind at least a general idea of what establishment might mean. However, neither Symon nor Barton articulated that idea. Symon and Barton appeared to be saying something rather more profound than simply that the Commonwealth would lack power to bring about the establishment of any religion. They appeared to be saying that religious establishment was a concept inconsistent with the very idea of the *Constitution*. In what way it was inconsistent, they did not spell out.

There were some slightly more precise comments. During a discussion on whether a clause prohibiting laws concerning religion was necessary at all, Barton said that 'a church could not receive the funds of the Commonwealth' under federal spending powers.[15] Barton's comment was in response to a question by the New South Wales premier and delegate, George Reid. Reid had asked: 'I suppose that money could not be paid to any church under this *Constitution*?' and Barton's comment was the reply.[16] Barton's comment was an explanation of the effect of the Commonwealth's spending powers and not directly an explanation of the meaning of any part of section 116. However, the fact that Reid asked his question during debate on section 116 suggests that Reid may have been thinking that Commonwealth funding of religious bodies could amount to 'establishment.' There is some American support for this idea. In his *Handbook of American Constitutional Law*, Black wrote that 'in general, and even without constitutional prohibitions, the compulsory support, by taxation or the appropriation of public funds, of religious establishments or religious instruction, would be contrary to the principles of religious freedom.'[17] Black did not

12 Ibid 1772.
13 Ibid.
14 Ibid 1776.
15 Ibid 1772.
16 Ibid.
17 Black, above n 10, 453.

directly connect this proposition to the establishment clause, although it is in a section of his book dealing with the First Amendment's religion clauses.

Reference works at the time on American constitutional law offered no clear definition of establishment that might be imputed to Convention delegates, even assuming that delegates had read the relevant passages in those works. Black's *Handbook of American Constitutional Law*, with which Higgins and Barton may have had at least some familiarity, either as the 'little handbook' or as a reference work, offered this definition:

> A church is by law "established" in a state when it is an institution of the state, under the direct protection and patronage of the state, to the exclusion of other churches or sects, when it is supported by general and public taxation, when its laws, ordinances, and doctrines are a part of the municipal law of the state, so that persons may be punished by the civil authorities for disobedience of them, and when its chief officers are officers of the state or appointed by the civil authorities.[18]

The British jurist, James Bryce in *The American Commonwealth*, with which the delegates to the Federal Convention were familiar,[19] did not offer any clear definition of establishment. However, Bryce described the abolition of public 'maintenance of churches', the withdrawal of 'special ecclesiastical privileges' and the withdrawal from a church of 'a measure of State favour' as instances of 'disestablishment.'[20] Bryce also seems to have contemplated a distinction between 'establishment' and 'endowment', writing: 'No voice has ever since been raised [in the United States] in favour of reverting – I will not say to a State establishment of religion – but even to any State endowment, or State regulation of ecclesiastical bodies.'[21] Although his view of establishment was not clearly articulated, it seems that Bryce had a broader understanding of establishment than Black in that Bryce appears to accept that a situation less than a religion being a state institution may amount to establishment.

There is nothing in the course of the debate at the Federal Convention to suggest that the delegates preferred one of these views to the other. Indeed, very few words were uttered about the meaning of establishment, and those words have all been noted above.

It seems likely that the framers of the *Constitution* understood the notion of establishing any religion only at a very high level of generality to involve institutional connections of some sort between the state and religions. The precise meaning of this part of section 116 was not something Convention delegates gave much thought to.

18 Ibid.

19 This book is included in Sir Richard Baker's *A Manual of Reference to Authorities for the Use of the Members of The National Australasian Convention* (WK Thomas & Co, 1891). See also Matthew Stubbs, 'A Brief History of the Judicial Review of Legislation under the Australian Constitution' (2012) 40 *Federal Law Review* 227, 239: 'James Bryce's *The American Commonwealth*, first published in 1888, provided the Framers with their chief distillation of the experience of the most comparable model of federal government' citing John Williams, 'The Emergence of the Commonwealth Constitution' in H P Lee and George Winterton (eds), *Australian Constitutional Landmarks* (Cambridge University Press, 2003) 1,14, 24–5 and J A La Nauze, *The Making of the Australian Constitution* (Melbourne University Press, 1972) 18, 273: '[Bryce's book was] quoted or referred to more than any other single work; never criticized, it was regarded with the same awe, mingled with reverence, as the Bible would have been in an assembly of churchmen.'

20 James Bryce, *The American Commonwealth* (Liberty Fund, first published 1888, 1995) 697.

21 Ibid 698.

Religious observance

The principal mischief section 116 was intended to address was the possibility that the Commonwealth might have power to impose religious observances such as by enacting Sunday closing laws. This is what both Higgins and the Seventh Day Adventists were particularly worried about. As Higgins told the Convention on 2 March 1898, a prohibition against laws imposing religious observances 'is rendered necessary' by the example of the United States Congress' closing of the Chicago Exhibition on Sundays and the United States Supreme Court's decision in *Church of the Holy Trinity*.[22] Despite the centrality of this clause to the whole debate on section 116, the Convention did not carefully consider its meaning.

Higgins was of the view that a law that did no more than require, either directly or indirectly, Sunday closing to involve or constitute the imposition of an observance. Indeed, it was such a law – the statutory provision concerning the Sunday closing of the Chicago Exhibition – that excited Higgins and that formed a significant element of his argument about why section 116 was necessary.[23] Given that Higgins' argument was ultimately successful and that he made the point about Sunday closing laws repeatedly and in strong terms, the Convention as a whole must have understood Sunday closing to involve or constitute an observance. Indeed, there are statements by other delegates expressing such an understanding. For instance, in speaking in support of the clause, New South Wales delegate Bernhard Wise referred to the American statute closing the Chicago Exhibition on Sundays as 'dealing with Sunday observance.'[24] Similarly, New South Wales delegate William Lyne referred to laws regulating the Sunday trading of 'places of public resort' such as museums and art galleries as being a matter of 'Sunday observance.'[25]

What is significant, however, is that none of the delegates to the Convention, including Higgins, appears to have turned his (and they were all men) mind to whether other things apart from Sunday closing might constitute an observance. There was, for example, no comment on whether the clause would prevent Commonwealth agencies from closing on Christmas Day or Good Friday.

Higgins did not understand his religious observances clause as preventing the enactment of Sunday closing laws generally. Rather, he explained that the clause prevented the enactment of religiously motivated Sunday closing laws. In speaking to the religious observances prohibition, Higgins noted that 'it has been said that this would prevent the imposing of a day of rest.' He responded to that suggestion, insisting that '[m]y amendment would not.'[26] He explained: 'It would not; it would simply prevent the imposing of a day of rest for religious reasons.'[27] It would be necessary, Higgins told the Convention, to look to

22 *Official Record of the Debates of the Australasian Federal Convention*, Melbourne, 2 March 1898, 1769.
23 See ch 5.
24 *Official Record of the Debates of the Australasian Federal Convention*, Melbourne, 2 March 1898, 1773–4.
25 Ibid 1777.
26 *Official Record of the Debates of the Australasian Federal Convention*, Melbourne, 8 February 1898, 664.
27 Ibid.

the purpose underlying a particular law to determine whether the observance it imposed was a religious one or not. He said:

> A number of laws have been held to be unconstitutional in America because of their reasons and because of their motives. There was a funny case in San Francisco, where a law was passed by the state that every prisoner, within one hour of his coming into the prison, was to have his hair cut within one inch of his head. That looked very harmless, but a Chinaman brought an action to have it declared unconstitutional, and it turned out that the law was actually passed by the Legislature for the express purpose of persecuting Chinamen.[28]
>
> . . .
>
> I am trying to point out that laws would be valid if they had one motive, while they would be invalid if they had another motive. All I want is, that there should be no imposition of any observance because of its being religious.[29]

In other words, in Higgins' view of the effect of the religious observances clause, a Sunday closing law motivated by secular reasons would be valid whereas such a law motivated by religious reasons would be invalid. Here, purpose has the function of determining whether an observance is a religious or non-religious observance. Higgins did not explain how a court should go about determining the motivation behind a particular law. Nor did Higgins provide any explanation as to what the situation would be if a Sunday closing law was motivated by both religious and secular reasons.

In accepting that not all Sunday closing laws would amount to laws imposing religious observances Higgins was seemingly at odds with the Seventh Day Adventists. W A Colcord, the senior Seventh Day Adventist with whom Higgins was in correspondence at the time of the Convention,[30] devoted two chapters of his 1913 book *The Rights of Man, or Religion and the State: An Exposition of the Province of Civil Government and Religion, and a Plea for Civil and Religious Liberty* to arguing that 'all Sunday laws are religious' even those justified by apparently secular reasons. Colcord's argument was that a day of rest is by definition a Sabbath and therefore a religious institution and that a day of rest prohibits secular or civil activities.[31]

Beyond explaining that the religious observances clause was directed at religiously motivated Sunday closing laws, there was no further discussion of what the clause might

28 The 'funny case' Higgins referred to in his comments concerned a San Francisco ordinance popularly known as the 'Pigtail Ordinance' or the 'Queue Ordinance' (queue being another word for the pigtail), since it was targeted at Chinese residents of San Francisco who commonly wore that hairstyle. Ho Ah Kow, a Chinese resident of San Francisco, was imprisoned for failing to pay a fine and had his pigtail forcibly removed by prison authorities. Kow sued in tort and the prison authorities pleaded the ordinance as a justification. In *Ho Ah Kow v Nuna*, 12 F Cas 252 (1879) the Circuit Court of the United States, comprising a judge of the United States Supreme Court and a circuit judge, invalidated the ordinance on the ground that it denied Chinese people the equal protection of the laws contrary to the Fourteenth Amendment. The purpose of the law was a key factor in the finding of invalidity.

29 *Official Record of the Debates of the Australasian Federal Convention*, Melbourne, 8 February 1898, 664.

30 See Richard Ely, *Unto God and Caesar: Religious Issues in the Emerging Commonwealth, 1891–1906* (Melbourne University Press, 1976) 142–3.

31 W A Colcord, *The Rights of Man, or Religion and the State: An Exposition of the Province of Civil Government and Religion, and a Plea for Civil and Religious Liberty* (Echo Publishing Co, 1913) 226; see also chs 21, 22.

mean or to what else it might apply. The Convention's attention simply did not turn to that matter.

Free exercise

The Convention gave slightly more attention to the meaning of the free exercise clause than it did to the other clauses of section 116. Several delegates expressed concern that the prohibition against laws prohibiting the free exercise of religion might prevent the law from dealing with unacceptable practices done in the name of religion. The Convention discussed this matter but nothing else about the possible meaning of the free exercise clause.

On 7 February 1898, the Tasmanian Premier and delegate Sir Edward Braddon said of the prohibition on prohibiting the free exercise of religion in clause 109 that:

> It is quite possible that this might make lawful practices which would otherwise be strictly prohibited. Take, for instance, the Hindoos. One of their religious rites is the "suttee" and another is the "churruck" – one meaning simply murder, and the other barbarous cruelty, to the devotees who offer themselves for the sacrifice.[32]

Accordingly, Braddon suggested the insertion 'of some such words' as: 'But shall prevent the performance of any such religious rites, as are of a cruel or demoralizing character or contrary to the law of the Commonwealth.'[33] Braddon's concern was with ensuring that the law would be able to deal with unacceptable practices even if they were done in the name of religion. The next day, Braddon indicated that he would prefer the clause struck out altogether on the ground that it could not be certain that even with the insertion of such a proviso the law would not be impeded from dealing with unacceptable practices done in the name of religion.[34] On 8 February 1898, other delegates expressed similar concerns to those expressed by Braddon, mentioning the actions of 'faith healers' as a practice that might be permitted by the clause.[35]

On 2 March 1898, when Higgins' new clause to replace the deleted clause 109 came on for discussion, there was little discussion of the free exercise clause. Barton commented, in similar terms to those of Braddon, that clause 109 was struck out in part because it

> might be held to be too express in its terms, because there may be practices in various religions which are believed in by persons who may enter into the Commonwealth belonging to other races, which practices would be totally abhorrent to the ideas, not only to any Christian, but to any civilized community.[36]

However, the course of debate drifted away from the specifics of the clause, focussing instead on whether a clause denying the Commonwealth power in respect of religion was necessary. Ultimately, the Convention accepted the free exercise clause as a component of Higgins' wider provision. Delegates' fears as to the ability of the law to deal with 'abhorrent' practices done in the name of religion must therefore have been sufficiently allayed.

32 *Official Record of the Debates of the Australasian Federal Convention*, Melbourne, 7 February 1898, 657.
33 Ibid.
34 Ibid 662.
35 Ibid 658–9 (John Gordon), 659 (Josiah Symon).
36 *Official Record of the Debates of the Australasian Federal Convention*, Melbourne, 2 March 1898, 1771.

In part at least, those fears may have been allayed because the free exercise clause was not expressed to bind the States. Higgins emphasised that section 116 left the States free to interfere with religious practices as they saw fit.[37]

Another basis for the allaying of fears about the scope of the free exercise clause may have been an acceptance that the words 'free exercise' did not imply anarchy or lawlessness. After all, as Higgins had emphasised a number of times to the Convention, a prohibition against laws prohibiting the free exercise of religion could be found in the *United States Constitution*. Delegates would have known that American law was not impotent in dealing with unacceptable religious practices. Black addressed this question in his *Handbook of American Constitutional Law*. He wrote:

> In several of the states the constitutions provide that the guaranties of religious freedom are not to be held to excuse acts of licentiousness, or to justify practices inconsistent with the peace and safety of the state. Even without such provisions in the organic law, it would be clearly competent for the state to condemn and punish acts which are contrary to its policy and the established laws regulating the conduct of citizens, notwithstanding that a minority of the people professed a religion which tolerated or even commanded such acts. In other words, peculiarities of religious belief cannot be made a defense to prosecutions for breaches of the criminal laws.[38]

Whatever the case and whether or not delegates consulted Black's book, the Convention's discussion of the free exercise clause was limited to this pragmatic concern. The Convention's discussion did not extend to addressing the more general question of what the clause might mean.

In this, the Convention's position contrasted with that of Andrew Inglis Clark. In his memorandum explaining the proposed amendment to clause 109 that he had persuaded the Tasmanian House of Assembly to put forward to the Convention, Clark offered an interpretation of clause 109, which then provided 'A State shall not make any law prohibiting the free exercise of religion.' Clark wrote:

> [S]ection 109 secures religious equality for all the citizens of a State, so far as it prevents the State from placing the adherents of any form of religion under any disadvantage or restriction in the exercise of it in comparison with adherents of other forms of religion.[39]

Here, Clark seems to be suggesting that he understood the provision as in some way involving the idea of discrimination. Perhaps oddly, this passage appears to suggest that imposing an equal burden on the practice of all religions would not violate the clause. In his memorandum, Clark offered no further explanation of his understanding of the provision, including any explanation of why he considered it to involve the idea of discrimination.

Clark's analysis did not come up in the Convention because the Convention did not turn its attention to the general meaning of the free exercise clause. Delegates would

37 Ibid 1772 (Henry Higgins).
38 Black, above n 10, 454.
39 Reproduced in Williams, above n 1, 65–79.

have known that Clark's memorandum existed, but they did not necessarily read it or, if they did read it, may not have read the entire document. This would not be particularly surprising given that religion was not a first order issue for the Convention.

The Convention's discussion of the free exercise clause focussed only on whether the clause might prevent the Commonwealth from dealing with unacceptable practices done in the name of religion. The delegates had a pragmatic concern about a possible unintended consequence of the clause and discussed that but no more. The Convention did not give any attention to the meaning of the clause at any broader or general level such as Clark had attempted to do in his memorandum.

Religious tests

As with the other clauses of section 116, the Convention gave no careful consideration to what the religious tests clause might mean. However, Higgins did make some brief comments about the clause, addressed to a pragmatic concern about a possible unintended consequence.

On 7 February 1898, Higgins spoke to what was then his proposed provision, which included a prohibition against laws 'imposing any religious test or observance.'[40] As the previous chapter noted, Higgins commented that 'we must qualify that in some way, because it has been said that it would void our imposing of the ordinary oaths in the courts and elsewhere.'[41] Higgins expressed a similar concern on 8 February.[42]

The previous chapter noted that Higgins did not indicate where it had been said that a prohibition against imposing religious tests might affect ordinary oaths. It is possible that Higgins got that notion from Black's *Handbook of American Constitutional Law*. In that book appears this passage:

> At common law those persons only were competent to give evidence as witnesses in a court of law who believed in the existence of a Supreme Being who would punish false swearing. Without such belief, it was considered, there was no way of making the oath obligatory on the conscience of the witness. In a considerable number of the states, this rule has been done away with by constitutional provisions that no religious test shall be required as a qualification of a witness.[43]

If Black's work is the 'little handbook' to which Barton referred, Higgins must have come across this passage. If so, Higgins had a basis for believing that a religious oath can amount to a religious test.

It is also possible that Higgins got the idea that a prohibition against religious tests might affect ordinary oaths from the case of Charles Bradlaugh in the United Kingdom. Bradlaugh was an outspoken atheist and founder of the National Secular Society who was first elected to the House of Commons in 1880. Legislation required certain oaths to be taken before a person could sit and vote in Parliament. Cases involving Bradlaugh had

40 *Official Record of the Debates of the Australasian Federal Convention*, Melbourne, 7 February 1898, 654.
41 Ibid 656–7.
42 *Official Record of the Debates of the Australasian Federal Convention*, Melbourne, 8 February 1898, 660.
43 Black, above n 10, 455.

confirmed that atheists had no right to make an affirmation in lieu of the parliamentary oath[44] and that atheists could not lawfully take the parliamentary oath.[45] The laws concerning oaths imposed a religious test for membership of Parliament and Bradlaugh could not satisfy that test.

During the course of his career, Bradlaugh had been excluded from Parliament on a number of occasions due to his failure to take the relevant oaths, only to be re-elected at the resulting by-elections.[46] Bradlaugh was not mentioned in debate at the Federal Convention but his situation was referred to in public in connection with the drafting of the *Constitution*. Sydney's *Sunday Times*, in editorialising against the campaign for 'recognition' of God in the constitutional preamble, wrote:

> The present proposal to insert a recognition of the Deity may seem harmless enough on the face of it, but there is the very palpable danger of what it may lead to, and what claims may be hereafter based upon it.
>
> . . .
>
> It is not many years since Charles Bradlaugh was disgracefully persecuted by the British House of Commons on account of his opinions, which ran contrary to the recognition of the Deity implied by the necessity of taking the oath, and it is quite conceivable that history might repeat itself in this country.[47]

Higgins was concerned about the ability to require oaths 'in the courts and elsewhere.' It seems inconsistent then that in the provision he proposed on 2 March 1898, and which was approved by the Convention, he included a clause stating 'and no religious test shall be required as a qualification for any office or public trust under the Commonwealth.' The base of Higgins' concern seems to be a desire to preserve the requirement for office holders to take an oath. The new clause, modelled on the American religious tests clause, does not of itself overcome Higgins' concern. However, there does appear to be an explanation.

Higgins must have thought that whilst an oath requirement might be used to impose a religious test, the ability to permit affirmations as an alternative to oaths meant that the Commonwealth Parliament would be able to require office holders to pledge their loyalty without requiring the satisfaction of any religious test. There is evidence in support of this explanation. The Convention made provision for members of the Commonwealth Parliament to take either an oath or affirmation of allegiance. The option of an affirmation avoids there being any requirement of a religious test.[48]

Higgins must also have realised that his general concern was unfounded since the *United States Constitution* contains a similar provision. Higgins would have known that oaths and affirmations were required in the United States 'in the courts and elsewhere.' Higgins must have known this because the American religious tests clause forms part of a

44 *Clarke v Bradlaugh* (1881) 7 QBD 38.

45 *Attorney-General v Bradlaugh* (1885) 14 QBD 667.

46 On Bradlaugh, see, e.g., Bryan Niblett, *Dare to Stand Alone: The Story of Charles Bradlaugh, Atheist and Republican* (Kramedart Press, 2010); Walter Arnstein, *The Bradlaugh Case: A Study in Late Victorian Opinion and Politics* (Clarendon Press, 1965).

47 'Religion and the State', *Sunday Times* (Sydney), 25 July 1897, 4.

48 Luke Beck, 'The Constitutional Prohibition on Religious Tests' (2011) 35 *Melbourne University Law Review* 323, 345.

longer provision requiring certain office-holders to swear or affirm that they will support the *United States Constitution*:

> The Senators and Representatives before mentioned, and the Members of the several State Legislatures, and all executive and judicial Officers, both of the United States and of the several States, shall be bound by Oath or Affirmation, to support this Constitution; but no religious Test shall ever be required as a Qualification to any Office or public Trust under the United States.[49]

Since Higgins borrowed the language of his religious tests clause from the American clause, it is fair to assume that he had read the entirety of the provision containing that clause.

None of this, of course, constitutes anything approaching a full explanation by the Convention of what the religious tests clause might mean. The discussion in the Convention of the religious tests clause was, like the discussion of the free exercise clause, limited to a pragmatic concern about a possible unintended consequence. Discussion of the meaning of the clause went no further.

American jurisprudence

Higgins made much of the fact he was borrowing language from the United States Constitution for section 116. How much did delegates know of the relevant American jurisprudence? And were they intending that section 116 should import that jurisprudence to Australia?

Higgins told the Convention that 'most of this clause . . . is already in the *American Constitution*.'[50] This does not necessarily mean that Higgins understood the equivalent expressions in his provision to have the same meaning as the religion clauses of the United States. At no point during the course of the debate at the Federal Convention did any delegate mention any American case on the religion clauses of the *United States Constitution* or offer a summary or statement of any part of American jurisprudence on the subject. Attention simply did not turn to American jurisprudence. The 'funny case' from San Francisco to which Higgins referred in explaining the difference between religious and non-religious Sunday closing laws was a case about the equal protection clause of the Fourteenth Amendment.

It is entirely possible that neither Higgins nor any of the other delegates had read any cases dealing with the religion clauses of the *United States Constitution*. At the time of the Federal Convention, American courts had decided very few cases on the religion clauses of the *United States Constitution*.[51] However, it is possible that Higgins had read the relevant sections of Black's *Handbook of American Constitutional Law* that discuss those provisions. This does not mean that Higgins subscribed to the views expressed in that work. As noted

49 *United States Constitution* art VI cl 3.

50 *Official Record of the Debates of the Australasian Federal Convention*, Melbourne, 2 March 1898, 1769.

51 The explanation for this is that much of the modern American religion clause jurisprudence concerns challenges to State and municipal actions. Following decisions of the United States Supreme Court in the 1940s, the religion clauses, although expressed to bind only Congress, bind the States according to the Fourteenth Amendment 'incorporation' doctrine: *Cantwell v Connecticut*, 310 US 296 (1940); *Everson v Board of Education of Ewing*, 330 US 1 (1947).

above in the discussion of the establishment clause, reasons can be found for supposing that Higgins would not have accepted the definition of establishment offered by Black.

It is also doubtful that there was any broad appreciation of the general contours of the American legal position on the part of the Convention as a whole. During discussion on whether a provision such as section 116 might be necessary, Barton said:

> I do not think, whatever may be the result of any American case [referring to *Church of the Holy Trinity*], that any such case can be stretched for a moment in such a way as to give Congress power of passing any law to establish any religion. I do not suppose that there is a man in Congress who would suggest it; and I have no doubt that the same court that decided that the community was a Christian community would say that the United States Congress had no power to establish any religion.[52]

Barton was, of course, correct that such a proposition would never be asserted by an American court or suggested by a member of Congress. The simple reason for that is the First Amendment plainly says 'Congress shall make no law respecting the establishment of religion.'

An uncharitable analysis of Barton's comments might suggest that Barton was not aware of the text of the First Amendment. A more charitable analysis would suggest that the text of the First Amendment was not at the forefront of Barton's mind at the time of making what were off the cuff remarks. Either way, Barton's error is significant. It suggests that in preparing for the Convention, which would have involved research into the American constitutional position on various subjects, Barton gave little serious attention to questions of religion.

This is entirely unsurprising. If it had not been for Higgins, the Federal Convention most likely would never have discussed the possibility of a religion provision such as section 116.[53] Quite reasonably, Barton would have thought it unnecessary to prepare on the topic of religion. Barton, therefore, is unlikely to have been familiar in any serious way with the relevant American jurisprudence and commentary. If that is the case, it can hardly be assumed that Barton held any understanding that the Australian expressions had a similar meaning to the American expressions. Equally, of course, nor can an understanding that the Australian expression had a different meaning to the American expressions be imputed to Barton. Barton simply did not know what meaning the American expressions had.

Barton was not the only one lacking familiarity with the American position. In their *Annotated Constitution of the Commonwealth of Australia*, Quick and Garran could not fathom the necessity or utility of the religion clauses of the First Amendment. They wrote:

> No logical or constitutional reasons have been stated why such a negation of power which had never been granted and which, therefore, could never be legally exercised, was introduced into the instrument of Government. It does not appear that its necessity has ever been demonstrated.[54]

52 *Official Record of the Debates of the Australasian Federal Convention*, Melbourne, 2 March 1898, 1772.

53 Andrew Inglis Clark was not a delegate to the 1897–8 Convention and so, despite his enthusiasm for one, would not have been able directly to pursue the inclusion of a religion provision.

54 John Quick and Robert Garran, *Annotated Constitution of the Commonwealth of Australia* (Angus & Robertson, 1901) 952.

Quick and Garran considered the American religion clauses to be without any potential legal effect. Both men were at the Convention, Quick as a delegate and Garran as an officer. If in writing a learned treatise sometime after the Convention, with the benefit of research and contemplation, these leading legal minds could not understand the purpose of the religion clauses of the First Amendment it stands to reason that they also did not understand those clauses at the time of the Convention.

Ultimately, therefore, there is nothing to suggest that Higgins or any of the other delegates had any real knowledge of the relevant American jurisprudence. Indeed, there is strong evidence that three of the leading legal minds – Barton, Quick and Garran – had very little, if any, familiarity with the American legal position concerning the First Amendment. The understanding of the other delegates is unlikely to have been any better.

It follows that it is impossible to conclude that the Convention was attempting to import particular American legal analyses into the *Australian Constitution* by the inclusion of section 116. The simple reason for this conclusion is that none of the delegates was aware of any particular American legal analysis. However, the Convention might well have thought that it was copying the American provisions and thereby importing their meanings, of which they knew little. Whatever the case, the key conclusion is that no close attention was given to the meaning of the American provisions that were being paraphrased.

The Federal Convention was not concerned with precise meanings

A clear theme emerges from this overview of what the Convention thought about the meaning of section 116: the Convention did not give close attention to the meaning of the provision it was adopting as section 116. The Convention considered the meaning of section 116's language only to the limited extent of considering pragmatic concerns about particular, possible unintended consequences.

The Convention did not engage in any serious discussion of the establishment clause as none of the delegates appeared to have thought that the clause would have any operation and no potential unintended consequences sprang to mind. The discussion of the religious observances clauses was limited to a discussion of Sunday closing laws because the possibility of federal Sunday closing laws was the principal mischief the clause was intended to address. The discussion of the free exercise clause was limited to concerns about the ability of the Commonwealth to deal with unacceptable practices done in the name of religion because that might have been an unintended consequence. The discussion, such as it was, of the religious tests clause was limited to concern about whether the clause would prohibit oaths.

Given the confused nature of the debate about the need for a provision limiting the Commonwealth's legislative powers in respect of religion, it is perhaps not surprising that the Convention limited its discussion to pragmatic concerns. There does not appear to have been a sufficient understanding on the part of delegates of any of the issues actually in play to permit discussion in a more sophisticated or detailed manner. A sizeable number of delegates thought that section 116 was unnecessary because none of the things it prohibited could be done in the first place at the federal level. For those delegates, worrying about the precise meaning or nuances of the language of section 116 would have been unnecessary.

It is more difficult to identify an explanation for the lack of attention given by those delegates Higgins managed to persuade that section 116 might well be necessary. It is true that delegates generally lacked knowledge, for example about American jurisprudence, for a sophisticated discussion to take place. However, this does not provide a satisfactory explanation. There was a confused and unsophisticated discussion about the need for section 116. It might be considered odd that a similarly confused and unsophisticated discussion did not occur about the meaning of section 116.

Why was the Convention unconcerned with the precise meaning and operation of section 116? In the *DOGS case*, Stephen J wrote that section 116 'contains four quite distinct restrictions'[55] and that they operate as 'four specific restrictions' on power.[56] It is not necessarily the case that Higgins and the other delegates would share Stephen J's view that section 116's clauses are 'quite distinct' and 'specific.'

The issue is not one of whether the Convention understood the clauses of section 116 to be dealing with mutually exclusive mischiefs. Nothing said in the Convention speaks to that question one way or the other. The delegates may well have accepted, for example, that legislation imposing a requirement to participate in a particular religious observance as a condition to holding a public office[57] violated both the religious observances and religious tests clauses. The issue is different. The language of section 116 is incapable of achieving Higgins' general purpose of denying the Commonwealth power to legislate 'on the subject of' religion. Nevertheless, it remains possible that the Convention understood the language of section to achieve the purpose of denying legislative power on the subject of religion.

On one reading of the debates at the Federal Convention, Higgins and the other delegates did understand each of the four clauses of section 116 to be individual clauses prohibiting particular mischiefs. That is, they considered the clauses to be distinct and specific. If this was not the case, then it may be wondered why Higgins was worried about the effect of a prohibition against religious tests and why other delegates were concerned that the free exercise clause might prevent the Commonwealth from dealing with unacceptable practices done in the name of religion. This suggests that, to the limited extent that each clause was explored, it was explored on its own terms. This is not the only possible reading.

The previous chapter observed that Higgins must have known that the religion clauses of the *United States Constitution* did not constitute a complete denial of legislative power over religion to the Congress. Higgins must have wondered whether Congress might be able to legislate in respect of religion in ways additional to religious observances (the Sunday closing law), which was the only example he gave of a religious law enacted by Congress. But Higgins and the other delegates might have believed, albeit wrongly, that by adding to the American clauses a prohibition against imposing religious observances, the Commonwealth would indeed be denied power to legislate 'on the subject of' religion.

That the Convention may have believed section 116 to amount to a denial of power 'on the subject of' religion is a conclusion for which support can be found in the debates in the Convention. The Convention's general consensus was that the Commonwealth had no power at all to legislate 'on the subject of' religion. Higgins was able to persuade the other delegates that somehow the Commonwealth might well be able to legislate in respect of religion and that a clause such as he was proposing was, for those reasons, necessary.

55 *Attorney-General (Vic); ex rel Black v Commonwealth* ('*DOGS case*') (1981) 146 CLR 559, 605, see also at 609 'four distinct and express restrictions.'

56 Ibid 609.

57 The *Test Act 1672*, 25 Car 2, c 2 (Eng), for example, made holding various public offices conditional upon, among other things, participating in Anglican religious observances.

It was because Higgins was successful in that attempt at persuasion that delegates voted for section 116.

Higgins was only able to demonstrate, although in a confused and convoluted way, that the Commonwealth might have power to impose religious observances. He did not attempt to demonstrate that the Commonwealth might have power to enact any other particular examples of laws on the subject of religion. It is possible that none of the delegates could imagine many other ways in which the Commonwealth might legislate in respect of religion. The main possibility of laws concerning religion suggested by delegates involved the use of the races power to regulate the religious practices of people of non-white races, a possibility considered to be unobjectionable.[58] Higgins proposed the establishment and free exercise clauses principally because they were found in the *United States Constitution.* Moreover, the emphasis Higgins placed in his argument for section 116 on the need to ensure a 'safeguard against the passing of religious laws by the Commonwealth'[59] also suggests that the Convention's thinking might have focussed on denying power in respect of religion generally. This might also explain the heading to section 116, which states 'Commonwealth not to legislate in respect of religion.'

On this view, while each of section 116's clauses might well be distinct and specific, the Convention may well have considered them in combination to amount to a complete denial of power to the Commonwealth to legislate 'on the subject of' religion. If this is what the Convention thought then the Convention did not need to turn its attention in any serious way to the question of the precise meaning of the words of section 116. The Convention appears to have understood the provision as prohibiting the Commonwealth from legislating 'on the subject of' religion. The Convention's attention needed only to address pragmatic concerns about possible unintended consequences. This it did.

58 *Official Record of the Debates of the Australasian Federal Convention*, Melbourne, 2 March 1898, 1776–7 (Charles Kingston).

59 Ibid 1734.

9 Section 116 as a safeguard against religious intolerance

What is the point of section 116?

What kind of provision is section 116 of the *Constitution*? What is its point? So far, this book has not addressed this question. So far, the book has addressed a series of causal questions: how and why did section 116 come to be included in the *Constitution*? How did it come to take the form that it does? What did the framers of the *Constitution* think its words meant?

Causal questions yield causal explanations. However, another type of question and explanation is also important: constitutive questions and explanations. The international relations theorist Alexander Wendt[1] explains that answers to constitutive questions – constitutive theories – provide 'insight into what it is that instantiates some phenomenon, not why that phenomenon comes about.'[2] Constitutive questions are about the identity of phenomena rather than the causes of phenomena.[3] Wendt explained that '[c]onstitutive theories provide explanations. These explanations are not causal, but they are explanations just the same.'[4]

What kind of provision is section 116? is a constitutive question. Constitutional law scholar Nicholas Aroney explains that legal theorising, including in constitutional law, is often a response to constitutive questions.[5] The language of constitutive questions is rarely used and other terminology tends to be more common. In constitutional law, the idea of underlying principles, for example, is broadly equivalent. To refer to just one of numerous scholars who have discussed the idea of underlying principles in constitutional law, Jack Balkin explains that underlying principles function to 'support and help explain the point of the [constitutional] text.'[6] Underlying principles understood in this sense are constitutive theories of constitutional provisions.

Ascribing an underlying principle to a constitutional provision in the sense of offering a constitutive theory of that provision is not the same thing as identifying the intentions of the framers of the provision. Those intentions might be relevant to developing the constitutive theory but they are not the same thing as the constitutive theory or underlying principle.

1 Alexander Wendt, 'On Constitution and Causation in International Relations' (1998) 24(5) *Review of International Studies* 101, 104–8.
2 Wendt, above n 2, 105.
3 Ibid 106.
4 Ibid 108.
5 Nicholas Aroney, 'Explanatory Power, Theory Formation and Constitutional Interpretation: Some Preliminaries' (2013) 38 *Australian Journal of Legal Philosophy* 1, 13–4.
6 Jack M Balkin, *Living Originalism* (Belknap Press, 2011) 260.

A constitutive theory of the foundations of a constitutional provision deals with a broader field of analysis than original intentions and purposes.

Wendt and Aroney's example of the constitutive question 'what is the nature of the European Union?' demonstrates the point. Suppose the intention of those who designed and founded the European Union was to create an emerging federation. Those intentions will be relevant to answering the constitutive question, but other factors, perhaps the broader political context or the quality of the designers' work, might mean that the European Union is in fact an international organisation, a consociational confederation or a supranational system of multilevel governance, for example.

Just as a constitutive theory of the foundations of a constitutional provision is different from the intentions of constitutional framers, so too a constitutive theory of the foundations of a constitutional provision is different from a doctrinal interpretation of the meaning of the provision the theory seeks to explain. Whilst a constitutive theory of the foundations of a constitutional provision might be relevant to the meaning of a constitutional provision, it is not the same as that meaning. In the context of discussing the *United States Constitution*, Balkin explains this point when he writes:

> Suppose that a principle underlying the Second Amendment's right to bear arms is the promotion of public safety. Once can promote public safety in many ways, however, including confiscating all privately held arms from the citizenry. Nevertheless, that would contradict the textual grant of a right to bear arms and so it is not a permissible application of the underlying principle [in the task of constitutional interpretation].[7]

The 'promotion of public safety' constitutive theory of the Second Amendment is a different phenomenon from the legal meaning or doctrinal interpretation of that constitutional provision. The same is true generally of constitutional provisions and constitutive theories of them.

The question *what kind of provision is section 116?* therefore is a constitutive question. Answering that question explains the point of section 116 at a conceptual level.

The neutrality theory

An explanation of the point of section 116 already exists in the literature. Proposed by former scholar and now judge of the Victorian Court of Appeal Stephen McLeish, it may be called the *neutrality theory*.

McLeish advances the neutrality theory in a 1992 article entitled 'Making Sense of Religion and the *Constitution*: A Fresh Start for Section 116.'[8] McLeish puts the theory in these terms:

> [U]nderlying s 116 there exists a general conception of state neutrality toward religion, reflected both in the avoidance of religious preferences and in respect for the autonomy

7 Balkin, above n 6, 271. The Second Amendment reads: 'A well regulated Militia, being necessary to the security of a free State, the right of the people to keep and bear Arms, shall not be infringed.'

8 Stephen McLeish, 'Making Sense of Religion and the *Constitution*: A Fresh Start for Section 116' (1992) 18 *Monash University Law Review* 207.

> of individuals in matters of religion, especially as participants in the wider community. It will be convenient to use the term 'neutrality' to embrace this joint conception of neutrality, participation and autonomy.[9]

In similar terms, McLeish writes that 'the impulse animating s 116 is the preservation of neutrality in the federal government's relations with religion so that full membership of a pluralistic community is not dependent on religious positions and divisions are not created along religious lines.'[10]

The general purpose of McLeish's article was to put forward 'the conception underlying the section' as a sound basis on which to approach the task of interpreting section 116.[11] McLeish argues that the neutrality theory requires that section 116 be 'construed as a guarantee of civil liberty' such that the task for courts is less about determining whether a challenged law can be characterised or described as a 'law for establishing any religion', for example, and more about assessing its impact on individuals.[12] The point of significance here is that the neutrality theory has an individual rights focus.

Although McLeish does not use the terminology, the neutrality theory is a constitutive theory of the foundations of section 116. McLeish's view of the need for such a theory is apparent in his remark that the 'text [of section 116] fails to suggest a principled rationale for its existence.'[13] The neutrality theory of section 116's 'underlying conception', 'animating impulse' or 'principled rationale' is a constitutive theory of the origins of section 116.

The idea of neutrality is also an important feature of the American jurisprudence and scholarship of the religion clauses of the First Amendment. Indeed, it is a widely-accepted constitutive theory of those clauses.[14] McLeish draws on this American pedigree in fleshing out the neutrality theory of the origins of section 116. After stating the neutrality theory as extracted above, McLeish asks 'what does this "neutrality" mean in practice?' and provides this answer:

> It will be argued . . . that recent American jurisprudence concerning the kind of neutrality the *United States Constitution* demands in this area is a useful starting point for an Australian approach responding to the animating principles of s 116. By this means, we may seek to flesh out the identified conception and give meaning to the text.[15]

Two key features of American neutrality jurisprudence and scholarship are relevant here. The first is that the idea of neutrality is conceptually rich. In fact, the idea of neutrality is so rich that the American scholar Douglas Laycock has been able to develop a taxonomy of the various principal conceptions of neutrality toward religion advanced in the American case law and academic literature.[16] These are 'formal neutrality', 'substantive neutrality'

9 Ibid 223.
10 Ibid 208.
11 Ibid.
12 Ibid 210.
13 Ibid 212.
14 See, e.g., Douglas Laycock, 'Formal, Substantive, and Disaggregated Neutrality Toward Religion' (1989–1990) 39 *DePaul Law Review* 993.
15 McLeish, above n 8, 223.
16 Laycock, above n 14.

and 'disaggregated neutrality.' Formal neutrality is the idea that religion should not be used as a standard or criterion for governmental action or inaction.[17] Substantive neutrality is the idea that government should 'minimize the extent to which it either encourages or discourages religious belief or disbelief, practice or nonpractice, observance or nonobservance' such that religion 'should proceed as unaffected by government as possible.'[18] Disaggregated neutrality towards religion is the idea that any governmental action that either advances or inhibits religion is objectionable even where there is some counterbalance to the action advancing or inhibiting religion.[19]

The second point to note about the idea of neutrality in American jurisprudence and scholarship is that the theory is routinely defended by reference to American history. Indeed, one American scholar has described American religion clause jurisprudence as 'one of the most history-laden of any area of [United States] constitutional law' and noted that 'nearly every decision of note [by the United States Supreme Court] regarding the meaning of the Establishment and Free Exercise Clauses has revolved around the country's religious history.'[20]

McLeish justifies the neutrality theory as a constitutive theory of the origins of section 116 by reference to Australian history. McLeish begins his analysis with some historical background, presenting an overview of official policies regarding religion during the early colonial period in Australia.[21] The discussion traverses in brief outline such matters as public payment of clergy at the beginning of colonial settlement, the introduction and subsequent withdrawal of public funding of denominational schools and the introduction and enforcement of Sunday closing laws. McLeish concludes that in the latter part of nineteenth century the 'dominant mood' in colonial Australia was one of 'anti-sectarian endorsement of religion.'[22]

McLeish then turns to consider the drafting of the *Constitution*. He begins by noting that questions of religious freedom and religion/government relationships were not central issues in the general federation debate.[23] McLeish briefly considers the 1891 Australasian Convention and its adoption of one of the two religion provisions from Andrew Inglis Clark's draft constitution prepared for consideration by delegates to that convention.[24] As earlier chapters noted, the 1891 Australasian Convention adopted Clark's provision denying the States power to prohibit the free exercise of religion but not Clark's other, much broader, provision denying the Commonwealth power to establish, support or give preferential recognition to any religion as well as to prohibit the free exercise of religion. McLeish explains that the 1891 Australasian Convention adopted this course because it believed that the Commonwealth lacked power to do any of those things rendering the federal provision unnecessary.[25]

After some brief comments concerning the political process that led to the 1897–8 Federal Convention, McLeish offers a brief overview of the effort to achieve recognition

17 Ibid 999.
18 Ibid 1001–2.
19 Ibid 1007.
20 Steven G Gey, 'More or Less Bunk: The Establishment Clause Answers that History Doesn't Provide' [2004] *Brigham Young University Law Review* 1617, 1617.
21 McLeish, above n 8, 213–7.
22 Ibid 217.
23 Ibid.
24 Ibid.
25 Ibid.

of God in the constitutional preamble and the reaction to that effort.[26] The discussion places emphasis on the idea that the Convention agreed to include recognition of God in the preamble to attract votes for the *Constitution* from religious voters and to include section 116 to attract votes from secular and non-religious voters. McLeish explains the course of debate in the Convention regarding the need for section 116, stating that Higgins feared that 'a reference to religion in the preamble could indicate an implicit federal power to make laws respecting religion.'[27]

McLeish concludes his discussion of the drafting of the *Constitution* by describing its religious inclusions as 'calculated pragmatism.'[28] He concludes that the Convention temporarily shifted 'its focus on federal relations and turned its attention to the individuals to be governed under the new arrangements, even if only to secure their assent to the scheme rather than through any loftier sentiments.'[29]

McLeish concludes that '[t]wo distinct themes appear from the historical materials.'[30] The first is a theme of anti-sectarianism.[31] The second is a theme 'that religion had come to be regarded as a personal matter with which the state should not interfere.'[32] These themes, McLeish argues, combine and give rise to the neutrality theory.

The safeguard against religious intolerance theory

This chapter proposes an alternative constitutive theory of the foundations of section 116. It may be called the *safeguard against religious intolerance theory.*

The word 'safeguard' is apt. Higgins used the word repeatedly in the course of advocating section 116 at the 1897–8 Federal Convention[33] and it fairly captures the point of section 116. The *Macquarie Dictionary* offers this definition of 'safeguard': 'something serving as a protection or defence, or ensuring safety.'[34] A safeguard is always a safeguard *against* something. In this case, it is a safeguard against religious intolerance.

The concept 'intolerance', as used here, is not the binary opposite of 'tolerance.' Rather, these concepts sit at either end of a continuum. If these concepts were binary opposites then 'safeguard against religious intolerance' would be the conceptual equivalent to 'guarantee of religious tolerance.' There is some grey between the black and white of intolerance and tolerance.

To make this point requires an exploration of what 'religious intolerance' means. Jeremy Waldron and Melissa Williams offer a useful starting point in their introduction to an edited collection organised by the American Society for Political and Legal Theory, considering the idea of toleration.[35] They explain that religious toleration can be understood generally as occurring when the state does not attempt to change or suppress a set of

26 Ibid 217–21.
27 Ibid 219.
28 Ibid 221.
29 Ibid.
30 Ibid.
31 Ibid 222.
32 Ibid.
33 *Official Report of the National Australasian Convention Debates*, Melbourne, 2 March 1898, 1734, 1779 (Henry Higgins).
34 Arthur Delbridge, John Bernard, David Blair, Susan Butler, Pamela Peters and Colin Yallop (eds), *Macquarie Dictionary* (Macquarie Library, revised 3rd ed, 2002) 1662.
35 Melissa S Williams and Jeremy Waldron, *Toleration and Its Limits* (New York University Press, 2008).

religious beliefs and practices or impose penalties for holding or following them even if the state does not endorse them.[36] Following Waldron and Williams, intolerance exists when the state attempts to change or supress a set of religious beliefs and practices or imposes penalties for holding or following them. This is intolerance as a lack of restraint.[37]

Describing the concept intolerance in these terms is not to suggest that section 116 necessarily operates in practice to prevent intolerance understood in this way. The safeguard against intolerance theory is a constitutive theory of the origins of section 116 and not a doctrinal interpretation of the constitutional provision's legal operation and effect. In this respect, section 116 may be described as partial in the sense that it is incomplete. Section 116 does not give full effect to its general purpose of denying the Commonwealth power 'on the subject of' religion. A law concerning religion might not be captured by one or more of section 116's clauses.[38] Section 116 is also partial in the sense that, notwithstanding Higgins' original proposal and his views expressed in private correspondence that the proper scope of the provision was to apply it to the States, section 116 is not expressed to bind the States.

Nevertheless, establishing a religion, imposing a religious observance, prohibiting the free exercise of a religion and imposing a religious test for public office are instances of intolerance in the sense explained above. Religious establishment is intolerant because it frames those who are not members of the established religion as outsiders and not full members of the community, which is a form of penalty for not adhering to the established religion. Imposing a religious observance has a similar effect as well as being an attempt to change the religious practices of individuals. Prohibiting the free exercise of religion is explicitly the suppression of religious practices. Imposing a religious test for public office plainly penalises individuals who do not adhere to favoured religious beliefs or who adhere to disfavoured religious beliefs by denying them access to public office.

There is a rich and vast philosophical literature on tolerance generally.[39] Not all is relevant to the key concept of 'intolerance' understood, in the context of religion, as sitting at the opposite end of a continuum to 'tolerance.'[40] However, there are three key insights from the philosophical literature on tolerance that are relevant to the safeguard against religious intolerance theory.

36 Ibid 4.

37 Ibid 20.

38 Examples include the power of the Australian Human Rights Commission under the *Australian Human Rights Commission Act 1986* (Cth) s 31 to inquire into acts and practices that may constitute discrimination on the ground of religion.

39 For an overview see, e.g., Catriona McKinnon, *Toleration: A Critical Introduction* (Routledge, 2006); Richard H Dees, *Trust and Toleration* (Routledge, 2004); Hans Oberdiek, *Tolerance: Between Forbearance and Acceptance* (Rowman & Littlefield, 2001); Melissa S Williams and Jeremy Waldron, *Toleration and Its Limits* (New York University Press, 2008); Anna Galeotti, *Toleration as Recognition* (Cambridge University Press, 2005); Ingrid Creppell, *Toleration and Identity: Foundations of Early Modern Thought* (Routledge, 2002); Michael Walzer, *On Toleration* (Yale University Press, 1999); Susan Mendus (ed), *The Politics of Toleration in Modern Life* (Edinburgh University Press, 1999); David Heyd (ed), *Toleration: An Elusive Virtue* (Princeton University Press, 1998).

40 The modern Western philosophical tradition of religious tolerance is often traced back to John Locke's 'A Letter Concerning Toleration' originally published in 1689: Richard H Dees, *Trust and Toleration* (Routledge, 2004) 10. Dees, however, notes that the philosophical discussion of the idea is much older than Locke. See also Oberdiek, above n 39, 69 noting Thomas Aquinas' thirteenth century discussions of toleration and noting that classical writers also discussed the concept. See also Perez Zagorin, *How the Idea of Religious Toleration Came to the West* (Princeton University Press, 2003).

The first insight is the distinction drawn in the literature between the subject or agent of tolerance and the object of tolerance. The subject or agent of tolerance is who or what is doing the 'tolerating', whereas the object of tolerance is who or what is tolerated.[41] The same distinction holds for intolerance.

This distinction is relevant to the safeguard against religious intolerance theory. The subject or agent of intolerance is, plainly enough, the Commonwealth. The objects of intolerance are both individuals and groups of individuals identified by reference to their religious status or affiliation. The object of intolerance in the safeguard against religious intolerance theory is not limited to individuals. The history discussed in this book shows that the object of intolerance must extend to groups. Indeed, Higgins' principal example of the mischief of a Commonwealth power on the subject of religion was the power's ability to authorise the Commonwealth to legislate for religious observances and the impact of such laws on groups like the Seventh Day Adventists. Sabbath observance is communal activity for Seventh Day Adventists, involving communal religious worship, as it is for other religious groups, and not simply an individual matter.

The second key insight from the philosophical literature is the distinction often drawn between toleration and tolerance. Where this distinction is drawn, toleration is understood to be a transitive concept in the sense that it requires an object.[42] Toleration in the transitive sense prompts the question: toleration of what? In other words, toleration is about action. Tolerance, on the other hand, is not necessarily transitive requiring an object.[43] Tolerance is a virtue in the sense of an attitude or character trait.[44] It is possible for a person or institution to possess tolerance but to occasionally do something intolerant. It is also possible for a person or institution not to possess tolerance but to act in a tolerant way.[45] Whilst the words can be, and regularly are, used without seeking to draw this distinction, the conceptual distinction nevertheless exists. It will always be a question of context whether the use of 'tolerant' or 'tolerance' involves this conceptual distinction. Equivalent distinctions hold for 'intolerant' and 'intolerance', with the obvious qualification being that intolerance is a vice rather than a virtue.

The safeguard against religious intolerance theory uses the word intolerance simply as the grammatically appropriate form of the transitive concept intolerant. The transitive concept is action or practice. The emphasis on action and practice is consistent with the history of section 116's origins. There is a theme of pragmatism and caution running through the relevant history, inconsistent with the notion that section 116 gives the Commonwealth some sort of philosophical character trait or attitude. The 1897–8 Federal Convention adopted section 116 chiefly as a pragmatic matter to ensure that the Commonwealth would have no power on the subject of religion, notwithstanding the general view that no such power existed in the first place. The theme of pragmatism and caution is also reflected in the Convention acceding to the demands of the Protestant churches

41 Oberdiek, above n 39, 40; Jeremy Waldron and Melissa S Williams, 'Introduction' in Melissa S Williams and Jeremy Waldron, *Toleration and Its Limits* (New York University Press, 2008) 1, 4, put the distinction in terms of agents of toleration and the objects of toleration. Preston King, *Toleration* (Frank Cass, New ed, 1998) 60ff uses the concepts of the tolerators and the tolerated as well as agents and objects.

42 Oberdiek, above n 39, 23.

43 Ibid 24; Nick Fotion and Gerard Elfstron, *Toleration* (University of Alabama Press, 1992) 9.

44 Oberdiek, above n 39, 24.

45 Ibid.

for recognition of God in the preamble whilst at the same time acceding to the demands, like those of the Seventh Day Adventists, for a provision prohibiting religious laws.

Section 116 is also pragmatic in the sense that it was adopted based on a concern about the practical operation of Commonwealth laws. The whole point of Higgins' poorly articulated argument in favour of section 116 was that the Commonwealth would be able to do certain things if there was no section 116. The fear of the Seventh Day Adventists was that the Commonwealth would be able to, and would in fact, do certain things. The Convention as a whole thought the Commonwealth could not do anything religious but adopted section 116 to make sure.

This pragmatism also speaks to the way in which the origins of section 116 can be described as non-theorised. The provision is not the result of a constitutional culture in which theoretical speculation about the nature of the state or about the proper role of religion in society was prominent.

To complete this description of the safeguard against religious intolerance theory – which might more fully be described as the partial and pragmatic safeguard against religious intolerance theory – it is useful to make explicit something that is implied by the preceding discussion. The safeguard against religious intolerance theory does not involve demands on private individuals. Waldron and Williams point out that much of the richness of the philosophical literature on toleration arises from the fact that the meaning of toleration is deeply disputed.[46] Versions of tolerance, these authors point out, may or may not be 'unilateral and asymmetrical'[47] in the sense that 'toleration is a one-way relationship from high to low.'[48] The obverse concept of 'intolerance' may also be asymmetrical. It is an asymmetrical version of intolerance that is relevant for the safeguard against religious intolerance theory. Asymmetry of this kind is implied by the concept 'safeguard' and follows from the fact that section 116 limits the powers of the Commonwealth as the subject or agent of intolerance without reposing any limitations or demands on the objects of intolerance. For instance, obliging the state to refrain from religiously intolerant actions does not oblige ordinary citizens to refrain from religiously intolerant actions.

Comparing the two theories

The *neutrality theory* and the *safeguard against religious intolerance theory* are different. There are three principal contrasts.

The first contrast is structural. The neutrality theory has a positive conceptual direction whereas the safeguard against religious intolerance theory has a negative conceptual direction. The idea of conceptual direction concerns whether a theory is positive, obliging action, or negative, obliging inaction. The distinction, which is a matter of continuum rather than dichotomy, is between whether a theory seeks to postulate a particular state of affairs or whether it postulates the avoidance of a particular state of affairs with no further preference as to what state of affairs actually obtains.

The word 'neutrality' itself does not necessarily suggest whether a theory with that label has a positive or negative conceptual direction. It is necessary therefore to look at

46 Waldron and Williams, above n 41, 4.

47 Ibid 20.

48 Ibid.

the substance of the theory to determine its conceptual direction. McLeish puts the theory in these terms:

> [U]nderlying s 116 there exists a general conception of state neutrality toward religion, reflected both in the avoidance of religious preferences and in respect for the autonomy of individuals in matters of religion, especially as participants in the wider community. It will be convenient to use the term 'neutrality' to embrace this joint conception of neutrality, participation and autonomy.[49]

On the one hand, 'avoidance of religious preferences' suggests an obligation of inaction. On the other hand, 'respect for the autonomy of individuals' suggests an obligation of action and postulates a particular state of affairs. However, the neutrality theory as a whole, with what McLeish calls 'civil rights' and 'civil liberties' perspectives, is not ambiguous as to its conceptual direction. While rights can be read as obliging inaction in the sense of an obligation to refrain from actions that would violate rights, rights can also be read as obliging action to promote or facilitate them. It is this sense that has conceptual predominance in the neutrality theory. In this vein, McLeish writes of a 'requirement of accommodation of religious beliefs and practices.'[50]

The neutrality theory has a positive conceptual direction; it is certainly more than half way along the continuum from negative to positive. The neutrality theory postulates a particular state of affairs and seeks to imbue the Commonwealth with a particular virtue or character trait. The particular state of affairs is, in McLeish's words, 'the preservation of neutrality in the federal government's relations with religion so that full membership of a pluralistic community is not dependent on religious positions and divisions are not created along religious lines.'[51] The virtue or character trait is neutrality.

By contrast, the safeguard against religious intolerance theory has a negative conceptual direction. The theory postulates the avoidance of a particular state of affairs – in this case, religious intolerance – with no further preference as to what state of affairs actually obtains. In the safeguard against religious intolerance theory section 116 is a shield not a sword. The theory aims at preventing vice but not at imbuing with virtue.

The second point of contrast between the two theories concerns the richness or thickness of each theory's substantive content. The neutrality theory is a rich or thick theory with a lot of substantive conceptual content. The safeguard against religious intolerance theory is conceptually more modest with significantly less substantive conceptual content.

Two matters clearly demonstrate the conceptual thickness of the neutrality theory. The first is its American pedigree. The fact that it is possible for the American approaches to the concept of neutrality to be classified in a taxonomy such as Laycock's[52] demonstrates just how many variations and versions the concept has. The second is the fact that the neutrality theory has a positive direction. It is not conceptually modest to seek to bring about a particular state of affairs. By contrast, the negative direction of the safeguard against religious intolerance theory indicates its substantive conceptual modesty.

49 McLeish, above n 8, 223.
50 Ibid.
51 Ibid 208.
52 Laycock, above n 14.

The third point of contrast between the neutrality and safeguard against religious intolerance theories concerns the focus on individual rights. The neutrality theory has an individual rights focus.[53] By contrast, the safeguard against religious intolerance theory does not have an individual rights focus.

There is a key point of similarity between neutrality and safeguard against religious intolerance theories. Both theories are consistent with the two themes McLeish identifies from his overview of Australian colonial history regarding religion, as part of the rationale for the neutrality theory: anti-sectarianism and the idea that religion was a personal matter with which the state should not interfere. These themes are also consistent with the safeguard against intolerance theory. The consistency between these themes and the idea of the state refraining from religious intolerance has long been recognised. In 1689 in 'A Letter Concerning Toleration', John Locke argued that because the care of souls is not the business of government, governmental interference in religious matters and attempts to suppress unfavoured religious groups causes civil unrest.[54] Locke's prescription for social harmony was religious toleration.[55]

Why the neutrality theory is wrong

There are five principal reasons why the neutrality theory cannot be accepted as a coherent and convincing constitutive theory of the origins of section 116.

A significant weakness in the neutrality theory is its positive direction and conceptual richness or thickness in terms of its substantive content. These features of the neutrality theory are not supported by and are inconsistent with key features of the origins of section 116. The relevant history requires that a coherent and persuasive constitutive theory of the foundations of section 116 have a negative direction and be conceptually modest in terms of its substantive content.

The 1897–8 Federal Convention was not interested in bringing about a particular state of affairs by inserting section 116. Its principal objective was to deny legislative power to the Commonwealth on the subject of religion. The Convention was seeking to avoid a particular state of affairs. As McLeish himself points out, there was repeated reference by Higgins to the word 'safeguard.'[56] Indeed, the Convention paid little attention to the meaning of the language it adopted as section 116. The Convention's attention to the meaning of the words of section 116 was limited to pragmatic concerns about possible unintended consequences such as the free exercise clause having the effect of permitting objectionable religious practices. The Convention gave no serious attention to general issues about separation of religion and government, as might be expected if the Convention had been trying to ensure that any particular state of affairs concerning

53 Other commentators have referred to section 116, in the course of doctrinal discussions of its meaning, as being concerned with individual rights: Joshua Puls, 'The Wall of Separation: Section 116, the First Amendment and Constitutional Religious Guarantees' (1998) 26 *Federal Law Review* 139, 139; Wojciech Sadurski, 'The Action-Belief Dichotomy and Freedom of Religion' (1989–1990) 12 *Sydney Law Review* 420, 245. See also Nicholas Aroney, 'Freedom of Religion as an Associational Right', (2014) 33 *University of Queensland Law Journal* 154, 154–5.

54 John Locke, *A Letter Concerning Toleration* (1689), <http://www.constitution.org/jl/tolerati.htm>.

55 McLeish does not mention Locke in his discussion of neutrality.

56 McLeish, above n 8, 222.

church and state relations should obtain in Australia. The course of the debate at the Convention requires that a constitutive theory of the foundations of section 116 have a negative direction.

Not only is the conceptual direction of the neutrality theory a significant weakness in the theory, so too is the substantive content of neutrality. The substantive content of the neutrality theory is at odds with the history of the origins of section 116. The principal focus of the Convention was on denying legislative power, the chief political protagonists in the recognition campaign and anti-recognition campaign were often thinking at cross-purposes, and the Convention paid little attention both to the precise meaning of the words it inserted into the *Constitution* as section 116 and to the conceptual importance of the constitutional recognition of God to which it had agreed. If, as McLeish says, section 116 was inserted principally as an 'exercise in symbolism'[57] then it is inconsistent for a constitutive theory of its foundations to have such a rich or thick conceptual content.

Moreover, there is nothing in the relevant history to support importing American conceptual debates about the meaning of neutrality into a constitutive theory of the foundations of section 116 of the *Australian Constitution*. The Convention knew little, if anything, of the case law on the religion clauses of the *United States Constitution* and the Convention gave no attention whatsoever to the purposes for which those clauses were inserted into the *United States Constitution*. Indeed, even after the Convention concluded and an opportunity for further research presented itself, John Quick and Robert Garran expressed bafflement as to why the religion clauses of the First Amendment had ever been adopted by the Americans.[58] The American case law and the historical purposes for adopting the First Amendment are relevant to the contemporary debates about the meaning of neutrality in the United States. It makes little sense for those matters, of which the framers of the *Australian Constitution* were unaware, to inform the content of a constitutive theory of section 116 in the way McLeish says they inform the content of the neutrality theory. The relevant Australian history, which differs from the history of the adoption of the United States Bill of Rights and its First Amendment, does not support adopting American thinking about the idea of neutrality for the purposes of a constitutive theory of the foundations of section 116 of the *Australian Constitution*.

The relevant Australian history requires a substantively minimalist constitutive theory of the origins of section 116, and the neutrality theory is not substantively minimalist. The Convention was seeking to deny the Commonwealth power 'on the subject of' religion, because that was a subject over which power was not intended to be conferred and because delegates were persuaded that the existence of such a power might be misused. The Convention aimed at preventing vice and not at imbuing the Commonwealth with virtue. The precise language of section 116 was not the result of careful deliberation or a considered

57 Ibid.

58 John Quick and Robert Garran, *Annotated Constitution of the Commonwealth of Australia* (Angus & Robertson, 1901) 952:

> The prohibition contained in the first amendment was one of the ten articles in the so-called "American Bill of Rights" adopted after the establishment of the Union, in order to satisfy popular demands and sentiments. No logical or constitutional reasons have been stated why such a negation of power which had never been granted and which, therefore, could never be legally exercised, was introduced into the instrument of Government. It does not appear that its necessity has ever been demonstrated.

choice of words, as might be expected if a conceptually rich theory of the origins of the provision was to be appropriate.

A conceptually rich theory might be useful in the task of constitutional interpretation, since it would provide a lot of content that might inform the meaning of the provision in question in individual cases. Given that McLeish's broader purpose is to use the underlying conception of section 116 in presenting a new interpretation of its clauses this might, in part, explain his adoption of such a theory but it does not make the theory persuasive.

This suggests a second problem with the neutrality theory. The fact that McLeish seeks to flesh out and give further conceptual content to the neutrality theory by reference to recent American jurisprudence indicates a disconnect between the neutrality theory and its stated rationale. The methodology for providing the rich or thick substantive content to the neutrality theory is anachronistic and inconsistent with the theory's purpose. McLeish wants to use American jurisprudence for two distinct purposes. The first purpose is to flesh out the neutrality theory. The second purpose is to interpret the text of section 116. The problem here is with the order in which McLeish's analysis takes place. The underlying principle, constitutive theory, underlying conception or animating impulse of a constitutional provision has content prior to and separate from the doctrinal interpretation of the constitutional provision. McLeish's purpose is to interpret the text of section 116 in light of its underlying conception. That conception must exist and have content prior to and separate from the interpretation; otherwise it cannot be used in the subsequent task of interpretation. It is analytically confused to give meaning to the underlying conception by means of interpreting the provision in accordance with that conception.

The third principal reason why the neutrality theory is questionable as a coherent and convincing constitutive theory of the origins of section 116 is its disconnectedness or lack of consilience with the broader theoretical framework of Australian constitutionalism existing at the time of the *Constitution's* drafting.[59] Aroney explains that the explanatory adequacy of a theory about a particular aspect of a constitution is greater when the theory has 'consilience . . . with cognate theories that deal with related aspects of the constitution' and 'consilience with wider theories that deal with aspects of the political or social context in which the constitution operates.'[60] Consilience in this sense refers to the coherent integration of a theory with other theories.[61]

As well as telling the story of how in 1894 Robert Shannon was sentenced to the stocks for Sabbath breaking, Chapter 1 examined broad matters of Australian constitutionalism forming the philosophical context in which the *Australian Constitution* was drafted. The chapter explained that, in contrast to the position in the United States, Australian constitutionalism did not give conceptual primacy to individual rights and that Australian constitutionalism was not deeply suspicious of governmental power. The chapter also explained how Australian constitutionalism was non-theorised in the sense that questions of political and constitutional theory were, on the whole, not actively engaged in by the framers of

59 For the importance of theories having consilience or being integrated with coordinate or subordinate theories of phenomena, see also Aroney, 'Explanatory Power, Theory Formation and Constitutional Interpretation', above n 5, 10; Nicholas Aroney, 'Towards the Best Explanation of the *Constitution*: Text, Structure, History and Principle in *Roach v Electoral Commissioner* (2011) 30 *University of Queensland Law Journal* 145, 148.

60 Aroney, 'Towards the Best Explanation', above n 76, 149.

61 Ibid 148.

the *Australian Constitution*. The neutrality theory lacks consilience with these features of Australian constitutionalism.

The neutrality theory gives conceptual primacy to individual rights and its richness or thickness sits uncomfortably with the non-theorised nature of Australian constitutionalism, as does its positive conceptual direction. By postulating a state of affairs where the state avoids religious preferences, respects individual autonomy in religious matters and ensures that religious grounds do not prevent participation in the life of the general community, the neutrality theory reflects a deep suspicion of what governmental power is capable of in respect of religion. More than postulating the avoidance of a state of affairs considered objectionable, the neutrality theory postulates that the opposite state of affairs obtains.

It is true that Higgins' argument for section 116 reflects some degree of suspicion of governmental power and that reference was made in the course of the debate in the Federal Convention on section 116 to individuals' 'rights with respect to religion.'[62] However, the suspicion of governmental power reflected in Higgins' argument for section 116 is far from being as deep as that of the neutrality theory. Higgins' remarks must also be understood in the context of the debate's principal focus, which was denying legislative power on a subject that was not intended to be granted to the Commonwealth. More significantly, Higgins' comments and the debate as a whole should be situated in the broader philosophical context of Australian constitutionalism. The neutrality theory has more consilience with American constitutionalism than it does with Australian constitutionalism. Indeed, McLeish appears to recognise the issue of consilience in acknowledging that 'the framework surrounding the provisions [i.e. the Australian and American religion clauses] is notably different' given that the American religion clauses form part of a Bill of Rights and section 116 does not.[63] This is a significant conceptual problem with the neutrality theory.

The fourth reason why the neutrality theory is questionable as a coherent and convincing constitutive theory of the origins of section 116 concerns difficulties with the claimed historical basis of the theory. Parts of the historical explanation given for the neutrality theory are inaccurate and pertinent aspects of the relevant history are missing from the analysis. McLeish contends that Higgins proposed section 116 at the 1897–8 Federal Convention out of a belief that 'a reference to religion in the preamble could indicate an implicit federal power to make laws respecting religion.'[64] McLeish is far from alone in holding this interpretation of Higgins' argument for section 116. However, that interpretation of Higgins' argument does not withstand detailed scrutiny. Higgins recognised, and explained to the Convention, albeit in a rather convoluted manner, that the Commonwealth's express powers would be wide enough to authorise laws on the subject of religion. On this basis, the neutrality theory is based, in part, on a misunderstanding.

Other pertinent parts of the history of the adoption of section 116 are ignored or glossed over in the defence of the neutrality theory, and this is significant because they tend not to support the neutrality theory. The neutrality theory purports to explain a range of historical material but that history is presented at a very high level of generality. Indeed, the historical analysis presented in defence of the neutrality theory does not consider in any

62 *Official Record of the Debates of the Australasian Federal Convention*, Melbourne, 7 February 1898, 654 (Henry Higgins).

63 McLeish, above n 8, 209.

64 Ibid 219.

detail the particulars of section 116's drafting history, ignoring the detail both of its textual evolution and what the Federal Convention might have understood the provision's terms to mean. These features of the foundations of section 116 are relevant to any constitutive theory of those foundations. The defence of the neutrality theory does seek to situate the inclusion of section 116 in broader historical context, but that context is limited to noting that the idea for section 116 arose principally as a reaction to the campaign for constitutional recognition of God. McLeish does not discuss the Convention's understanding of the religious words of the preamble and their potential conceptual significance. Nor does the defence of the neutrality theory consider the implications of the fact that the precise form of words for constitutional recognition of God was not as important to the churches campaigning for recognition of God as it was for at least some members of the Convention who were concerned that 'the least objectionable'[65] form of words be adopted.

Significantly, given its importance as the immediate political context in which the issue of section 116 arose, the defence of the neutrality theory does not involve discussion of the broader aims of the recognition movement or explain that the campaign for recognition of God in the *Constitution* was part of a broader and longstanding movement by colonial church leaders for public recognition of God and religion more generally. This context is an important feature of the origins of section 116 for which the neutrality theory does not account. It is also relevant to a constitutive theory of the origins of section 116 that the key political actors outside the Convention – those leading the recognition campaign and counter-campaign – held differing conceptual understandings of the nature of the political state and of constitutions and lacked a common understanding as to what their debate was fundamentally about. The relevant history is far more detailed and nuanced than McLeish's overview of it would suggest, and it does not support a constitutive theory with a focus on individual rights or a positive conceptual direction.

The fifth reason why the neutrality theory does not provide a coherent and convincing constitutive theory of the origins of section 116 is that the rationale given for the theory does not require or compel the theory. In his rationale for the neutrality theory, McLeish emphasises what he calls the 'calculated pragmatism'[66] of the Convention in inserting religious words in the preamble and agreeing to section 116 as a means of garnering votes for the *Constitution*. He also describes the insertion of section 116 as 'an exercise in symbolism to reassure those concerned about government interference with or imposition of religion.'[67] Moreover, McLeish writes of section 116 being inserted to deny possible implied legislative powers. If all of this correct, then it is difficult to reconcile with the neutrality theory's rejection of the notion that section 116 'is concerned primary with legislative power rather than civil rights.'[68] The neutrality theory places conceptual emphasis largely on secondary considerations rather than on the primary mischief the Convention was seeking to address, which was the scope of Commonwealth legislative power.

The two themes McLeish derives from his overview of colonial history regarding religion do not compel a civil rights-emphasising theory. The themes of anti-sectarianism and the

65 *Official Record of the Debates of the Australasian Federal Convention*, Melbourne, 2 March 1898, 1737 (Edmund Barton).

66 McLeish, above n 8, 221.

67 Ibid 222.

68 Ibid 208, 211.

idea that religion was a personal matter with which the state should not interfere are also consistent with a conceptual emphasis on limiting the scope of Commonwealth power.

Why the safeguard against intolerance theory is right

It remains to defend the safeguard against religious intolerance theory as a coherent and convincing constitutive theory of the origins of section 116.

The above critique of the neutrality theory goes some way towards mounting a defence of the safeguard against religious intolerance theory, demonstrating that a coherent constitutive theory of the foundations of section 116 needs to have a negative direction and be conceptually modest in terms of its substantive content. The comparison of the neutrality and safeguard against religious intolerance theories above indicated that the safeguard against religious intolerance theory possesses these structural features.

Unlike the neutrality theory, the safeguard against religious intolerance theory does not suffer from a lack of consilience with the features of Australian constitutionalism. One of these features was that Australian constitutionalism did not give conceptual primacy to rights. Since the safeguard against religious intolerance theory does not have an individual rights focus there is consilience with this feature of Australian constitutionalism. A second feature of Australian constitutionalism was its essential lack of suspicion of governmental power. The above critique of the neutrality theory's positive direction explained that only a constitutive theory of the foundations of section 116 with a negative direction would be consistent with this feature of Australian constitutionalism. In respect of the safeguard against intolerance theory, that critique also explained that while Higgins' argument for section 116 reflects some degree of suspicion of governmental power it was not such as to be inconsistent with Australian constitutionalism's lack of suspicion of governmental power. The broader and principal focus of events at the Federal Convention was on ensuring that the Commonwealth would not have power to make laws on the subject of religion because it was not intended that the Commonwealth should possess power to legislate on the subject of religion. Concern that the existence of such a power might lead to religious intolerance must be understood in this broader context and is consistent with the idea of preventing a vice, not imbuing with a virtue.

Similarly, the negative conceptual direction and comparatively more modest substantive content of the safeguard against religious intolerance theory sit comfortably with the non-theorised nature of Australian constitutionalism and its lack of concern with philosophical questions about the nature of the state. The fact that the notion of safeguard reflects a degree of suspicion of governmental power is not inconsistent with Australian constitutionalism's essential lack of suspicion of governmental power. The framers of the *Australian Constitution* did not adhere to any utopian view that governmental power was incapable of misuse. The degree of suspicion reflected in the safeguard against religious intolerance theory is less profound than that reflected in the neutrality theory. It is also far more pragmatic, concerned principally with questions of the scope of legislative power, albeit concerned with those questions due partly to fears about the potential for religiously oppressive laws.

The general theme of pragmatism running through the history of the origins of section 116 also points to the safeguard against religious intolerance theory. While the Seventh Day Adventists were in part seeking to have the Constitution reflect their theological views about the relationship between religion and government, they pursued their campaign with the principal pragmatic goal of ensuring they could not be subjected to federal

Sabbath observance laws. The Convention's decision to include section 116 in the Constitution and the debates on that question both in the Federal Convention and in the colonial legislatures focused on whether there was a need for 'a sufficient safeguard against the passing of religious laws by the Commonwealth.'[69] Higgins' more general antagonism towards the Councils of Churches included his belief that their constitutional recognition of God campaign was a disguised campaign 'to bring about religious oppression.'[70] Higgins' general aim and the Convention's decision aimed at preventing a particular state of affairs.

The theme of pragmatism also characterises how the Convention chose and thought about the language of section 116. The Convention simply copied language from America and added the religious observances clause to cover the principal mischief of Sabbath observance laws. To the extent that the Convention gave any real attention to the meaning of section 116 that attention was limited to pragmatic concerns about potential unintended consequences. The reason for this was that the delegates at the Convention seem to have believed that the limited language of section 116 amounted in some way to a complete denial to the Commonwealth to legislate 'on the subject of' religion. The Convention was seeking to prevent a particular state of affairs, not to ensure that a particular state of affairs obtained and not to imbue the Commonwealth with any virtue.

The safeguard against religious tolerance theory coherently and convincingly explains the point of the section 116.

69 *Official Record of the Debates of the Australasian Federal Convention*, Melbourne, 2 March 1898, 1734 (Henry Higgins).

70 'The Parliamentary Elections. Mr H B Higgins at the Exhibition Theatre. An Enthusiastic Reception.' *Geelong Advertiser* (Victoria), 2 October 1897, 2, 3.

10 H V Evatt's attempts to amend section 116 in the 1940s

Evatt's determination to expand section 116

The story of the origins of constitutional religious freedom in Australia does not end with the *Australian Constitution* coming into force on 1 January 1901. Constitutional provisions can be amended. This is exactly what Hebert Vere 'Doc' Evatt tried unsuccessfully to do twice in the 1940s.

Evatt had an impressive career. He held a doctorate in constitutional law, published several books and after a short time as a lawyer was elected to the New South Wales Legislative Assembly for the Labor Party. Evatt's career in State politics was short. He accepted appointment as a justice of the High Court in 1930 and served for a decade before stepping down in 1940 to enter federal politics. During his federal political career he served as Attorney-General and Minister for External Affairs for nearly a decade under the prime ministerships of John Curtin, Frank Forde and Ben Chifley, was the third president of the United Nations General Assembly helping to draft the *Universal Declaration of Human Rights*, and from 1951 was Leader of the Opposition for almost a decade after Chifley died shortly after losing government to Sir Robert Menzies' coalition. He left politics to become Chief Justice of the New South Wales Supreme Court.

It was during his time as Attorney-General that Evatt tried twice to amend section 116.

From shield to sword: the 1942 Referendum Bill

The first official proposal to alter section 116 occurred in 1942 during the Second World War. As Attorney-General in the Curtin Labor Government, Evatt sought to alter section 116 as part of sweeping package of constitutional reform. The proposals were officially Government proposals but, in reality, were a project of Evatt's.

On 1 October 1942, Evatt introduced the *Constitution Alteration (War Aims and Reconstruction) Bill 1942* into the House of Representatives.[1] The alteration to the *Constitution* proposed by the Bill was extraordinary in its breadth. It would have conferred on the Commonwealth Parliament plenary power to legislate on any subject.

1 Commonwealth, *Parliamentary Debates*, House of Representatives, 1 October 1942, 1338–41.

The Bill proposed to insert a new section 60A into the *Constitution.* Sub-section (1) would provide:

> The Parliament shall have full power to make laws for the peace, order and good government of the Commonwealth, its territories and all places under its jurisdiction or control for the purpose of carrying into effect the war aims and objects of Australia as one of the United Nations, including the attainment of economic security and social justice in the post-war world, and for the purpose of post-war reconstruction generally.

To make clear that this was a grant of general plenary power to the Commonwealth Parliament, unconfined as to subject matter, sub-section (2) would provide:

> Without limiting the generality of the foregoing sub-section, it is hereby declared that the power of the Parliament shall extend to all measures which in the declared opinion of the Parliament will tend to achieve economic security and social justice, including security of employment and the provision of useful occupation for all the people, and shall include power to make laws with respect to [fourteen listed subject matters].

Sub-section (3) would provide that 'All the powers conferred upon the Parliament by this section maybe exercised notwithstanding anything contained elsewhere in this Constitution.' Limitations on power contained elsewhere in the *Constitution* would no longer constrain federal legislative power. More profoundly, the combined effect of sub-sections (2) and (3) would be to make the Parliament the final judge of whether a law was within power. Such questions would no longer be determined by the High Court.

At the First Reading of the Bill in the House of Representatives,[2] Evatt gave what has become known as his 'horse and buggy speech' explaining the general purpose of his proposals. He told Parliament:

> When the war is over, Australia will be confronted with the greatest task of economic rehabilitation in its history. Problems of employment, of housing, of health and child welfare, of vocational training, and of markets and price stability, will call for enterprise and statecraft of the highest order. The whole history of the Commonwealth Constitution shows that these problems cannot be solved without wider powers in the hands of the central government . . .
>
> [T]he peace-time powers of the Commonwealth, though numerous and detailed, are hedged round with severe limitations. Although they were written down in the 1890s, many of the words and phrases were simply transcribed from the American Constitution of 1787. The general approach belongs to the horse and buggy age of social organization. This is especially true of the economic powers that are so vital an element in a modern industrial community. For instance, "trade and commerce" is so divided between the Commonwealth and the State authority that neither can deal effectively with it. Such topics as production, employment, investment, industrial conditions, are either

2 Commonwealth, *Parliamentary Debates*, House of Representatives, 1 October 1942, 1338–41.

> not committed to the national government at all, or are granted in jealous, limited, qualified and indirect terms. The Constitution of 1900 is outmoded.[3]

Evatt's Bill would have affected section 116 in contradictory ways. Among the subjects listed in sub-section (2) was

> (h) carrying into effect the guarantee of the four freedoms, that is to say –
>
> i freedom of speech and expression;
> ii religious freedom;
> iii freedom from want; and
> iv freedom from fear.

On the one hand, proposed section 60A(3) denied effect to section 116. It would no longer limit the scope of federal legislative power. On the other hand, proposed section 60A(2)(h)(ii) would grant the Commonwealth power to give effect to religious freedom.

The specific mention in sub-section (2) of religious freedom as a topic of legislative power was superfluous in substance since the general terms of proposed section 60A(1) were obviously wide enough to encompass that topic. Evatt said as much in his speech. He told Parliament:

> Though individual subject-matters of power are also enumerated, they are given by way of illustration and not by way of limitation. In many cases, the objective of policy is indicated in the list of particular subject-matters. Honourable members will note that this list, which will be found in sub-section 2, includes power for guaranteeing "the four essential human freedoms", to use President Roosevelt's famous phrase. At all points it is made clear that what the Parliament is asking for is power to carry out in peace-time the social and economic aims that the United Nations have declared in time of war. Surely those ideals for which our fellow countrymen have fought and died are worth embodying in the fundamental law of our Constitution.[4]

Whilst legally superfluous, the mention of religious freedom as a topic of legislative power is conceptually important. Evatt's thinking was obviously different to the 1897–8 Federal Convention. The Federal Convention was not seeking to ensure that any particular state of affairs regarding religion-government relations should obtain but was seeking to avoid a situation of religious intolerance on the part of the Commonwealth. By contrast, Evatt was seeking power to bring about – 'carry out' and 'carry[] into effect' – a particular state of affairs. The constitutional religion clauses would no longer represent a shield against Commonwealth action interfering with religious freedom but would become a sword wielded by the Commonwealth to bring about religious freedom in practice.

3 Ibid 1338–9.
4 Ibid 1341.

There was a moral imperative to Evatt's sword. In his speech, Evatt also told Parliament:

> This country, like all the other United Nations, has pledged itself to the task of achieving the broad objectives embodied in the Atlantic Charter and in the historic declaration of the four essential human freedoms – freedom of speech and expression, freedom of worship, freedom from want, freedom from fear – anywhere and everywhere in the world. These declarations are not legal instruments technically binding on Australia; they are far more. They are solemn pledges of our dedication as a nation to the great ends of economic security, social justice and individual freedom. Do we intend to carry out these pledges? The answer is, "Yes, we must". If so, the Australian nation, which is pledged as a nation, must be endowed as a nation with legislative powers to carry out the pledges within Australia and its territories.[5]

The sword reverts to a shield: the 1942 Convention

In Parliament, Evatt's Bill did not proceed past the first reading stage in the House of Representatives. The Curtin Government decided that debate should not proceed in the face of increasing opposition to the Bill.[6]

Instead, the Government convened a special conference, later described as a Convention, comprising 24 members to discuss the Bill and the broader question of Commonwealth powers necessary for post-war reconstruction. The Convention consisted of eight members of the House of Representatives (including Evatt) and four members of the Senate, equally representative of the Government and the Opposition. It also consisted of the Premier and Leader of the Opposition of each State.

Evatt planned to dominate the Convention's thinking before it even started. In preparation for the Convention, Evatt brought together a group of 30 senior public servants, academics and lawyers.[7] The purpose was to write a book under Evatt's direction. A few weeks later, a 188-page book entitled *Post-War Reconstruction: A Case for Greater Commonwealth Powers*[8] was ready for distribution to the members of the Convention when it met. The book was 'a curious mixture of emotional political appeals and argument', according to one member of the team that wrote it.[9] On its first day, the Convention agreed to delay the start of its second day of proceedings so that members would have time to read the book.[10]

The book contains further discussion of Evatt's proposals, but in the context of planned changes by Evatt to the Bill. Those planned changes included continuing the judicial review jurisdiction of the High Court and only exempting the proposed new powers from the

5 Ibid 1339.
6 Sir Paul Hasluck, *The Government and the People 1942–1945* (Australian War Memorial, 1970) 524.
7 Ken Buckley, Barbara Dale and Wayne Reynolds, *Doc Evatt: Patriot, Internationalist, Fighter and Scholar* (Longman Cheshire, 1994) 196; Hasluck, above n 6, 524.
8 H V Evatt, *Post-War Reconstruction: A Case for Greater Commonwealth Powers* (Commonwealth Government Printer, 1942).
9 Hasluck, above n 6, 526.
10 Convention of Representatives of the Commonwealth and State Parliaments on Proposed Alteration of the Commonwealth Constitution, *Record of Proceedings*, Canberra, 24 November 1942, 11.

limitation in section 92 of the *Constitution* concerning freedom of interstate trade and commerce, but not from other limitations such as section 116.

The book discussed what 'religious freedom' as a constitutional expression might mean. The relevant section of the book commenced by suggesting that the proper meaning of the constitutional expression is one for the United Nations: 'No formal definition of the four freedoms has as yet been made by the United Nations. The following tentative definitions are suggested.'[11] This suggestion is important. It speaks clearly to Evatt's general aim in proposing the Bill:

> [T]he two tasks – building a new world order and building a better Australia – should go hand in hand. A study of the international declarations and agreements summarized herein will show that the United Nations recognize that a lasting peace can be assured only if certain economic and social ends are attained. The attainment of those ends requires some legislative action within each and every territory. Essentials of peace such as full employment, development of national resources, adequate social services, improved standards of living and the enjoyment of the 'four freedoms' can, in the final issue, be realized only through the legislatures of the nations. In that sense, social justice must always begin at home.[12]

Evatt was not only trying to fashion a sword to be wielded by the Commonwealth to bring about a particular state of affairs, and in this he differed from the Federal Convention. The Bill, including its religious freedom power, would also be the mechanism by which Australia contributed to building a new world order. Also unlike the Federal Convention with its focus on the Australian situation, Evatt's desired state of affairs was to be understood in the context of emerging international human rights notions rather than any domestic Australian notions of the proper scope of religious freedom or the relationship between religion and government.

This explains why Evatt 'tentative definitions' are presented with an unlawyerly level of generality. The book offered up this explanation of what religious freedom might mean:

> *Freedom of religion* – means (a) that freedom of conscience and the free profession and practice of religion are, subject to public order and morality, guaranteed to every citizen; (b) that no person shall be subject to any disability or be required to take any oath on account of his religion or religious belief, and no religious test shall be imposed in respect of the appointment to or holding of any public office; (c) that no law shall be made for establishing any religion or for imposing any religious observance or for prohibiting the free exercise of any religion.[13]

None of (a), (b) or (c) really amounts to a definition. Points (a), (b) and (c) appear to be transcriptions from other constitutional texts. The words of definition (a) appear in both article 44 of the *Constitution of Ireland 1937* and section 46(1) of the Tasmanian *Constitution Act 1934.* The words of definition (b) also appear in section 46(2) of the Tasmanian *Constitution Act 1934.* The words of definition (c) are obviously taken from

11 Evatt, above n 8, 83.
12 Ibid 42.
13 Ibid 83.

section 116 of the *Australian Constitution*. As with the 1897–8 Federal Convention, the precise meaning of the constitutional religion provision was not given close attention by Evatt. For Evatt, this was because the provision was intended to import into the *Australian Constitution* a concept originating elsewhere.

As Evatt had mentioned in his First Reading Speech in Parliament, the origins of that concept lay in a speech by the American President Franklin Roosevelt. Indeed, and so there could be no doubt as to his inspiration, Evatt had included the relevant parts of Roosevelt's 1941 annual message to the United States Congress in which Roosevelt articulated the idea of the 'four freedoms' as an appendix to the book.[14] Moreover, Evatt intended the provision to be understood in light of emerging international human rights norms, which did not have a settled meaning. As the book explained, '[n]o formal definition of the four freedoms has as yet been made by the United Nations.'[15]

Evatt's lack of attention to the meaning of his religion provision seems to have had little to do with the fact that its meaning would have had no legal consequence given that the Bill proposed to grant the Commonwealth a general plenary power. Whilst Evatt told Parliament in his First Reading Speech that the subject-matters listed in proposed section 60A(2) are 'given by way of illustration and not by way of limitation', he said the contrary in the book prepared under his direction. Before discussing the religious freedom clause, Evatt discussed the free speech clause. In that discussion he wrote that '[i]ndirectly . . . the paragraph, by implication, would, it is submitted, operate to limit, in favour of the citizen, the general powers conferred by sub-section (1).'[16] The same would be true, Evatt argued, of the religious freedom provision. He wrote:

> It has been suggested that the overriding effect given by sub-section (3) of new section 60A to laws made in the exercise of the powers conferred by that section might possibly give the Commonwealth Parliament power to override the present guarantee in section 116. This is an impossible conclusion because, as already suggested, the power is to carry into effect the guarantee of the four freedoms, not to deny or destroy any of them.[17]

This argument is simply untenable given that sub-section (2), in which the four freedoms are listed as topics of legislative power, commences: 'Without limiting the generality of the foregoing sub-section.'

As a former High Court judge and leading legal mind, Evatt must have recognised that his argument was legally unsound. The book's discussion of the four freedoms power concludes by stating that 'it is important that all doubts on these great topics should be removed: and it can be taken for granted that at the proper time and in the proper place full opportunity for clarification and amendment will be given.'[18] Evatt plainly did not direct too much attention to the meaning of his religion provision or, indeed, to the textual form it should take.

14 Ibid 163–5.
15 Evatt, above n 8, 83.
16 Ibid 84.
17 Ibid 85.
18 Ibid 85.

Indeed, in the book Evatt acknowledges that he did not give close attention to the precise form of words his religion clause took. The book contains a section entitled 'Some Questions and Answers.' One of the participants in the book's drafting later described that section as containing the 'sort of thing [that] may be good stuff on the hustings but . . . scarcely what might be expected from an Attorney-General preparing for a Constitutional Convention.'[19] Question 65 was posed and answer in this way:

> *Q* – Well, what about the 'four freedoms'? No doubt they are not irrelevant; but are they not superfluous, as being included in other items? And is not their mention here rather a placard than an exposition?
>
> *A* – It has already been answered that these paragraphs are illustrative. Of course, if you wish to be disrespectful to an illustration, you can call it a placard. But the point is that these 'four freedoms' are a graphic illustration of the war aims that has [sic] caught the imagination of the world, and perhaps illustrate those aims better than other forms of words could do. And there is nothing rhetorical about them, in any uncomplimentary sense: they are a plain straightforward description, not beneath the dignity of Parliamentary language. Long abandoned is the notion that statutes must be couched in the pompous jargon dear to the old-time draftsman; and if a homely illustration helps to illustrate the meaning, why should it not be used just as one might use a diagram or a map or a formula?[20]

Evatt was obviously open to textual refinement.

In the few weeks between the drafting of this answer and the start of the Convention, Evatt thought some more about the form his religion clause should take. On the Convention's first day, Evatt announced that the Government had changed its mind on the form the four freedoms provision should take. Regarding religious freedom, Evatt announced:

> Instead of empowering the Commonwealth Parliament to pass laws carrying into effect the guarantee of religious freedom, we think it much safer to include a direct constitutional guarantee applicable as against either the Commonwealth or any State. This is done by providing that section 116 of the Constitution, which at present binds only the Commonwealth, shall bind the States also.[21]

Evatt came to the Convention ready with the proposed text. He proposed that section 116 be amended so that it would read:

> Neither the Commonwealth nor a State may make any law for establishing any religion, or for imposing any religious observance, or for prohibiting the free exercise of any religion, and no religious test shall be required as a qualification for any office or public trust under the Commonwealth or a State.[22]

19 Hasluck, above n 6, 526.

20 Evatt, above n 8, 105.

21 Convention of Representatives of the Commonwealth and State Parliaments on Proposed Alteration of the Commonwealth Constitution, *Record of Proceedings*, Canberra, 24 November 1942, 8.

22 Ibid 12.

This approach, Evatt told the Convention, would make the freedom 'more secure.'[23] This was a significant change on Evatt's part. Evatt had changed from proposing a sword to bring about a state of affairs to proposing a shield to prevent a state of affairs.

There was almost no discussion of the religion provision at the Convention. The only significant comment came from the Opposition's Robert Menzies, at the time a backbencher, who thought, like many of the delegates at the 1897–8 Federal Convention, that constitutional guarantees of religious freedom were unnecessary in Australia.[24]

Debate on the religion provision proved unnecessary. The Convention agreed to a plan by which the States would refer power to the Commonwealth under section 51(xxxvii) of the *Constitution* to legislate in respect of various matters relating to post-war reconstruction. The four freedoms were not among those matters since, as Evatt later explained, 'it would have been impossible to include them in a State Act of Parliament under the machinery of reference by State legislatures adopted by the Constitution Convention.'[25] However, the plan for all the States to refer power failed: New South Wales and Queensland passed legislation in the agreed form, as did Victoria, but the Victorian legislation would come into effect only if the other States passed the agreed legislation; South Australia and Western Australia passed modified versions of the agreed legislation, and the Tasmanian Parliament rejected the legislation.[26]

Evatt tries and fails again: the 1944 referendum

Lack of success in 1942 did not deter Evatt. On 10 February 1944, Evatt introduced the *Constitution Alteration (Post-War Reconstruction) Bill 1944* into the House of Representatives. The Bill proposed to alter the *Constitution* by granting the Commonwealth power to legislate in respect of fourteen subject matters for a period of five years after the end of the Second World War. The subject matters were substantially the same as those that the 1942 Convention had agreed the States should refer to the Commonwealth. The Bill as introduced did not include any provisions touching religion.

Evatt, however, was working behind the scenes to ensure that a broader guarantee of religious freedom would be proposed. On 9 March 1944, Evatt told the House of Representatives that the Cabinet had decided the Bill should be amended to include three 'safeguards.'[27] The Cabinet had agreed to these amendments at Evatt's instigation.[28] The first two safeguards would empower the Parliament to supervise the exercise by the Executive of delegated legislative powers and prohibit laws abridging freedom of speech or expression. The third safeguard would apply the prohibitions in section 116 to the States.

Evatt moved those amendments at about 2am on the morning of 16 March 1944 during a debate on the Bill that had lasted all the previous day and continued through the

23 Ibid 8.

24 Convention of Representatives of the Commonwealth and State Parliaments on Proposed Alteration of the Commonwealth Constitution, *Record of Proceedings*, Canberra, 25 November 1942, 25–6.

25 Commonwealth, *Parliamentary Debates*, House of Representatives, 9 March 1944, 1153 (Evatt).

26 Geoffrey Sawer, *Australian Federal Politics and Law 1929–1949* (Cambridge University Press, 1963) 140, 171.

27 Commonwealth, *Parliamentary Debates*, House of Representatives, 9 March 1944, 1152.

28 Meeting of full Cabinet held at 11am on Tuesday and Wednesday 7 and 8 December 1943 at Parliament House Canberra, Agendum 573a.

night.[29] The text of the amendment stated: 'Section one hundred and sixteen of this Constitution shall apply to and in relation to every State in like manner as it applies to and in relation to the Commonwealth.'[30] Evatt's amendment was agreed to without a division and without any substantive contributions by other members.[31]

In the House of Representatives, Evatt's speech on 9 March concerning his proposed amendments to the Bill repeated almost verbatim what he had written in his submission to Cabinet seeking approval to move the amendments.[32] Evatt's central point was that recent experience in Europe demonstrated the ease with which freedom of speech and religion could be 'swept away' and that their importance to democracy warranted their inclusion as constitutional safeguards.[33] He also pointed out that the legislative powers of the States were wider than those of the Commonwealth and that it was therefore anomalous that there was no constitutional safeguard against the use of those powers to interfere with religious freedom.[34]

Evatt also argued that Roosevelt's 'freedom of speech and expression' and 'freedom of every person to worship God in his own way' were 'fundamental freedoms which can and should be included to safeguard individual rights throughout Australia.'[35] Evatt viewed section 116 as principally about individual rights in a way that was not characteristic of the 1897–8 Federal Convention, which considered section 116 as principally about the scope of federal legislative power.

Evatt took up this theme again on 15 March. He told the House that 'British countries have tended to rely on Parliament itself' to protect individual rights.[36] His view, Evatt explained, had long been that it 'would be wise to follow the example set by the Constitution of the United States of America, and to give to two at least of the fundamental freedoms of citizenship the special protection of embodiment in the Constitution.'[37] Evatt's amendments were not so much about limiting Commonwealth legislative power as a matter of the proper distribution of powers between the Commonwealth and the States, as they were about protecting individual rights.

Evatt also told the House that he had received correspondence expressing support for his rights amendments from 'a tremendous body of non-partisan leaders of thought in this country, including church leaders of all denominations.'[38] If this is true, this would suggest a change of heart on the part of church leaders since applying section 116 to the States would be likely to prevent the sort of Sabbath observance laws advocated by their predecessors in the 1890s.

In moving his religion amendment, Evatt said: 'In the sphere of religious freedom, it is not proposed to adopt any new principle . . . The present proposal is to apply section

29 Commonwealth, *Parliamentary Debates*, House of Representatives, 15 March 1944, 1403 (Evatt). Hansard continues the day until the House adjourns, rather than starting a new day at midnight.

30 Ibid 1403.

31 Ibid 1407.

32 Meeting of full Cabinet held at 11am on Tuesday and Wednesday 7 and 8 December 1943 at Parliament House Canberra, Agendum 573a.

33 Commonwealth, *Parliamentary Debates*, House of Representatives, 9 March 1944, 1153–4.

34 Ibid 1154.

35 Ibid.

36 Commonwealth, *Parliamentary Debates*, House of Representatives, 15 March 1944, 1343.

37 Ibid.

38 Ibid.

116 to the States.[39] In explaining the origins of section 116 to Parliament, Evatt emphasised the provision's American pedigree. He said:

> Not all of our own section 116 is derived from the First Amendment. The prohibition against the imposition of a religious test as a qualification for office is based on a provision contained in Article VI in the Constitution of the United States of America. No prohibition against imposing a religious observance is found in the First Amendment. A similar phrase, however, is found in a number of the State constitutions.[40]

Evatt was not quite right. The motivation for the religious observances clause lies in the fears of the Seventh Day Adventists in Australia that recognition of God in the constitutional preamble might empower the Commonwealth to impose religious observances and in Higgins' convoluted argument in the 1897–8 Federal Convention that the Commonwealth's express powers could extend to laws on the subject of religion. In suggesting a form of words, neither Higgins nor any other delegate at the Federal Convention referred to any American State constitutions.

Evatt's homework for the parliamentary discussion of his amendments appears to have focussed on American jurisprudence. In his speech, Evatt spent most of his time traversing the American case law on religious freedom in some detail,[41] indicating some detailed research on that issue. However, Evatt appears not to have researched the history of section 116 in any detail. Quick and Garran's *Annotated Constitution of the Commonwealth of Australia* provides a brief, although somewhat erroneous, description of Higgins' argument as to the need for a religious observances clause. As a lawyer and former justice of the High Court, Evatt would have been familiar with that source. Had Evatt consulted Quick and Garran's work he may have rethought what appears to be little more than an assumption on his part that the origin of the religious observances clause lies with American State constitutions.

The facts that Evatt did not appear to consult Quick and Garran and focussed his thinking on American jurisprudence are important evidence of his conceptual focus. Evatt thought about his religion amendment through the prism of individual rights, a notion he was seeking to promote.

For the purposes of the referendum campaign, Evatt prepared a 59-page book entitled *Post-War Reconstruction: Temporary Alterations of the Constitution. Notes on the Fourteen Powers and the Three Safeguards.*[42] The passages in that book concerning religion said nothing new, simply repeating, mostly verbatim, passages from Evatt's speech on 15 March in Parliament.[43]

The Bill failed at the referendum held on 19 August 1944. It failed to obtain a national majority and majorities in favour were obtained in only Western Australia and

39 Ibid 1403–4.
40 Ibid 1404.
41 Ibid 1404–7.
42 H V Evatt, *Post-War Reconstruction: Temporary Alterations of the Constitution. Notes on the Fourteen Powers and the Three Safeguards* (Commonwealth Government Printer, 1944).
43 Ibid 48–53.

South Australia.[44] The campaign itself focussed principally on issues relating to the 'fourteen powers.'[45]

The official 'No' pamphlet was dismissive of Evatt's rights provisions. It stated that those provisions 'should not be taken too seriously. They were not in the Bill as it was introduced into Parliament but were inserted during an all-night sitting. They are designed to distract attention from the real objectives of the measure.'[46]

Despite being a peripheral issue in the context of the proposed constitutional amendments as a whole, the merits of Evatt's religion clause did receive a small amount of public attention. The Tasmanian *Advocate* newspaper of 29 July 1944 summarised the provision and printed for and against columns.[47] Evatt wrote the 'for' column and Robert Menzies, who had by this time become Leader of the Opposition, wrote the 'against' column.

Evatt commenced his case with an emphasis on the rights-basis of his proposal. He stated that '[r]eligious freedom is and should always be regarded as a foundational democratic right.'[48] He argued that it was anomalous that section 116 did not apply to the States because of the wider scope of their powers compared to the Commonwealth. It was even more anomalous, Evatt argued, referring to the franchise for and composition of those State Upper Houses at the time that did not have full adult suffrage and included appointed members,[49] because 'five State Parliaments are less democratic than that of the Commonwealth.'[50] Evatt emphasised that the proposal was not to give Australians religious freedom but to 'safeguard' that freedom 'as a measure of insurance.'[51] He expressed confidence that after the experience of the safeguard for five years the Australian people would give it 'a permanent place' in the Constitution.[52] Evatt also reassured readers that religious freedom would not be able to be 'used as a cloak for cruel or immoral practices.'[53]

Menzies was dismissive of the proposal in his 'against' column. It was, Menzies wrote, 'a quaint provision to put in a five year's amendment to the Constitution.'[54] Menzies' dismissiveness extended to sarcasm in explaining that democratic parliaments were sufficient to protect religious freedom:

> What is the reason for it? Is it that Dr Evatt has, through his investigation branch, discovered that State Parliament is intending to impair religious freedom? Of course not. If any State Parliament dreamed of taking such an action its membership would be very violently changed at the next election.[55]

44 Commonwealth Bureau of Census and Statistics, *Year Book Australia, 1944–45* (Commonwealth Government Printer, 1947) 61.
45 See generally Hasluck, above n 6, 535–40; W J Waters, 'The Opposition and the "Powers" Referendum, 1944' (1969) 4(1) *Politics* 42.
46 Reprinted in *Northern Argus* (Clare, South Australia), 11 August 1944, 8.
47 *Advocate* (Burnie, Tasmania), 29 July 1944, 2.
48 Ibid.
49 See Gareth Griffith and Sharath Srinivasan, *State Upper Houses in Australia* (New South Wales Parliamentary Research Service, Background Paper 1/2001).
50 *Advocate* (Burnie, Tasmania), 29 July 1944, 2.
51 Ibid.
52 Ibid.
53 Ibid.
54 Ibid.
55 Ibid.

The purpose of this provision, Menzies wrote, was 'simply that "Yes" advocates hope they will collect some votes' for the package of constitutional amendments from those who believe that by voting 'No' they would be voting to take away religious liberty.[56] Menzies continued, albeit not entirely accurately, given for example the experience of the Seventh Day Adventists during the 1880s and 1890s, that since the advent of self-government in the States, 'not one person in Australia has been prevented from expressing his own faith or worshipping in his own way.'[57] Menzies concluded his column by asking 'why should it be thought that all of a sudden, for no reason at all, this record is going to be besmirched by some iniquitous statute which only this hurried amendment to the Constitution could prevent?'[58]

The exchange between Evatt and Menzies is conceptually significant. Evatt approached the issue through the prism of individual rights and as a matter of principle. For him, the fact that religious liberty was not actually threatened was irrelevant; the broader principle was what mattered. For Menzies, such an approach was foreign to Australian constitutionalism. A focus on individual rights was not the proper way to think about constitutional provisions. Moreover, the matter should be approached pragmatically: the fact there was no danger to religious liberty spoke against the need for Evatt's religion provision.

The conceptual contrast between denying power and protecting individual rights can also be seen in Sir Isaac Isaacs' contribution to the public debate on Evatt's religion provision. In a letter to the editor of the *Sydney Morning Herald* in August 1944, Isaacs expressed his full support for the provision.[59] Isaacs pointed to 'some world-shaking events' which had led to the Atlantic Charter, to which Australia had acceded. He wrote that it 'has been made evident to the leading statesmen of the civilised world that among the safeguards for the future are the guarantees referred to [i.e. Roosevelt's 'four freedoms'].' Australia was, Isaacs argued, 'bound to honour that pledge' and the only way to do that under Australia's constitutional arrangements was to 'insert the guarantees in the Constitution that will bind the States as well as the Commonwealth.'

The views of Isaacs who, during his career, served as Attorney-General, Chief Justice of the High Court and Governor-General are noteworthy. It was Isaacs who, in the 1890s, introduced the constitutional recognition of God proposal into the Victorian Legislative Assembly.[60] Whilst Isaacs also ultimately voted at the 1897–8 Federal Convention for Higgins' provision that became section 116, he had earlier voted in favour of Symon's amendment to Higgins' provision, which would have limited the provision to a prohibition only against religious tests for public office. Isaacs' views had changed since the Convention where his concern had not been guarantees of rights.

Evatt's apparently limited research into the origins of section 116 also meant that he missed an opportunity to learn from how Higgins advocated in favour of section 116 at the 1897–8 Convention. Higgins ultimately succeeded in including section 116 in the

56 Ibid.
57 Ibid.
58 Ibid.
59 'What is this Freedom? Sir Isaac Isaacs's Views', *Sydney Morning Herald* (Sydney), 8 August 1944, 2.
60 Victoria, *Parliamentary Debates*, Legislative Assembly, 20 August 1897, 1696.

Constitution only because, through his convoluted argument, he was able to persuade other delegates that the Commonwealth might indeed have power to legislate on the topic of religion. Whether for the principal purpose of denying power, as for Higgins, or protecting individual rights as for Evatt, the need for a provision such as Higgins' or Evatt's in Australia, requires practical proof. It is unlikely to be a winning strategy to rest an argument on the grounds of principle.

That lesson was not heeded by those who came after Evatt seeking to expand section 116.

11 Post-war attempts to amend section 116

The Australian Constitutional Convention of 1973–1985

Following the defeat of the 1944 referendum, official attention was not given to amending section 116 until the Australian Constitutional Convention.[1] Between 1973 and 1985, the Australian Constitutional Convention met in the various State capitals. Its task was to review the *Constitution* and make proposals for its amendment. The idea for the Convention sprang from dissatisfaction by the States about Australia's constitutional arrangements leading to 'vertical fiscal imbalance' whereby the States have responsibility for large spending obligations in areas like health and education but lack the revenue raising capacity to properly fund those obligations. Delegates were appointed to represent the Federal, State and Territory Parliaments, as well as local government.

The Convention met for its first session in Sydney in September 1973 during the first year of the Whitlam Labor Government. The agenda paper listing topics for discussion included two items of relevance for section 116. Agenda item 10 concerned 'Constitutional guarantees under the Constitution, including guarantees of democratic processes of election for the Parliaments of the Commonwealth and the States.' Agenda item 15 concerned 'The Constitutional Provisions affecting Territories (ss 81, 92, 99, 116, 117, 118, Chapter VI and s 128).' Those items were not the subject of specific debate at the Sydney session.[2]

The Convention established four standing committees with responsibility for considering and preparing a report on the various agenda items. Agenda item 10 was referred to Standing Committee D and agenda item 15 was referred to Standing Committee B.

Both committees presented their reports at the Melbourne session of the Convention in 1975. Standing Committee D resolved to defer consideration of section 116 and make no recommendations regarding it.[3] The reason for the deferral was that the *DOGS case*,[4] – which

1 The Joint Standing Committee on Constitutional Review which operated from 1956 to 1958 did not consider section 116. For a brief discussion of the Australian Constitutional Convention see Cheryl Saunders, 'Historical Overview' in Heather McRea and Anne Mullins, *Australian Constitutional Convention 1973–1985: A Guide to the Archives* (Centre for Comparative Constitutional Studies, 1998); Legal and Constitutional Committee, Parliament of Victoria, *Second Report on the Australian Constitutional Convention* (1986). The Joint Standing Committee on Constitutional Review 1956–8 did not consider section 116.

2 *Official Record of Debates of the Australian Constitutional Convention*, Sydney, 7 September 1973, 295–349.

3 Australian Constitutional Convention, Standing Committee D, Report to Executive Committee, 1 August 1974, 32.

4 *Attorney-General (Vic); Ex Rel Black v Commonwealth* ('*DOGS case*') (1981) 146 CLR 559.

involved a claim that federal funding of non-government schools operated by religious groups violated the establishment clause of section 116 – was currently on foot in the High Court.[5] The Committee felt that proper consideration of the provision would require reflection on the High Court's judgment. Instead, the Committee simply summarised the five recommendations regarding section 116 provided to it in submissions from interested parties, including the plaintiffs in the *DOGS case*. The Combined State Education Organisations (Victoria) recommended to the committee: 'That this section . . . be amended to preclude financial aid for non-government schools.'[6] The Loyal Orange Institution of Victoria submitted: 'That this section remain unchanged.'[7] A Mrs Ureahin submitted: 'That this section be amended to provide that the Commonwealth of Australia is a secular State and no laws may be made that would establish, impose, favour or prohibit any religion and the free exercise thereof.'[8] The Movement for the Defence of Government Schools, the plaintiff organisation in the *DOGS case*, submitted that the section be repealed and replaced with:

> 116. A State shall not, nor shall the Commonwealth, make any law for establishing any religion, or for imposing any religious observance, or for prohibiting the free exercise of any religion, and no religious test shall be required as a qualification for any office or public trust under a State or under the Commonwealth.[9]

The final submission was from the Law Society of Western Australia, which submitted: 'That section 116 should bind the States.'[10]

Standing Committee B did consider the question of section 116 and its application to the Territories, and it made recommendations. It referred Item 15 to a sub-committee for report. In respect of section 116, the sub-committee explained in its report the uncertainty as it existed in the case law at the time about whether the Commonwealth's power to make laws for the territories section 122 was subject to limitations on power found elsewhere in the *Constitution*, including section 116. Accordingly, the sub-committee recommended 'that it should be put beyond doubt that section 116 applies in territories no less than in States.' The Standing Committee also commissioned a report on the constitutional issues relating to Item 15 from R D Lumb, a constitutional scholar.[11] Lumb's report canvassed the legal uncertainty regarding the scope of section 122 and suggested that 'the guarantee of freedom of religion probably applies to the Territories.'[12]

Standing Committee B adopted the sub-committee's recommendation. It recommended: 'That the *Constitution* be amended to make it completely clear that the provisions of section 116 have application in the territories.'[13] The Committee repeated that recommendation

5 Australian Constitutional Convention, Standing Committee D, Report to Executive Committee, 1 August 1974, 32.
6 Ibid.
7 Ibid.
8 Ibid.
9 Ibid.
10 Ibid.
11 Australian Constitutional Convention, Standing Committee B, Report to Executive Committee, 1 August 1974, append L.
12 Ibid 67.
13 Ibid 15.

in also recommending that 'the constitutional guarantees contained in section 51(xxxi), section 80, section 92, section 116, section 117 and section 118 should be made to expressly apply to and in relation to mainland territories.'[14] The first recommendation simply appeared in a list of recommendations. The second recommendation, along with some recommendations on other matters, was prefaced with the explanation that the recommendation arose because the Committee was 'of the opinion that the Northern Territory should forthwith be granted the maximum degree of autonomy that it is possible to grant under section 122.'[15]

This short explanation reveals much about the purpose of the recommendation. The recommendation was not one motivated by notions of religious freedom or individual rights. The motivation was a desire to put the territories, or at least the Northern Territory, in a comparable position to the States.

Whitlam's attempt to extend section 116 to the States

Gough Whitlam was a reformer and the Convention was another opportunity for another reform. At the Melbourne session of the Convention, Northern Territory Majority Leader and leader of the Country Party there, Goff Letts moved: 'That this Convention recommends that the Constitution be amended in relation to mainland Territories so as to ensure that the provisions of section 116 apply in such Territories.'[16] Letts pointed out that this was consistent with the recommendation of Standing Committee B.[17] Letts' motive was the same as the Standing Committee's. Letts said: 'if there are any doubts about the rights and responsibilities of Territorians as compared with people in the rest of Australia this should be put beyond doubt.'[18]

The Prime Minister, Gough Whitlam, saw an opportunity for wider constitutional reform and sought to amend Lett's motion. Whitlam moved that the words 'and in relation to the States, so as to ensure that the provisions of that section apply to the laws of the States' be added.[19] Whitlam suggested that '[i]f there is an argument for a constitutional guarantee in these matters, then not only should that guarantee apply' to federal legislation but also territory and State legislation.[20] He declared: the 'Australian Constitution has very few guarantees . . . Let us make them of universal application.'[21]

Whitlam also justified his proposal by reference to the situation in the United States. He pointed out that there 'a similar guarantee, from which the one in the Australian Constitution is derived' applies to Congress as well as the State legislatures. He thought it 'proper that a comparable provision be made in Australia.'[22] Whitlam was approaching section 116 from a very different angle to the Standing Committee and Letts. Rather like Evatt in the 1940s, Whitlam's motivation focussed on a concern to protect individual rights.

14 Ibid 16.
15 Ibid.
16 *Official Record of Debates of the Australian Constitutional Convention*, Melbourne, 25 September 1975, 127.
17 Ibid.
18 Ibid 128.
19 Ibid.
20 Ibid.
21 Ibid 128–9.
22 Ibid 129.

Colin Jamieson, a Labor delegate from the West Australian Parliament, suggested that debate on the matter be adjourned to allow closer consideration of the issue.[23] Jamieson's concern was that applying section 116 to the States would have potentially undesirable consequences. He was concerned that it might invalidate State laws permitting children to be made wards of the State for the purpose of allowing blood transfusions where parents refuse to grant their consent for such a procedure due to religious beliefs.[24] These potential consequences needed careful consideration, Jamieson argued. A motion to adjourn the debate on the item until the next session of the Convention was agreed to without further debate.[25] Later during the Melbourne session, Whitlam's amendment to the motion was agreed to without further debate.[26]

At the Hobart session of the Convention in October 1976 debate resumed on the resolution, which read:

> That this Convention recommends that the Constitution be amended in relation to mainland Territories so as to ensure that the provisions of section 116 apply in such Territories and, in relation to the States, so as to ensure that the provisions of that section apply to laws of the States.[27]

James Pead, an independent member of the Australian Capital Territory Legislative Assembly, moved that the resolution be adopted.[28] He argued that whilst section 116 might limit the Commonwealth's power to legislate for the territories, the matter should be put beyond doubt.[29] Pead also noted concerns about applying section 116 to the States, such as had been raised at the Convention's previous session by Jamieson, but concluded that 'in spite of whatever difficulties there might be, it cannot be denied that individuals should have the constitutional guarantees that the motion proposes.'[30]

A New South Wales delegate, John Maddison, moved that the resolution be amended to delete its attempt to apply section 116 to the States, but did not speak to his amendment.[31] Alan Hunt of Victoria explained that the Victorian delegation thought that Maddison's amendment 'springs from a misplaced fear about the position of the States.'[32] It would, Hunt said on behalf of the Victorian delegation, be 'pressing State rights much too far to say that the States should make their own decisions about religious freedom.'[33] He rejected fears about undesirable consequences if the States were to be subject to the provision: 'in countries where a provision of this nature does exist,' Hunt said, 'this does not in any way interfere with the State laws relating to questions such as health, law and order, justice or anything of the kind.'[34] Hunt concluded his remarks with an indication

23 Ibid 129–30.
24 Ibid 129.
25 Ibid 130.
26 Ibid 153.
27 *Official Record of Debates of the Australian Constitutional Convention*, Hobart, 29 October 1976, 178.
28 Ibid.
29 Ibid.
30 Ibid.
31 Ibid 179.
32 Ibid.
33 Ibid.
34 Ibid.

that he was viewing the matter through the prism of individual rights: 'Surely this should be a matter guaranteed by the Constitution to all citizens.'[35] Hunt took an individual rights view of what section 116 should be about.

Alan Greenwood of Queensland spoke next. He pointed to the United States where, he lamented, schools are unable to have prayers.[36] He explained that while section 116 as it applied to the Commonwealth was unproblematic given the limited scope of federal legislative power, the same was not true in respect of the States. '[A]s soon as section 116 is extended to the State', Greenwood explained, 'a problem arises because in most States the Education Departments encourage religious instruction of various types in their schools.'[37] Greenwood's view was that the section should be left entirely unaltered since any expansion of its scope was 'fraught with very real dangers.'[38] Accordingly, he was in favour of Maddison's amendment to delete the attempt to extend section 116's application to the States.[39]

The next speaker was the now former Prime Minister Gough Whitlam, who spoke only briefly. He described Greenwood's argument as 'patently absurd' and said that intellectual consistency would demand that Greenwood move for the deletion of section 116 from the *Constitution*, which he had not done.[40] '[T]here is nothing more noble than at least the freedom of religion', Whitlam said, opposing Maddison's amendment and supporting the motion.[41]

The final speaker was Senator Peter Durack who explained that the Commonwealth Government was opposed to any extension of section 116 and thus happy to support Maddison's amendment of the motion but determined to oppose the motion as whole.[42] The Commonwealth's concerns were, like Greenwood's, pragmatic. The Commonwealth believed that 'in the present state of interpretation or non-interpretation of section 116 by the High Court, there is a real concern that it could be interpreted in such a way as to affect the provision of State aid to independent schools.'[43] Accordingly, depending on the interpretation of section 116 adopted, to extend the scope of section 116 'could have serious effects or even more serious effects than it would if simply confined to the Commonwealth.'[44]

Durack also seems to have suggested that the Commonwealth Government viewed section 116 as a guarantee of individual rights. The Government 'strongly support the guarantees of freedom of religion', Durack said.[45] 'However, we believe the proper approach would be to look at section 116 and endeavour to amend it in such a way as to guarantee freedom of religion to all Australians and bind all Governments in Australia to a guarantee of that kind.'[46] Concluding his remarks, Durack explained that the Government believed

35 Ibid.

36 Ibid. Presumably, this was a reference to *Engel v Vital*, 370 US 421 (1962) in which the United States Supreme Court held that school-sponsored prayers in public schools violated the establishment clause of the First Amendment.

37 Ibid 180.

38 Ibid.

39 Ibid.

40 Ibid.

41 Ibid.

42 Ibid.

43 Ibid.

44 Ibid.

45 Ibid.

46 Ibid 181.

that section 116 was not 'a suitable instrument to effect a guarantee of religious freedom for all Australians.' Durack did not give any indication of what a suitable provision might look like.

The Convention then divided on Maddison's amendment, rejecting it, before dividing on the unamended motion, agreeing to it with 45 delegates in favour and 33 opposed.[47]

Although the Convention agreed that section 116 should be expanded to bind the States nothing came of the proposal. Section 116 was not discussed further at any subsequent session of the Convention and the Convention itself was discontinued following its 1985 Brisbane session.

The Constitutional Commission of 1985–1988

In December 1985, the Attorney-General in Bob Hawke's Labor Government, Lionel Bowen, announced that the Commonwealth Government would establish a Constitutional Commission to review the *Constitution*. The Commission comprised Sir Maurice Byers, a former Commonwealth Solicitor-General, as chairman, with constitutional law professors Enid Campbell and Leslie Zines, former Labor Prime Minister Gough Whitlam and former Liberal Victorian Premier Sir Rupert Hamer as members.

The Commission's Terms of Reference required it to inquire into and report on the revision of the *Constitution* to, among other things, 'ensure that democratic rights are guaranteed.'[48] To assist in its task, the Commission appointed a number of advisory committees including an Individual and Democratic Rights Advisory Committee.

In June 1986, the Individual and Democratic Rights Advisory Committee released an Issues Booklet and called for public submissions. The Advisory Committee released its report in 1987.[49]

The Committee recommended the expansion of section 116 so that it would apply to the States and to all governmental institutions.[50] It recommended the addition of the words 'or a State' and the deletion of the words 'make any law for', such that section 116 would read:

> The Commonwealth or a State shall not establish any religion, or impose any religious observance, or prohibit the free exercise of any religion, and no religious test shall be required as a qualification for any office or public trust under the Commonwealth or a State.[51]

The Advisory Committee's discussion of its recommendation to expand section 116 occupies barely more than a page of its report.[52] Echoing concerns raised at the Australian Constitutional Convention, the Advisory Committee noted that an extension of section 116

47 Ibid.

48 The Terms of Reference are set out in Constitutional Commission, *First Report of the Constitutional Commission* (Australian Government Publishing Service, 1988) vol II, 678.

49 Constitutional Commission, *Report of the Advisory Committee on Individual and Democratic Rights under the Constitution* (Australian Government Publishing Service, 1987).

50 Ibid xvi, 53.

51 Ibid 53.

52 Ibid 52–3.

to bind the States might have implications for 'legitimate State activities' such as the regulation of schools. The Advisory Committee was confident, however, that the courts 'will be able to differentiate between legitimate religious pursuits and activities which properly become subject to regulation.'[53]

The Advisory Committee stated that extending the scope of section 116 to the States '*might* affect a state government's legislative capacity.'[54] The use of the word 'might' is odd since the whole point of extending the scope of section 116 would surely be to limit the legislative capacity of the States.

The Advisory Committee justified its recommendation to delete the words 'make any law for' in two sentences:

> The Committee has taken the view that consistent with its general approach to limits on excesses of governmental power, all forms of governmental conduct, including both legislative and executive actions, should be reasonably restricted. For instance, in order to make it clear that the actions of departmental officials interfering with the conduct of the religious affairs of a congregation would be clearly prohibited, the restraint on power should not be limited merely to the passing of 'laws'.[55]

The Advisory Committee did not directly mention the possibility of expanding the provision to apply expressly to the Territories. However, in a separate part of its report it recommended amending section 122 to provide that the grant of power in that provision was 'subject to this Constitution' thereby overcoming any uncertainty as to whether the Commonwealth's power under that section was constrained by limitations on its power such as section 116.[56]

The Advisory Committee also made a recommendation that would have the effect of limiting section 116. It thought that the *Constitution* be amended to include an 'opt-out' clause that would allow the State and Federal Parliaments to legislate notwithstanding the limitation on power contained in section 116, among other limitations, if a Parliament really wanted to. The Advisory Committee recommended a new section 117A that would read:

> The Parliament of the Commonwealth or of a State may expressly declare in a law that the law shall operate notwithstanding a provision included in sections
>
> . . .
>
> 116
>
> . . .
>
> Such declaration and any re-enactment thereof shall have effect for 3 years after it comes into force or such shorter period as may be specified in the declaration.[57]

53 Ibid 52.
54 Ibid (emphasis added).
55 Ibid 53.
56 Ibid 105.
57 Ibid 38. The 'opt-out' clause was modelled on the so-called 'notwithstanding clause' (s 33) of the *Canadian Charter of Rights and Freedoms*, which provides:

> (1) Parliament or the legislature of a province may expressly declare in an Act of Parliament or of the legislature, as the case may be, that the Act or a provision thereof shall operate notwithstanding a provision included in section 2 or sections 7 to 15.

The Advisory Committee explained that the idea of parliamentary supremacy justified an 'opt-out' provision[58] 'Occasions may arise', the Advisory Committee explained, 'when the courts interpret the inevitably general words of the Constitution in a way in which a Parliament considers inappropriate or simply wrong.'[59] The Advisory Committee also thought that the opt-out provision would lessen any opposition to its other recommendations by State Governments.[60]

The Advisory Committee's rather cursory discussion of its recommendations concerning section 116 is not necessarily evidence that the matter was not the subject of careful thought. In the preface to its report, the Advisory Committee explained that it 'viewed its task as being practical, rather than theoretical' and had 'prepared what it believes to be a "practical" report.'[61] The Advisory Committee emphasised that it 'has been at pains to avoid the drafting of an academic document' so that the report is accessible to a wide audience.[62] This approach, however, makes it difficult to work out the underlying reasoning.

Nevertheless, the Advisory Committee devoted a chapter of its report to discussing the conceptual framework informing all of its recommendations.[63] The Advisory Committee explained that the American or European concept of a Bill Rights 'has never formed part of the Australian constitutional framework.'[64] By contrast, the 'Australian approach has been to limit the power of Governments rather than to proclaim the rights of citizens.'[65] The Advisory Committee decided to frame its thinking consistently with this view of Australian constitutional tradition, rejecting an approach of declaring positive rights and embracing the 'concept of restraints on governmental power.'[66]

The Constitutional Commission released a First Report in April 1988. The report recommended amending section 116 so that it would apply also to the States and Territories and omitting the words 'make any law for' so that it had an operation beyond the making of statutes.[67] Section 116 would then read:

> The Commonwealth, a State or a Territory shall not establish any religion, impose any religious observance or prohibit the free exercise of any religion, and no religious

(2) An Act or a provision of an Act in respect of which a declaration made under this section is in effect shall have such operation as it would have but for the provision of this Charter referred to in the declaration.
(3) A declaration made under subsection (1) shall cease to have effect five years after it comes into force or on such earlier date as may be specified in the declaration.
(4) Parliament or the legislature of a province may re-enact a declaration made under subsection (1).
(5) Subsection (3) applies in respect of a re-enactment made under subsection (4).

58 Ibid 37–8.
59 Ibid 37.
60 Ibid.
61 Ibid xii.
62 Ibid.
63 Ibid ch 5.
64 Ibid 30.
65 Ibid 31.
66 Ibid 32.
67 Constitutional Commission, *First Report of the Constitutional Commission* (Australian Government Printing Service, 1988) vol II, 620.

> test shall be required as a qualification for any office or public trust under the Commonwealth, a State or a Territory.[68]

The Commission commenced its discussion of section 116 with a brief historical overview. It noted that the provision was modelled on provisions of the *United States Constitution* and outlined the 'standard account' of Higgins' argument for the provision at the 1897–8 Federal Convention.[69] In this respect, the Commission's views were more historically situated than were Evatt's in the 1940s.

The Commission then turned to consider the present scope of section 116, describing it as 'one of the few guarantees of rights and freedoms' expressly provided for in the *Constitution*.[70] The Commission explained that the words 'make any law' indicated that section 116 did not expressly limit the powers of the executive government and that the word 'for' gave rise to questions about the role purpose plays in determining the scope of the provision.[71]

The Commission wrote that there were five main issues concerning section 116. These were:

> (a) Are the religious freedoms of Australians adequately protected under the common law in the States?
> (b) Is it appropriate to extend the guarantees in section 116?
> (c) Would the proposed alteration to section 116 produce any problems regarding the distinction between educational and religious activities?
> (d) Is it important to include the Territories in the section?
> (e) Should the operation of section 116 be extended beyond the making of a statute?[72]

These 'five main issues' are not entirely coherent. Issue (c) is phrased in a way that assumes the answer to (b) is 'yes', and issues (d) and (e) appear to be specific forms of issue (b). In any case, the Commission did not go on to address these issues in any systematic way in its report as the listing of the issues might suggest it would.

The Commission's report summarises previous proposals for amending section 116; namely, the Post-War Reconstruction and Democratic Rights referendum, the discussions at the Australian Constitutional Convention, and the Advisory Committee's recommendations.[73] The Commission's report then discusses the public submissions it received commenting on the Advisory Committee's recommendations.[74] It explained that a majority of public submissions favoured amending section 116 'broadly in terms recommended by the Advisory Committee.'[75]

The Commission identified four main arguments arising from those submissions. The first was, in the Commission's words, that '[f]reedom of religion is of the essence of a free society

68 Ibid 620.
69 Ibid 621–2.
70 Ibid 623.
71 Ibid.
72 Ibid 652.
73 Ibid 625–9.
74 Ibid 629–32.
75 Ibid 632.

and its constitutional guarantee should be extended to the States.'[76] The second main argument identified was that 'Australia is a multi-cultural society and it would be appropriate for the Constitution to prohibit discrimination against the religions of ethnic and other minority groups.'[77] The third main argument arising from public submissions was that '[w]hile freedom of religion is of fundamental importance, it must operate within reasonable limits prescribed by law.'[78] The final main argument the Commission identified was that '[d]iscrimination should not be permitted on the ground of freedom of religion.'[79]

Without turning to discuss what it had identified as the 'five main issues' concerning section 116, the Commission then set out its reasons for its recommendations.[80] The reasoning was straightforward. The Commission explained that the 'values that underlie our political tradition demand' religious freedom. The Commission took the view that that freedom should 'be consistent throughout the Federation' and should 'apply in every place and to every Government.'[81]

The Commission also explained that the multicultural makeup of contemporary Australia meant that the 'reasons the Framers of the Constitution had for limiting section 116 to the Commonwealth are no longer compelling.'[82] This is curious reasoning. The Commission did not identify what reasons the framers had for limiting section 116 to the Commonwealth. This makes it difficult for the Commission to have known whether the modern multicultural makeup of Australia actually posed a challenge to the framers' reasoning.

Turning to the specifics of its recommendations, the Commission explained that deleting the words 'make any law' would ensure that executive action would be subject to the guarantees in section 116.[83] As for deleting the word 'for', the Commission explained that doing so 'would assist the courts in arriving at a reasonable interpretation' of the free exercise clause.[84] This comment was not further elaborated. Nowhere in the Commission's discussion is there any suggestion that 'for' had led to unreasonable interpretations of that clause. The Commission emphasised that deleting 'for' would not alter the result in the *DOGS case*, which held that public funding of non-government schools operated by religious groups did not amount to establishing any religion.[85] Presumably, however, the Commission meant that deleting 'for' would prevent any interpretation that section 116 prohibited only laws that have the express purpose of doing one of the things mentioned in the provision rather than also prohibiting laws that have the effect of doing one of the things mentioned even if the law has some other purpose.

The 1988 rights and freedoms referendum

Less than a fortnight after the Commission released its First Report, Attorney-General Bowen introduced four Bills into the House of Representatives proposing to amend the

76 Ibid 629.
77 Ibid 630.
78 Ibid.
79 Ibid 631.
80 Ibid 632–3.
81 Ibid.
82 Ibid 632.
83 Ibid 633.
84 Ibid.
85 Ibid.

Constitution in respect of parliamentary terms,[86] the electoral system,[87] local government[88] and rights and freedoms. The *Constitution Alteration (Rights and Freedoms) Bill 1988* proposed changes to section 80 relating to trial by jury, to section 51(xxxi) relating to compensation for compulsory acquisition of property, and to section 116.

One of the members of the Constitutional Commission later explained that the Government's decision to hold a referendum before the Commission delivered its final report arose from a desire that a referendum should be held in Australia's bicentennial year.[89]

The Bill proposed to replace the text of section 116 as recommended by the Constitutional Commission so that it would provide:

> The Commonwealth, a State or a Territory shall not establish any religion, impose any religious observance or prohibit the free exercise of any religion, and no religious test shall be required as a qualification for any office or public trust under the Commonwealth, a State or a Territory.[90]

The Bill's explanatory memorandum was brief in its explanation of the proposed amendment. In short, sharp sentences it stated that the proposed section applied to the Commonwealth, the States and the Territories, that the prohibitions were not confined to laws but extended to cases of executive action and that there was 'no change that would render the decision in [the *DOGS case*] inapplicable to the new section.'[91]

Bowen's Second Reading Speech was similarly brief.[92] He told Parliament that the purpose of the Bill was to 'strengthen three fundamental rights and freedoms already in the Constitution.'[93] As for the proposed amendment to section 116, Bowen explained that it would apply the 'safeguards' in section 116 to the States and Territories and apply them also to executive action.[94] He justified the proposed changes in a single sentence: 'If religious freedom warrants constitutional protection, the guarantee should apply uniformly to Commonwealth, State and Territory governments.'[95]

The Shadow Attorney-General's speech reflected the Liberal/National Coalition's opposition to the proposed amendments. Peter Reith said that the various proposals for constitutional amendment 'are clearly not in the interests of the people of Australia and they must be rejected.'[96] He made a special point of criticising the Commission process. 'The Commission is all about politics', Reith argued.[97] 'The trouble is that the Commission has

86 Constitution Alteration (Parliamentary Terms) Bill 1988 (Cth).
87 Constitution Alteration (Fair Elections) Bill 1988 (Cth).
88 Constitution Alteration (Local Government) Bill 1988 (Cth).
89 Enid Campbell, 'Fashioning and Refashioning the Constitution' (2001) 24(3) *University of New South Wales Law Journal* 620, 627.
90 Constitution Alteration (Rights and Freedoms) Bill 1988 (Cth) cl 4.
91 Explanatory Memorandum, Constitution Alteration (Rights and Freedoms) Bill 1988, 6.
92 Commonwealth, *Parliamentary Debates*, House of Representatives, 10 May 1988, 2390 (Bowen).
93 Ibid 2390.
94 Ibid.
95 Ibid.
96 Commonwealth, *Parliamentary Debates*, House of Representatives, 17 May 1988, 2444.
97 Ibid.

never had a mandate from the people and its report carries no more weight than the views of any other so-called experts.'[98]

Reith outlined some general objections to the Bill. He complained that the Bill was presented as a 'package': Reith argued that it should be split in three so that a voter could vote yes or no to each individual proposal. Reith also objected that the proposals were unnecessary since the freedoms concerned were not under threat. He argued that constitutional guarantees of rights were ineffectual for protecting rights and pointed to Russia as an example of a country that had written protections for rights that were useless in practice. Reith complained that constitutional rights provisions transferred political power away from elected parliaments to unelected judges. He also argued that constitutional rights guarantees were foreign to the general purpose of the *Australian Constitution* in providing the framework for government.[99]

Reith then turned briefly to specific objections to each of the three proposals in the Bill. The amendment to section 116 'would open a Pandora's Box', Reith claimed, and 'is playing with fire.'[100] Reith's concerns were about how the expanded section 116 might work in practice. The expansion, he said, had the problem of possibly 'validating extreme practices conducted under the guise of religion' and 'limiting or preventing normal religious observance in many aspects of our Australian way of life.' Alluding to the *DOGS case*, Reith said he was concerned about how the amendment 'will affect the management of our government school systems, let alone the difficult issue of funding of non-government schools.'

In the Senate, debate focussed principally on whether deleting the words 'make any law for' would have the effect of undermining the result in the *DOGS case*.[101] This concern was unfounded, as government Senators tried to explain.[102] The reasoning in the *DOGS case* rested on the meaning of 'establishing' and not on the effect of the words 'make any law for.'

The referendum campaign as it concerned the *Constitution Alteration (Rights and Freedoms) Bill* largely followed the themes outlined by Bowen and Reith in Parliament. This was reflected in the official 'Yes' and 'No' cases prepared by members of Parliament for and against the proposals[103] and published by the Australian Electoral Commission.[104] The 'Yes' case emphasised the desirability of applying a 'guarantee of religious freedom' consistently throughout the country against all levels of government and to extending it to executive action.[105] The 'Yes' case also emphasised that the proposal would not affect government funding of religious schools or hospitals or allow people to commit harmful acts in the name of religion.[106]

98 Ibid.

99 Ibid.

100 Ibid.

101 Commonwealth, *Parliamentary Debates*, Senate, 31 May–1 June 1988, 3271ff.

102 Ibid.

103 *Referendum (Machinery Provisions) Act 1984* (Cth) s 11(1).

104 Australian Electoral Commission, 'Yes or No? Referendums. Saturday 3 September 1988. The Cases For and Against' (Australian Electoral Commission, 1988).

105 Ibid 22–3.

106 Ibid 23.

The 'No' case argued that amending section 116 would create legal uncertainty and, as in America, fill the courts with cases arguing about the meaning of the provision.[107] Not only was that uncertainty unnecessary since there was no threat to religious freedom in Australia, it was also potentially dangerous since it might result in new legal interpretations prohibiting government funding of religious schools and allowing offensive practices done in the name of religion to occur.[108] There was also the related risk, the 'No' case claimed, that by expanding section 116 and thus defining religious freedom in more detail, the proposal would endanger and weaken the religious rights already possessed by Australians.[109]

Concern that the proposed alteration of section 116 would potentially reopen the result in the *DOGS case* led the Australian Catholic Bishops Conference to issue a statement urging a 'no' vote and to some non-government schools writing letters to the parents of their students urging a 'no' vote.[110]

During public debate on the Government's referendum proposals, the Constitutional Commission released its final report in two volumes on 30 June 1988.[111] Its discussion of section 116 and recommendations for its alteration were the same as in its first report.[112]

At the referendum held on 3 September 1988, voters rejected each of the four Bills. The *Constitution Alteration (Rights and Freedoms) Bill* suffered the worst defeat of any referendum in Australian history.[113]

The day after the referendum, Attorney-General Bowen described constitutional reform as a lost cause.[114]

More insightfully, a newspaper editorialised that one 'lesson politicians are having difficulty in learning is that the Australian voter is content with a Constitution that has served this nation for 88 years.'[115] Higgins managed to persuade the decision makers at the Federal Convention that there was a practical need for section 116; Evatt and Bowen could not persuade Australian voters as the decision makers that there was a practical need to expand section 116.

107 The fact that the proposals for amendment arose from the Constitutional Commission was also an issue. The Coalition had suggested that it might disband the Commission if it won the 1987 general election and, according to Brian Galligan, after not winning that election, 'waged an effective campaign of denigration with the result that the Commission never achieved legitimacy': Brian Galligan, 'Australia's Rejection of a Bill of Rights' (1990) 28(3) *Journal of Commonwealth and Comparative Politics* 344, 364.

108 Australian Electoral Commission, above n 104, 25–6.

109 Ibid.

110 Campbell Sharman, 'The 1988 Referendums and their Context' in Brian Galligan and J R Nethercote, *The Constitutional Commission and the 1988 Referendums* (Centre for Research on Federal Financial Relations, 1989) 105, 113.

111 Constitutional Commission, *Final Report of the Constitutional Commission* (Australian Government Printing Service, 1988).

112 Constitutional Commission, *Final Report of the Constitutional Commission* (Australian Government Printing Service, 1988) vol 2, 609–17.

113 Brian Galligan, 'The 1988 Referendums and Australia's Record on Constitutional Change' (1990) 43 *Parliamentary Affairs* 497; House of Representatives Standing Committee on Legal and Constitutional Affairs, Parliament of Australia, *Constitutional Change: Select Sources on Constitutional Change in Australia 1901–1997* (1997) 113–4.

114 Lenore Taylor, 'Referendum buoys Liberals for State poll', *The Canberra Times* (Canberra), 5 September 1988, 1.

115 'The people say No to the lot', *The Canberra Times* (Canberra), 4 September 1988, 6.

12 The future of section 116

How does section 116 provide a safeguard against religious intolerance?

If the point of section 116 of the *Australian Constitution* is to provide a safeguard against religious intolerance on the part of the Commonwealth, *how* in practice does section 116 provide that safeguard?

At a simple level, section 116 provides that safeguard in four ways: by forbidding federal laws for establishing any religion, by forbidding federal laws for imposing any religious observance, by forbidding federal laws for prohibiting the free exercise of any religion, and by forbidding religious tests as a qualification for any office or public trust under the Commonwealth. At a more complex level, section 116 provides that safeguard by constraining and regulating Commonwealth power to channel and discipline political judgment.[1] How does it do this?

Constitutional language constrains and regulates because it is binding. But not all constitutional language is the same. The American constitutional theorist Jack Balkin distinguishes between three types of constitutional norms that constrain and regulate in different ways. *Rules* are determinate and require little practical or evaluative judgment to apply to particular situations.[2] The *Australian Constitution* includes many rules. For example, the requirement that each original State must have at least six senators is a rule and so is the requirement that each original State must always have the same number of senators.[3] There is no possibility, unless the *Constitution* is amended, for Victoria to ever be limited to having five senators. Reasonable minds cannot differ on how this rule applies to any particular situation.

Standards are different. Standard are norms that 'require considerable practical or evaluative judgment to apply to concrete situations because they contain vague terms or terms that involve questions of degree.'[4] Standards require the development of doctrines to structure the 'practical and evaluative' judgment they require.[5] Balkin gives as an example

1 Jack Balkin, *Living Originalism* (Harvard University Press, 2011) 29.

2 Jack Balkin, 'The Framework Model and Constitutional Interpretation', in David Dyzenhaus and Malcolm Thorburn (eds), *Philosophical Foundations of Constitutional Law* (Oxford University Press, 2016) 241, 251.

3 *Australian Constitution* s 7.

4 Balkin, 'The Framework Model and Constitutional Interpretation', above n 2, 251.

5 Ibid.

of a standard the prohibition on 'unreasonable searches and seizures' in the Fourth Amendment of the *United States Constitution*.[6] Development of constitutional doctrine is necessary in order to be able to apply that prohibition in any particular case. Where a standard applies, it is conclusive of the matter. In this example, if a particular event amounts to an unreasonable search or seizure according to the prevailing legal doctrine, the legal answer is clear: that search or seizure was unconstitutional. Reasonable minds might, however, differ as to whether a standard is met.

The distinction between rules and standards is not black and white: rules and standards exist along a continuum.[7] Increasing degrees of practical judgment are required along that continuum. *Principles* exist at the very opposite end of the continuum to rules. Where principles apply to a situation they are not always conclusive but simply one factor that must be balanced against other competing considerations. Balkin gives the example of the 'equal protection of the laws' guarantee of the Fourteenth Amendment to the *United States Constitution*.[8] The provision is highly abstract and obviously does not require equality in all respects. Applying principles like this to particular situations requires 'considerable practical reasoning.'[9]

So constitutional language constrains and regulates power, and channels and disciplines political judgment by employing rules, standards and principles. The language of section 116 was not the subject of careful consideration by those who drafted and adopted it. In situations such as this where the framers of constitutional language 'did not think very deeply or at all about why they used rule-like and principle-like language',[10] Balkin explains that 'we must try in good faith to *ascribe* an economy of freedom and constraint, trust and distrust, from the text we have been handed, using the familiar modalities of legal argument.'[11]

Section 116 does not channel and discipline political judgment by imposing rules. None of its four clauses is a rule in the sense just explained. Practical and evaluative judgment is required to determine whether any of section 116's clauses applies in a particular situation. Its clauses must therefore be either standards or principles.

The best view is that section 116 contains three standards and one principle. The establishment, observance and religious tests clauses each provide standards. The free exercise clause is much further along the continuum from rules than the other three clauses. It does not, because it simply cannot, mean what it literally says. A federal law that forbids killing people burdens the free exercise of any religion that practises human sacrifice. Such a law cannot be constitutionally valid unless the free exercise clause is a principle.

The fact that this hypothetical law amounts to forbidding the free exercise of any religion that practises human sacrifice does not determine the legal outcome in the same way that a law that amounts to establishing a religion, for example, does determine the legal

6 *United States Constitution* amend IV 'The right of the people to be secure in their persons, houses, papers, and effects, against unreasonable searches and seizures, shall not be violated.'
7 Balkin, 'The Framework Model and Constitutional Interpretation', above n 2, 251.
8 Ibid.
9 Balkin, *Living Originalism*, above n 1, 350.
10 Ibid 47.
11 Ibid.

outcome. Determining what amounts to establishing a religion requires practical and evaluative reasoning, and reasonable minds might plausibly differ on that question. But once a law is determined to amount to establishing a religion the outcome is necessarily constitutional invalidity. The same is not true of the free exercise clause. The fact that a federal law prohibiting murder burdens the free exercise of religions that practise human sacrifice does not necessarily lead to constitutional invalidity.

In applying standards and principles, the necessary practical and evaluative reasoning involves employing the full range of modalities of constitutional argument that may be applicable to the particular case. In a case concerning the establishment clause, it may be necessary to look at general legal history to see how the concept has been used in other contexts. In a case involving the religious tests clause, it may be necessary to draw textual analogies to ensure the construction of the word 'under' in 'under the Commonwealth' corresponds with the construction of that word in section 44's disqualification of officers 'under the Crown' from sitting in Parliament.

Another of the familiar modes of constitutional argument relies on the purpose of constitutional provisions.[12] This type of reasoning underlies the prevailing doctrine in respect of section 92 of the *Australian Constitution*, which requires that 'trade, commerce, and intercourse among the States, whether by means of internal carriage or ocean navigation, shall be absolutely free.' In the leading case of *Cole v Whitfield*, the High Court relied upon history to discern the point of s 92 in order to develop the construction that section 92 prohibits discriminatory burdens of a protectionist kind.[13] In other words, although not explicitly employing the language of rules, standards and principles, the High Court understood the concept 'absolutely free' as a principle. That principle was fleshed out in *Cole v Whitfield* by employing the subsidiary standards 'discriminatory burden' and 'protectionist kind' that were developed by looking to, among other strands to the legal reasoning, the history and underlying point of s 92.

The point is that the practical and evaluative reasoning required in applying standards and principles can employ subsidiary rules, standards and principles. These are usually called doctrine, but they are rules, standards and principles nevertheless because they channel and discipline decision-making. Courts and lawyers develop these subsidiary rules, standards and principles using the full range of modes of constitutional argument.

What subsidiary rules, standards or principles to inform the practical and evaluative reasoning necessary to apply each of section 116's clauses to particular situations can be derived from the origins and point of section 116?

Section 116 is concerned with the practical operation of laws

Chapter 9 argued that section 116 is not simply a safeguard against religious intolerance but is a *pragmatic* safeguard against religious intolerance on the part of the Commonwealth. Section 116 is concerned with the practical operation of laws.

A focus on the practical operation of laws arises from the concept of intolerance. Chapter 9 showed how the safeguard against religious intolerance theory does not use the

12 *Cole v Whitfield* (1988) 165 CLR 360.
13 Ibid.

concept of intolerance in the sense of the vice or character trait. Rather, it uses the concept of intolerance in the transitive sense of being about action or practice.

A focus on the practical operation of laws also arises from the theme of pragmatism that runs through the history of section 116's inclusion in the *Constitution.* The Seventh Day Adventists were worried that the Commonwealth could, and would, *do* certain things – in particular, enact Sabbath observance laws – that would harm them. Higgins managed to convince the Federal Convention that the Commonwealth might indeed have power to *do* things like that. And the consensus position of the Federal Convention was that the Commonwealth should not have power to *do* such things.

The idea that section 116 is concerned with the practical operation of laws is contrary to the High Court's existing doctrine on the meaning of section 116. This is most evident in the High Court's 1981 decision in *Attorney-General (Vic); Ex Rel Black v Commonwealth.*[14] The case is sometimes called the *DOGS Case* because it was instigated by a group called the Association for the Defence of Government Schools, which used the acronym DOGS. The case involved a challenge to various Commonwealth statutes setting up a scheme of federal funding of non-government schools, including schools operated by churches and religious groups. Among other things, the plaintiffs argued that those statutes contravened the establishment clause of section 116 to the extent that they authorised the provision of Commonwealth funds to those non-government schools owned or operated by churches and other religious groups. A majority of the High Court held that the statutes did not violate the establishment clause of section 116.

The doctrine developed by the High Court in the *DOGS Case* about how to apply section 116 includes the idea that section 116 is concerned only with the purpose of laws. The High Court held that it is only laws with the purpose of doing one of the things prohibited by section 116 that will be unconstitutional; it does not particularly matter if a law in fact does one of the things prohibited by section 116. In other words, according to the High Court, section 116 constrains and regulates only the purposes for which the Commonwealth might act regardless of the practical consequences of the Commonwealth's actions.

Chief Justice Barwick was emphatic that improper purpose is essential to invalidity under section 116 and that this was the consequence of the presence of the word 'for' in the provision. He distinguished the language of s 116 from the language of the religion clauses of the First Amendment, writing:

> The divergence in language to which I have earlier referred is apparent from the use of the word "respecting" in the American text and the word "for" in s 116. What the former may fairly embrace, quite clearly the latter cannot: and that is so, in my opinion, even without placing critical significance on the purposive nature of the Australian expression and the lack of such an element in the American text.[15]

In the context of the establishment clause, Barwick CJ explained that '[t]he law must be a law *for* it, i.e., intended and designed to set up the religion as an institution of the Commonwealth.'[16]

14 *Attorney-General (Vic); Ex Rel Black v Commonwealth* (1981) 146 CLR 559.
15 Ibid 579.
16 Ibid 583.

Chief Justice Barwick went further than simply holding that improper purpose is essential for invalidity under section 116. He also held that invalidity attaches only to a law whose sole purpose is a purpose prohibited by s 116 and not to laws that have additional non-prohibited purposes. He wrote: 'because the whole expression is "for establishing any religion", the law to satisfy the description must have that objective as its express and, as I think, single purpose.'[17] Chief Justice Barwick gave no reasons for his conclusion that a law with multiple purposes, one of which was prohibited by s 116, would not be invalid.

The other majority judges all adopted the improper purpose interpretation of 'for' based on distinguishing section 116 from the religion clauses of the First Amendment. In doing so, these judges have all assumed that the language of section 116 was the subject of careful consideration by the Federal Convention when in fact, as Chapter 7 showed, it was not. Justice Gibbs wrote:

> More importantly, the words of s 116 did not reproduce verbatim those of the First Amendment. The latter speaks of a law "respecting an establishment of religion" and those words appear wider than those of s 116 which refer to "any law for establishing any religion" – words which look to the purpose of the law rather than to its relationship with a particular subject matter . . .[18]

Justice Stephen similarly wrote:

> [T]he First Amendment requires that "Congress shall make no law respecting an establishment of religion", a restriction of wider scope than s 116's prohibition of laws "for establishing any religion". To illustrate this wider scope one may use another of the restrictions in s 116, thus avoiding the effect of any preconception about the meaning of "establishing": a law which did no more than require all places of entertainment to be closed on Sundays would not be a law "for" imposing any religious observance whereas it might well be one "respecting" the imposition of some religious observance.[19]

Justice Wilson likewise wrote:

> Furthermore, it seems to me that the words "for establishing" are not comparable with the words "respecting an establishment". The former words convey the sense of "in order to establish", and speak quite specifically of the purpose of the law in terms of the end to be achieved. "Respecting" conveys the notion of "in respect of" a particular subject-matter . . .[20]

17 Ibid 579.
18 Ibid 599.
19 Ibid 609.
20 Ibid 653.

In his judgment, Mason J recognised that 'for' could mean 'with respect to' but held that it did not have that meaning in the context of s 116. He wrote:

> There is a second distinction between the language of s 116 and the First Amendment. We speak of any "law for establishing" any religion. The Americans speak of a law "respecting an establishment" of religion. In *Lamshed v Lake* (1958) 99 CLR 132, at p 141, Dixon CJ, when referring to s 122, equated "for" with "with respect to" in its application to the government of the Territory. Here, however, we are dealing, not with a grant of legislative power, but with a prohibition against the exercise of legislative power. In such a context "for" is more limiting than "respecting"; "for" connotes a connexion by way of purpose or result with the subject matter which is not satisfied by the mere circumstance that the law is one which touches or relates to the subject matter. In this respect the first prohibition in s 116 is narrower than its American counterpart.[21]

One strand of the practical and evaluative reasoning employed by the High Court to apply the establishment clause of section 116 to decide the *DOGS Case* is wrong. Contrary to what the High Court has said, section 116 is concerned with the practical operation of laws. This does not necessarily mean that the ultimate conclusion in the case is wrong: it just means – like a lucky high school student who gets the right answer to a problem in a maths exam but with errors in her working out – that their reasoning is wrong.

Nevertheless, the fact that the High Court's existing doctrine about the operation of section 116 is wrong still matters. The rules of precedent mean that the error will be repeated. Courts will continue to apply that doctrine in future cases unless it is corrected.

Section 116 should not be interpreted narrowly

The standards and principles employed by section 116 are capable of broad and narrow constructions. For example, what does 'establishing any religion' mean? Does it mean only setting up a national church? Or does it mean something broader about giving official imprimatur to religions and religious principles? A subsidiary principle that says 'the concepts employed by section 116 should be understood narrowly' or one that says 'the concepts employed by section 116 should be understood broadly' helps in answering that question: it channels and disciplines a court's reasoning process in deciding a case.

Section 116 is not only a pragmatic safeguard against religious intolerance, it is a partial safeguard against religious intolerance. It is partial in the sense that it limits only the powers of the Commonwealth. The States remain free, for example, to impose religious observances. This does not mean that section 116 should be interpreted narrowly. Section 116 should be interpreted broadly.

The general purpose of section 116 is, in Higgins' words, to provide 'a sufficient safeguard against the passing of religious laws by the Commonwealth'[22] His concern was

21 Ibid 615–6.

22 *Official Report of the National Australasian Convention Debates*, Melbourne, 2 March 1898, 1734 (Higgins).

broad: any laws on the subject of religion. Even Quick and Garran in their *Annotated Constitution of the Commonwealth of Australia*, and remembering that Quick was a player in securing constitutional recognition of God and hostile to section 116, understood that Higgins wanted to ensure that 'the power to deal with religion in every shape and form should be clearly denied to the Federal Parliament. These arguments were allowed to prevail, and the provisions of section 116 became part of the *Constitution*.'[23]

Chapter 7 showed there is a discordance between the expressed general purpose of section 116 to deny the Commonwealth power to make laws on the subject of religion generally and the language of section 116. The terms of section 116 do not amount to a complete denial to the Commonwealth of power in respect of religion. Nevertheless, effect can be given to that general purpose and the whole point of section 116 by adopting a principle that the concepts employed by section 116 should be understood broadly.

As with the idea that section 116 is concerned with the practical operation of laws, the *DOGS Case* shows that the principle that the concepts employed by section 116 should be understood broadly is contrary to the High Court's existing doctrine on the meaning of section 116.

A number of the majority judges in the *DOGS Case* said themselves that they were being deliberately narrow in their reasoning. Justice Gibbs said '[t]here is no reason to give [s 116] a liberal interpretation.'[24] Justice Wilson, with whom Mason J agreed,[25] stated what while grants of power 'should be construed with all the generality which the words used will admit . . . the same is not true of a provision which proscribes power.'[26]

In the *DOGS Case*, the High Court even thought that employing a principle of interpreting section 116 narrowly would give effect to the underlying point of section 116. Justice Wilson said: 'having regard to the other clauses which are contained in s. 116, and to the precise manner of their expression, I infer a legislative intent to adopt a narrow notion of establishment.'[27] Justice Gibbs,[28] Justice Stephen,[29] and Justice Mason[30] each also made this point. Courts should interpret the establishment clause narrowly, these judges said, because the framers chose to include only 'four specific restrictions of legislative power'[31] and intended that there could be no overlap between the clauses.

What makes this a very strange mode of constitutional reasoning is that, as Justice Wilson said in his judgment, 'it is not permissible to seek the meaning of section 116 in the convention debates.'[32] Justice Gibbs in his judgment emphasised that it is 'forbidden to consider the debates of our own Constitutional Conventions for the purpose of discovering

23 John Quick and Robert Garran, *Annotated Constitution of the Commonwealth of Australia* (Angus & Robertson, 1901) 952.
24 *Attorney-General (Vic); Ex Rel Black v Commonwealth* (1981) 146 CLR 559, 603.
25 Ibid 612.
26 Ibid 653.
27 Ibid 653.
28 Ibid 597.
29 Ibid 605, 609.
30 Ibid 616.
31 Ibid 609.
32 Ibid 654.

what the delegates thought was the meaning of a particular provision accepted by the Convention.'[33] As Chief Justice Barwick said in his judgment, 'the settled doctrine of the Court is that they are not available in the construction of the *Constitution*.'[34]

In other words, what the High Court did in the *DOGS Case* is infer the intentions of the framers of a constitutional provision by ascribing significance to the precise form of words they adopted and then apply those intentions in developing constitutional doctrine. The High Court did so while simultaneously asserting that it is a rule of constitutional interpretation that the court must not consider the history of a constitutional provision and the thinking of its framers. An inference was made, which was not permitted to be made, and was made without looking to any facts.

The High Court abolished the rule that reference to the debates at the Federal Convention is not permitted in constitutional interpretation shortly after the *DOGS Case*.[35] Had the High Court in the *DOGS Case* looked to the actual history of section 116, it would have found that the precise language of section 116 was not the result of a careful drafting decision. The High Court would also have found that there was a general intention to enact a broad denial of power to the Commonwealth on the subject of religion. There is simply no basis for the inference drawn by the High Court in the *DOGS Case*.

The correct principle to employed in structuring and disciplining the practical and evaluative reasoning necessary to apply section 116 in any particular case is that the concepts employed by the section should be interpreted broadly.

Section 116 should be interpreted to avoid religious intolerance on the part of the Commonwealth

If the point of section 116 is to provide a safeguard against religious intolerance on the part of the Commonwealth then an important subsidiary standard that should structure and discipline the practical and evaluative reasoning needed to apply section 116 is that section 116 should be interpreted to avoid religious intolerance on the part of the Commonwealth.

The safeguard against religious intolerance theory holds that intolerance exists when the state attempts to change or suppress a set of religious beliefs and practices or imposes penalties for holding or following them. Each of the key concepts employed by section 116 is readily understood in these terms. Religious establishment is intolerant because it frames those who are not members of the favoured religion as outsiders and not full members of the community, which is a form of penalty for not adhering to the favoured religion. Imposing a religious observance has a similar effect as well as being an attempt to change the religious practices of individuals. Prohibiting the free exercise of religion is explicitly the suppression of religious practices. Imposing a religious test for public office necessarily penalises individuals who do not adhere to favoured

33 Ibid 603.
34 Ibid 577–8.
35 *Cole v Whitfield* (1988) 165 CLR 360.

religious beliefs or who adhere to disfavoured religious beliefs, by denying them access to public office.

The High Court's existing case law on section 116 is not consistent with the idea that section 116 should be interpreted to avoid religious intolerance on the part of the Commonwealth. The High Court's 2012 decision in *Williams v Commonwealth*, sometimes called the *School Chaplains Case* makes this clear.

The *School Chaplains Case* involved a challenge to the constitutional validity of the National School Chaplaincy Program, which the Commonwealth had established in 2007. The *National School Chaplaincy Programme Guidelines* issued by the Commonwealth described it as 'a voluntary Programme that will assist schools and their communities to support the spiritual wellbeing of their students.'[36] The program allowed schools to apply for funding. The Commonwealth entered into contracts, called 'Funding Agreements', with chaplaincy provider organisations, which would hire chaplains to provide chaplaincy services at schools whose applications were successful.

The Guidelines defined 'school chaplain' as:

> a person who is recognised
>
> - by the local school, its community and the appropriate governing authority as having the skills and experience to deliver school chaplaincy services to the school and its community; and
> - through formal ordination, commissioning, recognised qualifications or endorsement by a recognised or accepted religious institution or a state/territory government approved chaplaincy service.[37]

This definition was incorporated into the contracts the Commonwealth used to implement the program.

Ron Williams, an atheist and father of children at a school with a chaplain engaged under the program, argued in the High Court that the program guidelines implemented a religious test for a public office or trust under the Commonwealth. The High Court unanimously rejected that argument.

The High Court did not hold that there was no religious test involved. Rather, the High Court held that the position of a school chaplain was not 'under the Commonwealth.'

Williams argued that the Commonwealth had effective control over the chaplains. Chaplains had to sign a code of conduct set out in the program guidelines and any breach of the code of conduct required that a chaplain immediately stop providing chaplaincy services. The Commonwealth would only make payments once it had received progress reports about the provision of chaplaincy services. The Commonwealth could also directly monitor the work of chaplains by conducting visits to schools and by seeking feedback about their work from school communities.

36 Department of Education, Science and Training (Cth), *National School Chaplaincy Programme Guidelines* (19 January 2007) 3.
37 Ibid 4.

The High Court did not think this was enough to make the position of chaplains 'under the Commonwealth.' Justices Gummow and Bell, with whom Chief Justice French and Justices Hayne, Crennan and Kiefel agreed, wrote:

> The chaplains engaged by SUQ hold no office under the Commonwealth. The chaplain at the Darling Heights State Primary School is engaged by SUQ to provide services under the control and direction of the school principal. The chaplain does not enter into any contractual or other arrangement with the Commonwealth. That the Commonwealth is a source of funding to SUQ is insufficient to render a chaplain engaged by SUQ the holder of an office under the Commonwealth.
>
> It has been said in this Court that the meaning of "office" turns largely on the context in which it is found, and it may be accepted that, given the significance of the place of s 116 in the Constitution, the term should not be given a restricted meaning when used in that provision. Nevertheless, the phrase "office . . . under the Commonwealth" must be read as a whole. If this be done, the force of the term "under" indicates a requirement for a closer connection to the Commonwealth than that presented by the facts of this case.[38]

The effect of this reasoning is that the Commonwealth can circumvent the religious tests clause of section 116 by outsourcing. It allows the Commonwealth to do indirectly what it is forbidden from doing directly. Had the Commonwealth employed the chaplains itself there would have been a breach of section 116. But because the Commonwealth chose to outsource chaplaincy services, the High Court allowed the Commonwealth to write into the outsourcing contracts that only people who satisfy a religious test may be employed.

The word 'under' is a standard. It requires practical and evaluative reasoning to determine whether it applies to a particular situation. Had that reasoning been structured and disciplined by the idea that section 116 should be interpreted to avoid religious intolerance on the part of the Commonwealth then the High Court's decision in the *School Chaplains Case* is likely to have been different.

Williams ultimately won his case, but on different grounds. The High Court held that legislation was required before the Commonwealth could fund the program and no such legislation existed.

The future of section 116

Section 116 of the *Australian Constitution* is unlikely to be amended to apply to the States. Every attempt at doing so has failed, with the most recent attempt suffering the worst defeat of any referendum in Australian history. Section 116 is not, however, without future prospects.

The High Court has seriously misunderstood the point of section 116, and the High Court's reasoning in section 116 cases is seriously flawed.

Section 116 has the potential to provide a pragmatic safeguard against religious intolerance on the part of the Commonwealth, if only the High Court understood its history. This book provides that history.

38 *Williams v Commonwealth* (2012) 248 CLR 156, [109]–[110].

Bibliography

Books and articles

Arlin M Adams and Charles J Emmerich, 'A Heritage of Religious Liberty' (1989) 137 *University of Pennsylvania Law Review* 1559.

A W Anderson, *Religious Liberty in Australasia: The Attitude of Seventh Day Adventists to Religious Legislation and to Military Service* (Signs Publishing Co, 1917).

Anon, 'Enjoining the Sunday Opening of the World's Fair' (1893) 27 *American Law Review* 571.

Walter Arnstein, *The Bradlaugh Case: A Study in Late Victorian Opinion and Politics* (Clarendon Press, 1965).

Nicholas Aroney, 'The Constitutional (In)Validity of Religious Vilification Laws: Implications for their Interpretation' (2006) 34 *Federal Law Review* 287.

Nicholas Aroney, 'Towards the Best Explanation of the *Constitution*: Text, Structure, History and Principle in *Roach v Electoral Commissioner* (2011) 30 *University of Queensland Law Journal* 145.

Nicholas Aroney, 'Explanatory Power, Theory Formation and Constitutional Interpretation: Some Preliminaries' (2013) 38 *Australian Journal of Legal Philosophy* 1.

Nicholas Aroney, 'Freedom of Religion as an Associational Right' (2014) 33 *University of Queensland Law Journal* 154.

Richard Baker, *A Manual of Reference to Authorities for the Use of the Members of The National Australasian Convention* (WK Thomas & Co, 1891).

Jack M Balkin, *Living Originalism* (Belknap Press, 2011).

Jack Balkin, 'The Framework Model and Constitutional Interpretation', in David Dyzenhaus and Malcolm Thorburn (eds), *Philosophical Foundations of Constitutional Law* (Oxford University Press, 2016).

Terence Ball (ed), *The Federalist with Letters of Brutus* (Cambridge University Press, 2003).

Luke Beck, 'The Constitutional Prohibition on Religious Tests' (2011) 35 *Melbourne University Law Review* 323, 345.

Henry Campbell Black, *Handbook of American Constitutional Law* (West Publishing Co, 1895).

Henry Campbell Black, *Handbook of American Constitutional Law* (West Publishing Co, 2nd ed, 1897).

William Addison Blackley (ed), *American State Papers Bearing on Sunday Legislation* (Religious Liberty Association, 1911).

James Bryce, *The American Commonwealth* (Liberty Fund, first published 1888, 1995).

Ken Buckley, Barbara Dale and Wayne Reynolds, *Doc Evatt: Patriot, Internationalist, Fighter and Scholar* (Longman Cheshire, 1994).

David F Burg, *Chicago's White City of 1893* (University Press of Kentucky, 1976).

Enid Campbell, 'Fashioning and Refashioning the Constitution' (2001) 24(3) *University of New South Wales Law Journal* 620.

Martin Chanock, *The Making of South African Legal Culture, 1902–1936: Fear, Favour and Prejudice* (Cambridge University Press, 2001).
Andrew Inglis Clark, 'Why I am A Democrat' in Marcus Haward and James Warden (eds), *An Australian Democrat: The Life, Work, and Consequences of Andrew Inglis Clark* (Centre for Tasmanian Historical Studies, 1995) 200.
Andrew Inglis Clark, 'Denominational Education' in Richard Ely (ed), *A Living Force: Andrew Inglis Clark and the Ideal of the Commonwealth* (Centre for Tasmanian Historical Studies, 2001) 145.
W A Colcord, *The Rights of Man, Or Religion and the State: An Exposition of the Province of Civil Government and Religion, and a Plea for Civil and Religious Liberty* (Echo Publishing Company, 1913).
Edward Countryman, *The American Revolution* (Hill and Wang, 1985).
Ingrid Creppell, *Toleration and Identity: Foundations of Early Modern Thought* (Routledge, 2002).
R W Dale, *Impressions of Australia* (Hodder and Stoughton, 1889).
Raoul Dederen (ed), *Handbook of Seventh Day Adventist Theology* (Review and Herald Publishing Association, 2000).
Richard H Dees, *Trust and Toleration* (Routledge, 2004).
Arthur Delbridge, John Bernard, David Blair, Susan Butler, Pamela Peters and Colin Yallop (eds), *Macquarie Dictionary* (Macquarie Library, revised 3rd ed, 2002).
A V Dicey, *Introduction to the Study of the Law of the Constitution* (Macmillan, 4th ed, 1893).
Richard Ely, 'Andrew Inglis Clark and Church-State Separation' (1975) 8 *Journal of Religious History* 271.
Richard Ely, *Unto God and Caesar: Religious Issues in the Emerging Commonwealth, 1891–1906* (Melbourne University Press, 1976).
Richard Ely, 'The Forgotten Nationalism: Australian Civic Protestantism in the Second World War' (1987) 11(20) *Journal of Australian Studies* 59.
Richard Ely, 'Protestantism in Australian History: An Interpretative Sketch' (1989) 5 *Lucas: An Evangelical History Review* 11.
Richard Ely, 'Andrew Inglis Clark on the Preamble to the *Australian Constitution*' (2001) 75 *Australian Law Journal* 36.
Richard Ely, 'Clark's "Why I am a Democrat"' in Richard Ely (ed), *A Living Force: Andrew Inglis Clark and the Ideal of the Commonwealth* (Centre for Tasmanian Historical Studies, 2001) 27.
Richard Ely, 'Protecting Commonwealth from Church: Clark's "Denominational Education", and Beyond' in Richard Ely (ed), *A Living Force: Andrew Inglis Clark and the Ideal of the Commonwealth* (Centre for Tasmanian Historical Studies, 2001) 140.
Carolyn Evans, *Legal Protection of Religious Freedom in Australia* (Federation Press, 2012).
H V Evatt, *Post-War Reconstruction: A Case for Greater Commonwealth Powers* (Commonwealth Government Printer, 1942).
H V Evatt, *Post-War Reconstruction: Temporary Alterations of the Constitution. Notes on the Fourteen Powers and the Three Safeguards* (Commonwealth Government Printer, 1944).
Max Farrand, *The Framing of the Constitution of the United States* (Yale University Press, 1913).
Gaines M Foster, *Moral Reconstruction: Christian Lobbyists and the Federal Legislation of Morality, 1865–1920* (University of North Carolina Press, 2002).
Nick Fotion and Gerard Elfstron, *Toleration* (University of Alabama Press, 1992).
Anna Galeotti, *Toleration as Recognition* (Cambridge University Press, 2005).
Brian Galligan, 'Australia's Rejection of a Bill of Rights' (1990) 28(3) *Journal of Commonwealth and Comparative Politics* 344.
Brian Galligan, 'The 1988 Referendums and Australia's Record on Constitutional Change' (1990) 43 *Parliamentary Affairs* 497.

Steven G Gey, 'More or Less Bunk: The Establishment Clause Answers that History Doesn't Provide' [2004] *Brigham Young University Law Review* 1617.

Howard Gillman, Mark A Graber and Keith E Whittington, *American Constitutionalism* (Oxford University Press, 2013) vol 1.

Howard Gillman, Mark A Graber and Keith E Whittington, *American Constitutionalism* (Oxford University Press, 2013) vol 2.

Alexander Gosman, 'Imperial Federation and Congregationalism' in *Jubilee of Congregationalism in South Australia: Report of the Intercolonial Conference Held in Adelaide, September 1887* (W R Thomas & Co, 1887) 82.

Edward G Gray and Jane Kamensky, *The Oxford Handbook to The American Revolution* (Oxford University Press, 2013) 447.

Steven Keith Green, The National Reform Association and the Religious Amendments to the Constitution, 1864–1876, (MA Thesis, University of North Carolina at Chapel Hill, 1987).

Gareth Griffith and Sharath Srinivasan, *State Upper Houses in Australia* (New South Wales Parliamentary Research Service, Background Paper 1/2001).

Robert T Handy, *Undermined Establishment: Church-State Relations in America, 1880–1920* (Princeton University Press, first published 1991, 2014 ed).

Andrew Harper, *Australia Without God: An Appeal to the Churches of Australia to Secure an Acknowledgement of God in the Australian Constitution* (Hutchinson, 1897).

Sir Paul Hasluck, *The Government and the People 1942–1945* (Australian War Memorial, 1970).

David Heyd (ed), *Toleration: An Elusive Virtue* (Princeton University Press, 1998).

Dan Himmelfarb, 'The Preamble in Constitutional Interpretation' (1991) 2 *Seton Hall Constitutional Law Journal* 127.

Michael Hogan, *The Sectarian Strand: Religion in Australian History* (Penguin Books, 1987).

Alonzo T Jones, *The Union of Church and State in the United States, a Protest: Review of the United States Supreme Court Decision in case no. 143, October term, 1891. The Rector, Church Wardens and Vestrymen of the Church of the Holy Trinity, Plaintiffs in error, vs. the United States. (February 29, 1892), and also certain Acts of Congress for the closing of the World's Columbian Exposition on Sunday* (Pacific Press Publishing Co, 1892).

Alonzo T Jones, *Appeal from the US Supreme Court Decision Making this "A Christian Nation" Review of the United States Supreme Court Decision in Case No.143–October Terms, 1891. The Rector, Church Wardens, and Vestrymen of the Church of the Holy Trinity, Plaintiffs in Error vs. the United States [February 29, 1892.] And also certain Acts of Congress for the closing of the World's Columbian Exposition on Sunday* (International Religious Liberty Association, 1893).

Geoffrey Kennett, 'Individual Rights, the High Court and the Constitution' (1994) 19 *Melbourne University Law Review* 581.

Preston King, *Toleration* (Frank Cass, New ed, 1998).

Milton Frederick Krause, *The Seventh Day Adventist Church in Australia: 1885–1900* (MA Thesis, The University of Sydney, 1969).

David N Laband and Deborah Hendry Heinbuch, *Blue Laws: The History, Economics and Politics of Sunday-closing Laws* (Lexington Books, 1987).

J A La Nauze, *The Making of the Australian Constitution* (Melbourne University Press, 1972).

P H Lane, *The Australian Federal System* (Lawbook Co, 1979).

Douglas Laycock, 'Formal, Substantive, and Disaggregated Neutrality Toward Religion' (1989–1990) 39 *DePaul Law Review* 993.

John Locke, *A Letter Concerning Toleration* (1689), <http://www.constitution.org/jl/tolerati.htm>.

Carl McCamish, 'The Use of Historical Materials in Interpreting the Commonwealth Constitution' (1996) 70(8) *Australian Law Journal* 638.

Catriona McKinnon, *Toleration: A Critical Introduction* (Routledge, 2006).

Stephen McLeish, 'Making Sense of Religion and the *Constitution*: A Fresh Start for Section 116' (1992) 18 *Monash University Law Review* 207.

Susan Mendus (ed), *The Politics of Toleration in Modern Life* (Edinburgh University Press, 1999).

John C Miller, *Origins of the American Revolution* (Stanford University Press, 1966).

William Harrison Moore, *The Constitution of the Commonwealth of Australia* (Legal Books, 2nd ed, 1910, republished 1997).

Reid Mortensen, 'Judicial (In)activism in Australia's Secular Commonwealth' in Christine Parker and Gordan Preece (eds), *Theology and Law: Partners or Protagonists* (ATF Press, 2005) 52.

Reid Mortensen, 'The Establishment Clause: A Quest for Meaning' (2014) 33 *University of Queensland Law Journal* 109.

J M Neasy, 'Andrew Inglis Clark Senior and Australian Federation' (1969) 15(2) *Australian Journal of Politics and History* 1.

F M Neasy and L J Neasy, *Andrew Inglis Clark* (University of Tasmania Law Press, 2001).

Bryan Niblett, *Dare to Stand Alone: The Story of Charles Bradlaugh, Atheist and Republican* (Kramedart Press, 2010).

Gerard O'Collins, *Patrick McMahon Glynn: A Founder of Australian Federation* (Melbourne University Press, 1965).

Patrick O'Farrell, *The Catholic Church and Community: An Australian History* (New South Wales University Press, 1992).

Hans Oberdiek, *Tolerance: Between Forbearance and Acceptance* (Rowman & Littlefield, 2001).

Clifford L Pannam, 'Travelling Section 116 with a US Road Map' (1963) 4 *University of Melbourne Law Review* 41.

Walter Phillips, *Defending "A Christian Country": Churchman and Society in New South Wales in the 1880s and After* (University of Queensland Press, 1981).

Ezra Parmalee Prentice, *The Commerce Clause of the Federal Constitution* (Callaghan and Co, 1898).

Joshua Puls, 'The Wall of Separation: Section 116, the First Amendment and Constitutional Religious Guarantees' (1998) 26 *Federal Law Review* 139.

John Quick and Robert Garran, *Annotated Constitution of the Commonwealth of Australia* (Angus & Robertson, 1901).

William Pember Reeves, *Social Experiments in Australia and New Zealand* (Cambridge University Press, first published 1902, 2011 ed) vol 1.

John Reynolds, 'A I Clark's American Sympathies and his Influence on Australian Federation' (1958) 32(3) *Australian Law Journal* 62.

Wojciech Sadurski, 'The Action-Belief Dichotomy and Freedom of Religion' (1989–1990) 12 *Sydney Law Review* 420.

Cheryl Saunders, 'Historical Overview' in Heather McRea and Anne Mullins, *Australian Constitutional Convention 1973–1985: A Guide to the Archives* (Centre for Comparative Constitutional Studies, 1998).

Geoffrey Sawer, *Australian Federal Politics and Law 1929–1949* (Cambridge University Press, 1963) 140.

Campbell Sharman, 'The 1988 Referendums and their Context' in Brian Galligan and J R Nethercote, *The Constitutional Commission and the 1988 Referendums* (Centre for Research on Federal Financial Relations, 1989) 105.

Eric Slauter, 'Rights' in Edward G Gray and Jane Kamensky, *The Oxford Handbook to The American Revolution* (Oxford University Press, 2013).

T P Stephenson, 'History of the Movement to Secure the Religious Amendment of the Constitution of the United States' in *Proceedings of the National Convention to Secure the Religious Amendment of the Constitution of the United States* (James B Rodgers Co, 1872).

Matthew Stubbs, 'A Brief History of the Judicial Review of Legislation under the Australian Constitution' (2012) 40 *Federal Law Review* 227.

Jeremy Waldron and Melissa S Williams, 'Introduction' in Melissa S Williams and Jeremy Waldron, *Toleration and Its Limits* (New York University Press, 2008).
Michael Walzer, *On Toleration* (Yale University Press, 1999).
W J Waters, 'The Opposition and the "Powers" Referendum, 1944' (1969) 4(1) *Politics* 42.
Alexander Wendt, 'On Constitution and Causation in International Relations' (1998) 24(5) *Review of International Studies* 101.
George Williams, *Human Rights under the Australian Constitution* (Oxford University Press, 2002).
John Williams, 'The Emergence of the Commonwealth Constitution' in H P Lee and George Winterton (eds) Australian Constitutional Landmarks (Cambridge University Press, 2003).
John M Williams, *The Australian Constitution: A Documentary History* (Melbourne University Press, 2005).
Melissa S Williams and Jeremy Waldron, *Toleration and Its Limits* (New York University Press, 2008).
Anne Winckel, 'Almighty God in the Preamble' (1999) 4 *The New Federalist* 78.
Perez Zagorin, *How the Idea of Religious Toleration Came to the West* (Princeton University Press, 2003).
Leslie Zines, 'Changing Attitudes to Federalism and its Purpose' in Robert French, Geoffrey Lindell and Cheryl Saunders (eds), *Reflections on the Australian Constitution* (Federation Press, 2003).
Leslie Zines, *The High Court and the Constitution* (Federation Press, 5th ed, 2008).

Cases

Australia

Attorney-General (Vic); Ex Rel Black v Commonwealth (1981) 146 CLR 559.
Cole v Whitfield (1988) 165 CLR 360.
Herald & Weekly Times Ltd v Commonwealth (1966) 115 CLR 418.
Huddart, Parker and Co v Moorehead (1909) 8 CLR 330.
Kruger v Commonwealth (1997) 190 CLR 1.
Krygger v Williams (1912) 15 CLR 366.
Murphyores Incorporated Pty Ltd v Commonwealth (1976) 136 CLR 1.
Williams v Commonwealth (No 1) (2012) 248 CLR 156.

United Kingdom

Attorney-General v Bradlaugh (1885) 14 QBD 667.
Clarke v Bradlaugh (1881) 7 QBD 38.

United States

Cantwell v Connecticut, 310 US 296 (1940).
Church of Holy Trinity v United States, 143 US 547 (1892).
Engel v Vital, 370 US 421 (1962).
Everson v Board of Education of Ewing, 330 US 1 (1947).
Helvering v Davis, 301 US 619 (1937).
Hepburn v Griswold, 75 US (8 Wall) 603 (1870).
Jacobson v Commonwealth of Massachusetts, 197 US 11, 22 (1905).
Mahon v Justice, 127 US 700 (1888).
National Federation of Independent Business v Sebelius, 567 US 519 (2012).

United States v Butler, 297 US 1 (1936).
World's Columbian Exposition v United States, 56 F 654 (7th Cir, 1893).

Legislative materials

Australia

Australasian Federation Enabling Act 1895 (NSW).
Australasian Federation Enabling Act 1896 (SA).
Australasian Federation Enabling Act 1896 (Tas).
Australasian Federation Enabling Act 1896 (Vic).
Australasian Federation Enabling Act 1896 (WA).
Australian Constitution.
Australian Human Rights Commission Act 1986 (Cth).
Constitution Act 1934 (Tas)
Constitution Alteration (Fair Elections) Bill 1988 (Cth).
Constitution Alteration (Local Government) Bill 1988 (Cth).
Constitution Alteration (Parliamentary Terms) Bill 1988 (Cth).
Constitution Alteration (Rights and Freedoms) Bill 1988 (Cth).
Explanatory Memorandum, Constitution Alteration (Rights and Freedoms) Bill 1988.
Referendum (Machinery Provisions) Act 1984 (Cth).

United Kingdom/England

Sunday Observance Act 1677, 29 Car 2 c 7.
Test Act 1672, 25 Car 2, c 2.

United States

23 Stat 332, c 164.
Act of 5 August 1892, 52 Cong Ch 381, 27 Stat 389.
Declaration of Independence.
United States Constitution.

Other

Canadian Charter of Rights and Freedoms
Constitution of Ireland 1937

Official reports and records

23 *Congressional Record* 5999 (Joseph Hawley) (1892, Senate).
23 *Congressional Record* 6003 (John Morgan) (1982, Senate).
Australian Bureau of Statistics, *Australian Historical Population Statistics 2014* (cat. no. 3105.0.65.001), <http://www.abs.gov.au/AUSSTATS%5Cabs@.nsf/0/632CDC28637CF57ECA256F1F0080EBCC?Opendocument> accessed 21 May 2016.
Australian Constitutional Convention, Standing Committee B, Report to Executive Committee, 1 August 1974.
Australian Constitutional Convention, Standing Committee D, Report to Executive Committee, 1 August 1974.

Australian Electoral Commission, 'Yes or No? Referendums. Saturday 3 September 1988. The Cases For and Against' (Australian Electoral Commission, 1988).
Commonwealth Bureau of Census and Statistics, *Year Book Australia, 1944–45* (Commonwealth Government Printer, 1947).
Commonwealth Department of Education, Science and Training, *National School Chaplaincy Programme Guidelines* (19 January 2007).
Commonwealth, *Parliamentary Debates*, House of Representatives.
Commonwealth, *Parliamentary Debates*, Senate.
Constitutional Commission, *Final Report of the Constitutional Commission* (Australian Government Printing Service, 1988).
Constitutional Commission, *First Report of the Constitutional Commission* (Australian Government Publishing Service, 1988).
Constitutional Commission, *Report of the Advisory Committee on Individual and Democratic Rights under the Constitution* (Australian Government Publishing Service, 1987).
Constitutional Committee, Minutes, 8 April 1897, National Archives of Australia, Series R213.
Convention of Representatives of the Commonwealth and State Parliaments on Proposed Alteration of the Commonwealth Constitution, *Record of Proceedings*, Canberra.
House of Representatives Standing Committee on Legal and Constitutional Affairs, Parliament of Australia, *Constitutional Change: Select Sources on Constitutional Change in Australia 1901–1997* (1997).
Legal and Constitutional Committee, Parliament of Victoria, *Second Report on the Australian Constitutional Convention* (1986).
New South Wales, *Parliamentary Debates*, Legislative Assembly.
New South Wales, *Parliamentary Debates*, Legislative Council.
Official Record of Debates of the Australian Constitutional Convention, Sydney, 1973.
Official Record of Debates of the Australian Constitutional Convention, Melbourne, 1975.
Official Record of Debates of the Australian Constitutional Convention, Hobart, 1976.
Official Record of the Debates of the Australasian Federal Convention, Melbourne, 1898.
Official Report of the National Australasian Convention Debates, Adelaide, 1897.
Official Report of the National Australasian Convention Debates, Sydney, 1897.
Official Report of the National Australasian Convention Debates, Melbourne, 1898.
Proceedings of the National Australasian Convention, Sydney, 1891.
Proceedings of the People's Federal Convention, Bathurst, November 1896 (Gordon and Gotch, 1896).
South Australia, *Parliamentary Debates*, House of Assembly.
South Australia, *Parliamentary Debates*, Legislative Council.
Tasmania, *Debates on the Draft Constitution Bill, as adopted by the Convention at Adelaide, March–May, 1897*, House of Assembly.
Tasmania, *Debates on the Draft Constitution Bill, as adopted by the Convention at Adelaide, March–May, 1897*, Legislative Council.
Victoria, *Parliamentary Debates*, Legislative Assembly.
Victoria, *Parliamentary Debates*, Legislative Council.
Western Australia, *Parliamentary Debates*, Legislative Assembly.
Western Australia, *Parliamentary Debates*, Legislative Council.

Newspapers and newspaper articles

'A Blow to Religion. Professor Rentoul on Petty Coteries', *The Argus* (Melbourne), 7 May 1897, 6.
Advocate (Burnie, Tasmania), 29 July 1944.
Argus (Melbourne), 30 June 1897.

'Council of Churches. Some Recommendations', *The Inquirer & Commercial News* (Perth), 5 March 1897, 16.
'Deputations. The Federal Bill. Recognition of God. Deputation to the Minister for Lands', *The Sydney Morning Herald* (Sydney), 23 July 1897, 3.
'Enforcing the Sunday Law', *Bible Echo* (Melbourne), 19 July 1897, 232.
P Glynn, Letter to the Editor, *South Australian Register* (Adelaide), 12 May 1897, 3.
'Governmental Recognition of God: What Does it Mean?', *Bible Echo* (Melbourne), 12 June 1897, 220.
'Hard Names v Logic', *Bible Echo* (Melbourne), 19 April 1897, 123.
'Is God to be Confessed in the Constitution?', *South Australian Register* (Adelaide), 17 April 1897, 6.
S M'Cullagh, 'Religious Persecution', *The Australian Star* (Sydney), 17 August 1894, 3.
'Meeting of the Council of Churches. Recommendations to the Convention', *The Advertiser* (Adelaide), 3 March 1897, 6.
P Moran, 'Address to Electors', *Freeman's Journal* (Sydney), 20 February 1897, 17.
'National Recognition of the Supreme Being. The Council of Churches', *The Australian Register* (Adelaide) 19 March 1897, 3.
Northern Argus (Clare, South Australia), 11 August 1944, 8.
'Our Petition', *Bible Echo* (Melbourne), 19 April 1897, 128.
'Parliament', *Sydney Morning Herald*, 5 August 1897, 5.
'Petitions', *Bible Echo* (Melbourne), 22 March 1897, 96.
'Petitions to Parliament: Which Shall We Sign?', *Bible Echo* (North Fitzroy), 12 July 1897, 221.
'Recognition of God', *Sydney Morning Herald* (Sydney), 3 August 1897, 5.
'Religion and the Federal Constitution', *Bible Echo* (Melbourne), 19 July 1897, 225.
'Religion and the State', *Sunday Times* (Sydney), 25 July 1897, 4.
'Religious Legislation or Religious Liberty: Which Shall it Be?', *Bible Echo* (Melbourne), 29 March 1897, 97.
'Sentenced to the Stocks', *National Advocate* (Bathurst), 11 August 1984, 2.
'Sentenced to the Stocks. The Sentence to be Remitted', *The Age* (Melbourne), 14 August 1894, 6.
'State Education', *Christian Colonist* (Adelaide), 29 June 1886, 6.
'Sunday Labor Prosecution', *Evening News* (Sydney), 9 August 1894, 4.
'Sunday Observance. The Seventh Day Adventists', *The Australian Star* (Sydney), 20 August 1894, 2.
L Taylor, 'Referendum buoys Liberals for State poll', *The Canberra Times* (Canberra), 5 September 1988.
'The Commonwealth Bill. Lecture By Professor Harper', *Sydney Morning Herald* (Sydney), 3 August 1897, 5.
'The Commonwealth Constitution. Recognition of God', *Sydney Morning Herald* (Sydney), 6 July 1897, 6.
The Convention', *The Advertiser* (Adelaide), 23 April 1897, 5.
'The Council of Churches', *Bible Echo* (Melbourne), 22 February 1897, 60.
'The Council of Churches', *Daily Telegraph* (Sydney), 3 March 1897, 8.
'The Council of Churches', *Sydney Morning Herald* (Sydney), 4 March 1897, 6.
'The Parliamentary Elections. Mr H B Higgins at the Exhibition Theatre. An Enthusiastic Reception.' *Geelong Advertiser* (Victoria), 2 October 1897, 2.
'The people say No to the lot', *The Canberra Times* (Canberra), 4 September 1988.
'The People's Federal Convention. A Week at Bathurst' *Sydney Mail and New South Wales Advertiser* (Sydney) 28 November 1896, 1140.
'The Stocks Case. Sentenced Remitted', *Evening News* (Sydney), 13 August 1894, 5.
'The Stocks. Shannon's Case', *Evening News* (Sydney), 11 August 1894, 4.

'The Stocks Case – Some Departmental Correspondence', *Newcastle Morning Herald and Miners' Advocate* (Newcastle), 11 August 1894, 5.

Untitled Article, *Sydney Morning Herald* (Sydney) 18 November 1896, 7.

'What is this Freedom? Sir Isaac Isaacs's Views', *Sydney Morning Herald* (Sydney), 8 August 1944, 2.

'What Religion in the Constitution Means', *Bible Echo* (Melbourne), 26 July 1897, 233.

Other

Australasian Union Conference Record, Volume 1, Nos 1 and 2, January and February 1898

Gale Cengage Learning, Fact Sheet, 'Making of Modern Law: Legal Treatises, 1800–1926' <http://www.gale.cengage.com/pdf/facts/momlTreaties.pdf>.

Gosman to Organising Committee, 'The Recognition of the Supreme Being – Resolution as Originally Drafted', undated, Astley Papers, CY3431, Mitchell Library, Sydney.

R L Hanson, 'Secularizing the American State, 1876–1905', Paper Presented at Indiana University Department of Political Science Political Theory Luncheon, 4–7, http://polisci.indiana.edu/about/news/Hanson_TheoryLuncheon.pdf.

Letter from W A Colcord to H B Higgins, 10 February 1898, in National Library of Australia, Papers of Henry Higgins 1851–1929, MS 1057, Series 1, Item 23.

Letter from W A Colcord to H B Higgins, 23 March 1898, in National Library of Australia, Papers of Henry Higgins 1851–1929, MS 1057, Series 1, Item 23C.

Loretta Re, 'Moore, Sir William Harrison (1867–1935)', *Australian Dictionary of Biography*, National Centre of Biography, Australian National University, <http://adb.anu.edu.au/biography/moore-sir-william-harrison-7645/text13367>.

Meeting of full Cabinet held at 11am on Tuesday and Wednesday 7 and 8 December 1943 at Parliament House Canberra, Agendum 573a.

Sir Samuel Griffith, *Successive Stages of the Constitution of the Commonwealth of Australia*, held in the State Library of New South Wales call number DLMSQ 198.

Index

For Product Safety Concerns and Information please contact our EU representative GPSR@taylorandfrancis.com
Taylor & Francis Verlag GmbH, Kaufingerstraße 24, 80331 München, Germany

www.ingramcontent.com/pod-product-compliance
Ingram Content Group UK Ltd.
Pitfield, Milton Keynes, MK11 3LW, UK
UKHW050753180926
475701UK00007B/1024
* 9 7 8 0 3 6 7 8 9 3 7 4 3 *